Bayard Taylor

Travels in Greece and Russia with an Excursion into Crete

Bayard Taylor

Travels in Greece and Russia with an Excursion into Crete

ISBN/EAN: 9783337169206

Printed in Europe, USA, Canada, Australia, Japan

Cover: Foto ©Andreas Hilbeck / pixelio.de

More available books at **www.hansebooks.com**

BAYARD TAYLOR'S TRAVELS.

Eldorado; OR, ADVENTURES IN THE PATH OF EMPIRE (Mexico and California). 12mo. Household edition . . $1.50

Central Africa. LIFE AND LANDSCAPE FROM CAIRO TO THE WHITE NILE. Two plates and cuts. 12mo. Household edition $1.50

Greece and Russia. WITH AN EXCURSION TO CRETE. Two plates. 12mo. Household edition . . . $1.50

Home and Abroad. A SKETCH-BOOK OF LIFE, SCENERY, AND MEN. Two plates. 12mo. Household edition . . $1.50

——(Second Series.) With two plates. 12mo. Household edition $1.50

India, China, and Japan. Two plates. 12mo. Household edition $1.50

Land of the Saracen; OR, PICTURES OF PALESTINE, ASIA MINOR, SICILY, AND SPAIN. With two plates. 12mo. Household edition $1.50

Northern Travel. SUMMER AND WINTER PICTURES OF SWEDEN, DENMARK, AND LAPLAND. With two plates. 12mo. Household edition $1.50

Views Afoot; OR, EUROPE SEEN WITH KNAPSACK AND STAFF. 12mo. Household edition $1.50

——Sq. octavo. Illustrated. Kennett edition . . $2.50

By-Ways of Europe. 12mo. Household edition . . $1.50

Egypt and Iceland in the Year 1874. 12mo. Household edition $1.50

BAYARD TAYLOR.

TRAVELS

IN

GREECE AND RUSSIA;

WITH AN EXCURSION TO CRETE

BY BAYARD TAYLOR.

HOUSEHOLD EDITION.

G. P. PUTNAM'S SONS
NEW YORK   LONDON
27 West Twenty-third St.   24 Bedford St., Strand
The Knickerbocker Press
1893

Entered, according to Act of Congress, in the year 1889, by
BAYARD TAYLOR,
In the Clerk's Office of the District Court of the United States for the Southern District of New York.

PREFACE.

THE reader will observe that in describing Greece, I have devoted myself to the physical aspects of the country, and the character and habits of its present population, rather than to its past history and classic associations. If, therefore, there are no new pictures in this volume, there may be, at least, some old and familiar subjects exhibited under new atmospheric effects. I should otherwise have hesitated to select a field which may be considered well-nigh exhausted, were it not that the country is still in a transition state, and every few years presents a new phase to the traveller's eye.

Owing to the pressure of other literary labors, this volume has been too rapidly prepared for the press, to allow me to add a special chapter on the Ethnology of Greece, as I had originally designed. I can only record my complete conviction of the truth of the views entertained by Fallmereyer, that the modern Greeks are a mongrel race, in which the Slavic element is predominant, and that the pure Hellenic blood is to be found only in a few localities.

The chapters relating to Russia must be considered as studies rather than finished pictures. They are an attempt to sketch the gay, bizarre, incongruous *external* forms of Russian life. Anything more could not be safely attempted without a longer residence in the country and a knowledge of the language—both of which I hope to accomplish at some future day. So far, however, as the Greek Church is concerned, it may be interesting to the reader to trace its character and influence in the two countries, which, with a common ambition, are far from having a common destiny.

BAYARD TAYLOR.

NEW YORK, *July,* 1859

CONTENTS

CHAPTER I.
Pictures from the Dalmatian Coast,

CHAPTER II.
Further from Dalmatia,

CHAPTER III.
First Days in Greece,

CHAPTER IV.
On the Acropolis,

CHAPTER V.
Winter Life in Athens,

CHAPTER VI.
A Greek Baptism,

CHAPTER VII.
The Court of King Otho,

CHAPTER VIII.
Greek Festivals, Religious and Civic,

CHAPTER IX.
An Excursion to Crete,

CHAPTER X.
A Cretan Journey,

CONTENTS.

CHAPTER XI
Our Imprisonment at Rhithymnos, ... 112

CHAPTER XII.
The Caverns, Mountains, and Labyrinths of Crete, . . 123

CHAPTER XIII.
Two Days with an Archbishop, . . . 137

CHAPTER XIV.
The Earthquake at Corinth, ... 148

CHAPTER XV
Argolis and Arcadia, ... 161

CHAPTER XVI.
Four Days among the Spartans, ... 169

CHAPTER XVII
Messenia, Elis, and Achaia, ... 186

CHAPTER XVIII.
Byron in Greece, ... 203

CHAPTER XIX.
The Haunts of the Muses, ... 216

CHAPTER XX.
Parnassus and the Dorian Mountains, ... 226

CHAPTER XXI.
The Frontier of Thessaly, ... 237

CHAPTER XXII.
Adventures in Euboea, ... 247

CHAPTER XXIII.
People and Government, ... 261

CHAPTER XXIV
Agriculture and Resources, ... 273

CHAPTER XXV.
Return to the North, . . . 281

CHAPTER XXVI.
Cracow, and the Salt Mines of Wieliczka, . . 289

CHAPTER XXVII.
A Glance at Warsaw, ... 303

CONTENTS.

	PAGE
CHAPTER XXVIII.	
A Journey through Central Russia,	315
CHAPTER XXIX.	
A Panoramic View of Moscow,	325
CHAPTER XXX.	
The Kremlin,	331
CHAPTER XXXI.	
A Visit to the Foundling Hospital,	348
CHAPTER XXXII.	
Moscow, In-doors and Out,	359
CHAPTER XXXIII.	
Railroads in Russia,	37
CHAPTER XXXIV.	
St. Petersburg and its Palaces,	381
CHAPTER XXXV.	
Tzarsko Selo, Paulovsk and the Islands,	594
CHAPTER XXXVI.	
Varieties of the Russian Capital,	407
CHAPTER XXXVII.	
Journey through the Baltic Provinces,	417

TRAVELS IN GREECE AND RUSSIA.

I.

GREECE.

CHAPTER I.

PICTURES FROM THE DALMATIAN COAST.

AFTER giving up the hope of enjoying a Siberian Winter, which had been my original intention, I determined to go as near as possible to the opposite extreme of avoiding the Winter altogether. But by the time we left Gotha (on the 4th of December, 1857) the season was already inaugurated. The first snow whitened the Thüringian hills; bitter blasts blew down upon us from the Hartz—the last chilly farewell of the forsaken North. Like a true German, he was not satisfied with one adieu, but must return again and again to prolong the sweet sorrow of parting. He accompanied us to Dresden, through the black and lowering passes of the Saxon Switzerland, over the open plains of Bohemia, and only left us for a while in the valley of the Danube to return with a more violent embrace, on the top of the Semmering

Alp. Finally, at the southern edge of the *Karst*, or table-land of Carinthia, where his rugged name of Boreas is Italianized into the Bora, we left him, and the little olive-trees in the gardens of Trieste welcomed us to the threshold of the South.

At Trieste, I determined to make the most of my southward voyage, by taking the Lloyd steamer of the Dalmatian and Albanian line, which would enable me to see something of one of the least frequented and most interesting of the Mediterranean shores. At noon, on the 12th, we were all three on board of the Miramar, Captain Mazarevitch, steaming out of Trieste under a cloudless sky and over a smooth blue sea, albeit the south-eastern wind, blowing over the Istrian mountains, was keen enough. Our vessel, although new, clean, and sufficiently comfortable, was painfully slow, and consequently we were not up with Pola, the famous amphitheatre whereof is plainly visible from the sea, until long after dark. Our comfort during the afternoon was our fine view of the Julian Alps, wheeling in a splendid arc around the head of the Adriatic, from Trieste nearly to Venice. During the night we crossed the mouth of the Gulf of Fiume, which you may remember as the only outlet of Croatia, much talked of during the Hungarian struggle, in connexion with the design of uniting the Slavic races with the Magyars, and securing a seaport for the new nation. I cheerfully testify that the Gulf of Fiume is as rough a piece of water as the Bay of Biscay, and this is all I know about it, for by sunrise we were at anchor in the harbor of Zara, the capital of Dalmatia.

Most gentlemen have heard of this place, from reading

on the labels of certain square, wicker-encased bottles—
"*Maraschino di Zara.*" Those who have dipped into history far enough will remember the famous sea-fight fought here during the Fourth Crusade, and the happy few who know Venice have not forgotten the famous picture in the Doge's Palace, wherein the son of Barbarossa is taken prisoner by the Venetians, the most flagrant case of lying which the world can produce—no such incident ever having occurred Zara, I suspect, looks pretty much as it did in those days Its long, crenelated walls and square bastions had a familiar aspect to me, from the aforesaid picture. Of its ancient history I need only say that it was the capital of the Roman province of Liburnia, and a place of some note in the days of Augustus.

The sun rose over the snowy range of the Velebich, which separates Dalmatia from the Turkish pashalik of Bosnia. The land, under the clearest illumination, looked intensely bare and stony. Around the harbor were olive orchards, with a spiry Italian cypress or two, and some leafless fig-trees. Dalmatian boatmen thronged the low quay, in front of the water gate, and hovered about the steamer, in their red caps, loose shirts and wide trowsers. The picture was neither Italian nor Oriental, yet with something of both, and there was enough of Frank innovation to give it a shabby air. I know nothing more slovenly and melancholy than the aspect of those Mediterranean ports which are in a transition state—where the old costume, habits, and ways of living have been for the most part given up, and those of Western Europe are still new enough to appear awkward and affected. The interior of the town produced the same impression; there was every where the same curious mixture of two heterogeneous elements. Only the country people, who had come in with their market-carts and were selling vegetables in the principal square, and some shaggy fellows, whom I took to be Morlaks, or Mountain Slaves, seemed to be purely Dalmatian, both in blood and habits. Their Slavic ancestry was to be seen at a glance. The deep-set eye, the heavy brow, the strong nose, and lengthened oval of the face—the expression of courage, calculation, and obstinacy—the erect, rather haughty form, and free, graceful carriage, are characteristics which belong to all the branches of this widely spread race. Some of the old men were noble figures; but the men, as elsewhere among the Slaves, were much handsomer than the women.

Zara is a little place, and one can easily see the whole of it in an hour. The streets are very narrow and crooked, but paved with heavy stone slabs, and kept perfectly clean. At one corner of the public square, stands a Corinthian pillar surmounted by a winged griffin, which is believed to have belonged to a temple of the age of Augustus. The Cathedral, a low building of marble, Byzantine in style, was founded by old Dandolo, who wintered here in 1202, on his way to take Constantinople. We went into a café to taste Maraschino on its native soil, but the specimen proved that the flavor of the liqueur is improved by banishment. It is made from the berries of a variety of wild cherry, called the *marasca*, whence the name.

We left at noon, and running along a coast which appeared barren, although every valley which opened to the sea was silver-gray with olive orchards, reached Sebenico a little before sunset. This is a wonderfully picturesque place, built along the side of a hill which rises steeply from the water, and dominated by three massive Venetian fortresses, behind which towers a bald, barren mountain. Our steamer was hauled in beside a mole which protects the little harbor, and we stepped ashore to see the place before dark. Crowds of grizzly, dirty men, dressed in wide trowsers and shaggy sheepskin jackets, stared at us with curiosity. A few of them begged in unintelligible Illyrian or bad Italian. The women, some of whom were quite pretty, wore a very picturesque costume, consisting of a crimson boddice, open to the waist in front, disclosing a snowy linen chemise, in which the full breast was enveloped, a petticoat of red or dark blue, and a gay handkerchief twisted through the long braids of their thick black hair.

The streets were so very narrow, steep, and dark, that we hesitated at first about plunging into such a suspicious labyrinth, but at last hit upon a lane which led us to the public square before the Cathedral, the only level piece of ground in the city. It is an artificial terrace, about halfway up the hill, and may be a hundred feet square. On one side is the Cathedral, a very quaint, squat old building of white marble, in a bastard Byzantine style; on the other a building resting on an arched corridor, which reminds you of Venice. Broad slabs of slippery marble paved the court, which we found utterly silent and deserted. As the yellow lustre of sunset struck upon the dome and the front of the fortress which frowned high over our heads, and a glimpse of purple sea glimmered afar through the gap by which we had ascended, I felt as if I had discovered some lost, forgotten city of the past, over which no wind of ruin had as yet blown. All was quaint and solemn, mellowed by the touch of age: had it been new, it would have been merely grotesque.

We mounted to the fort, whence there was a wide view of the coast, the sea, and the Dalmatian Islands. The fortresses appeared to be no longer kept up as defences, for which, indeed, they are now worthless. Sebenico is a poor place, and as proud as it is poor, if one may rely upon the statements made by a thriving brewer, who keeps a beerhouse on the quay. "There is no such thing as enterprise here," said he; "the country is capable of producing much more than it does, if the people were not so lazy. Here, for instance, are half-a-dozen old Venetian families, who consider themselves too nobly born to do anything, and who are gradually starving in their pride. After having sold everything except the family mansion, they then sell their plate piece by piece. What they will do when that is gone, I cannot tell. I am considered rich, because I earn more than I spend, but am despised by these gentry because I have a business. My father was once applied to by one of them, who wished to borrow money. He went to the house, but was refused admittance by the noble lady, who said: 'Stay in the street until my lord comes out.' Well, when my lord came, my father said to him: 'If my person is not worthy to enter your house, my money is not worthy to touch your fingers'—and so left him. These people would like to restore the Venetian rule, because they held offices then, and were somebodies; but if we were well rid of them, and could fill their places with Germans, not afraid to work, it would be better for Dalmatia." I have no doubt there is much truth in the brewer's remarks. Dalmatia seems to me as well adapted for the production of wine, oil, and silk, as any part of Southern Europe. Its present yield of wine, which is of excellent quality, amounts to 1,200,000 barrels annually. About 60,000 barrels of oil are produced, but as the number of olive trees in the province amounts to near three millions, and from two-and-a-half to five pounds of olives (according to the season) yield one pound of oil, there must be a great waste of raw material in the preparation of the article. Wheat and barley also thrive remarkably well. The value of the staples exported from the province amounts to about $2,000,000 yearly, which, for a population of 400,000, gives but $5 a head as the amount of their industry beyond what is required for their maintenance.

Early the next morning we started again, still favored with cloudless skies and sleeping seas. The tops of the shore hills rose bold and yellow above the olive terraces which belted their bases, and far inland rose pale-purple mountain chains, tipped with snow—the dividing ridge between Dalmatia and Bosnia. Towards noon, rounding a point of the coast and turning almost due eastward, the spires of Spalato (not *Spalatro*, as it is generally spelled) famous for its memories of Diocletian, twinkled before us. It lies on a little cove, at the head of a wide bay, landlocked by the islands of the Dalmatian Archipelago, and at the end of a gently sloping plain three or four miles long

The mountains here fall back, and form a graceful amphitheatre, at the head of which stood the old Roman city of Salona. Spalato is founded on the ruins of Diocletian's palace, the walls of which still contain the whole of the mediæval city. Every one has heard of Diocletian and his Dalmatian cabbages, but few know how much of his imperial hermitage has been spared by time. Let us go ashore and see.

CHAPTER II.

FURTHER FROM DALMATIA.

SPALATO ought properly to be called *Diocleziano*. In the front of the long row of houses facing the sea, we counted twenty-eight arches of the Emperor's palace, and we recognised, in the hexagonal structure behind the tall Venetian belfrey, the temple of Jupiter which stood within its walls. Landing in the midst of a wild, dirty, but very picturesque crowd of Dalmatians and Morlaks, we discovered an arched entrance into the mass of houses, in the centre of the ancient sea-front. A vaulted passage, ascending by irregular steps, led us into the midst of irregular ruins, among which the modern inhabitants are nested like bats, blackening with their fires and defiling with their filth the Roman arches and walls. A circular hall, the vaulted roof of which had fallen in, was evidently the vestibule to the architectural splendors of the inner court.

Beyond this, however, the picture suddenly changed. A portico, supported by four pillars—monoliths of red granite, with Corinthian capitals of white marble—and with a pediment sculptured in the most florid style, conducted us to the court of the palace, paved with marble, and surrounded by a colonnade of red granite, raised upon a lofty base. On the right hand, the massive portico of the temple of Jupiter now serves as the foundation of the lofty campanile, behind which stands the temple itself, almost entire in all its parts. On the left, a short distance behind the colonnade, is a smaller building of marble, with a very rich Corinthian cornice, which is generally supposed to have been a temple of Æsculapius, although some antiquaries regard it as the mausoleum of Diocletian. In front of the temple of Jupiter sits an Egyptian sphynx of black porphyry, with an inscription of the time of Amunoph III.—about fifteen centuries before Christ. The charm of the court is greatly enhanced by the suddenness with which it comes upon you, and by contrast with the tall, plain masses of the old Venetian houses which inclose it. The fact that it served as a public square to the inhabitants of the Spalato of the middle ages, which was built entirely within the palace-walls, has no doubt preserved it from ruin. The square is still called "*Piazza del Tempio.*"

We went into the temple, now the cathedral. The tawdry appurtenances of its present religion do not at all harmonize with the simple severity of the old. It is rather gloomy, the ancient vaulted dome having no aperture to admit light, like that of the Roman Pantheon. There is an external colonnade, which is gradually falling into ruin through neglect, and its condition shows that there is need of an appeal similar to that upon the outside of a church in Florence—"If you bear the name of Christians, oh respect the temple of the Lord!" Two large sarcophagi were lying between the columns. One of them had a cracked lid, a piece of which Braisted shoved aside, and diving into the interior, brought out a large thigh-bone, the owner of which must have been over six feet in height. There is an interior gallery, under the dome, which rests upon columns of porphyry and grey granite. This gallery is adorned with a frieze representing a hunt, whence some suppose the temple to have been erected to Diana instead of Jupiter. It is well known, however, that hunting subjects were used in the temples of various gods, at a later period. The execution is so very clumsy, that one can have no very exalted opinion of Diocletian's taste. I can only compare it to those monstrosities which were perpetrated under the name of sculpture, during the Greek Empire. In front of the temple of Æsculapius lies a sarcophagus, which is supposed to be that of Diocletian himself, and with more probability than usually belongs to such conjectures.

Braisted and I mounted to the summit of the campanile, and sat down to contemplate the landscape. It was a warm, still, cloudless day, and the rich plain behind, sloping back to the site of the ancient Salona, the blue harbor, inclosed by the purple Dalmatian islands, and the bald, lilac-tinted mountains, rising along the Bosnian frontier, formed so large, cheerful, and harmonious a picture, that we at once understood Diocletian's choice, and gave him full credit for it. "He was the only Roman Emperor who had good common sense," said B., with a positiveness from which there was no appeal. In the gardens around Spalato we noticed some cabbages, the descendants, probably, of those which Diocletian so ostentatiously shook under the nose of Maximinian. But in spite of his cabbages Diocletian was far from being a Diogenes in the purple. I looked down on he compact little town, and could easily trace the line of his palace-wall—an irregular parallelogram, 500 feet on the shortest side, and 670 on the longest. It was originally adorned with eighteen towers, and pierced with four gates, the main entrance. the *Porta Aurea* (golden gate), being on the side towards Salona. This has been recently excavated, and, except that its statues have fallen from their niches, is very well preserved. The other gates were named Silver, Bronze, and Iron. Within this space the Emperor had his residence and that of a large retinue, including his women, guards, and slaves, besides two temples, a theatre, bath, and halls for festivities. The Byzantine writer, Porphyrogenitus, who saw the palace in its perfect state, says: "No description can convey any idea of its magnificence." Who would not be willing to raise cabbages in this style? For my part, I should not object to a dish of such imperial sour-krout.

We left Spalato in the afternoon, and made for the port of Milne, on the island of Brazza, whose olive-streaked hills shimmered faintly in the west. This island is the largest in the Dalmatian Archipelago, producing annually 80,000 barrels of wine, and 10,000 of oil. It was celebrated by Pliny for its fine goats, a distinction which it still preserves. Brazza, I am informed, sent quite a number of emigrants to California. It is curious to observe how very closely the threads of commercial and social intercourse are knitted, all over the world. All civilized nations are rapidly becoming limbs of one vast body, in which any nerve that is touched in one is more or less felt by all. "Our business is very dull in Zara," said a Dalmatian to me, "on account of the crisis in America." "But the worst of the crisis there is already over," I said, "as well as in England." "Then we may hope that ours will not last long," said he. In Zante, and other Ionian islands, the people were greatly pinched, during the crisis of 1857, because the Anglo-Saxon race could not afford so many plum-puddings, and their currants remained unsold.

Rounding the western end of Brazza, a deep channel, terminating in a circular harbor, as regular as if cut by art, and sunk in the heart of the hills, opened unexpectedly on our right. This was Milne, the port of the island, a silent, solitary, tranquil place, which even our arrival did not appear to excite in the least. We halted here but a short time, and then sped away to Lesina, where Titian is said to have been banished for some years, through the strait where, in 1811, four English vessels defeated the French fleet of eleven, touched during the night at Curzola, and by the next sunrise were at anchor in the harbor of Ragusa. This is, historically, the most interesting point on the Dalmatian coast. A few scattering Greeks and Illyrians founded here, in the year 636, a little Republic—not bigger than the estate of many an English nobleman—which survived the fall of empires, and the political storms of nearly twelve hundred years. It was finally wiped out in January, 1808, by a decree of Napoleon, who bestowed upon Marshal Marmont, the commander of the French troops in Dal matia, the title of Duke of Ragusa. Tributary both to Venice and the Ottoman Empire, it still preserved its municipal independence; and, besides its commerce, which at one time employed 360 vessels and 4,500 sailors, found leisure to cultivate literature and the sciences. Cœur de Lion, returning from Palestine, was entertained as a guest by the Senate, after his shipwreck on the neighboring island of Lacroma, where he built a church to commemorate his escape. The Republic also sheltered King Sigismund of Hungary, after his defeat by Sultan Bajazet, and three times afforded succor to George Castriot, or Scanderbeg, the last gallant chieftain of the Grecian Empire. Ragusa, in short, has stood unharmed, like a bit of moss in the forest, while every tree has been blasted or uprooted, and many a chance sunbeam of history has struck athwart its secluded life. Napoleon, the Destroyer and Builder, set his foot upon it and crushed it at last.

The captain gave us two hours for a ramble on the shore, and we set out for Old Ragusa, which is between two and three miles distant. The present port is a landlocked basin, shut in by sweeping hills, which are feathered to their summits with olive groves, while the gardens below sparkle with their boskage of orange and lemon trees. The hills are dotted with country houses, many of them stately structures of the republican time, but all more or less dilapidated. Marks of the French and subsequent Russian invasion are seen on all sides. Roofless houses, neglected gardens, and terraced fields lying fallow, gave a melancholy air of decay to the landscape. Climbing a long hill from the harbor, we crossed the comb of a promontory, and saw the sea before us, while down in a hollow of the coast, on our left, swam in the blue morning vapors the spires and fortresses of Old Ragusa. Far above it, on the summit of the overlooking mountains, shone the white walls of another fort, the road to which ascended the steep slope in fourteen zigzags. It was a warm picture, full of strong color, and sharp, decided outline. Clumps of aloe clung to the rocks below; oranges hung heavy over the garden walls above, and in a sunny spot some young palms were growing. We only succeeded in reaching the outskirts of Old Ragusa, whence we overlooked the falling city, upon whose main street, paved with slippery marble, no horse is yet allowed to set his foot.

I did not find the Ragusan costumes—at least those which I saw—quite so picturesque as those of the other Dalmatian ports. The race, however, is mainly the same. Indeed, it has been ascertained that of all the inhabitants of Dalmatia, fifteen out of sixteen are of Slavic blood. They are a medium-sized people, but tough, hardy, and of considerable muscular strength. Their mode of life is quite primitive. Every family has its patriarchal head, and the sons bring their wives home to the paternal hut, until the natural increase crowds them out of its narrow bounds. The mother takes her unweaned infant to the field with her, and lays it down on a soft stone to sleep. They still cultivate witches, and believe in demons and magical spells. Among the Morlaks, the bridegroom, until very recently, was obliged to catch his bride in a public race, like Hypolitus, or the Tartar bachelors. Blood revenge, as among the Corsicans, exists in spite of the law, and the wandering bard, singing the exploits of his heroic ancestors, goes from village to village, as in the days of Homer.

Continuing our voyage southward along the coast, we reached in the afternoon the *Bocca di Cattaro*, the entrance to one of the wildest and most wonderful harbors in the world. Austria has held on with the tenacity of a terrier to all the Venetian settlements along the Adriatic upon which she could lay hands. Look at the map, and you will see how, from Zara to Budua, she has seized a strip of coast, between two and three hundred miles in length, while its breadth wavers between five and thirty miles. Bosnia, the Herzegowina, and Montenegro have now no communication with the sea, except through Austrian ports. In two places this strip is interrupted by narrow wedges of the Turkish territory, which come down to the sea—of course at points where no seaport can be created. Austria has taken good care of that. We swept close under a beetling cliff of mellow-tinted rock, up which rose, bastion over bastion, the heavy white walls of a fortress. The mouth of the bay is somewhat less than a mile in breadth, with an island, also fortified, lying athwart it. We entered a deep, land-locked sheet of water, shut in by mountains. In the south-east rose a lofty peak of the Montenegrin Alps, its summit glittering with snow. "Where do you suppose Cattaro lies?" asked the captain. "Somewhere in this bay," I answered. "No," said he, "it is just under yon snowy peak." "But how are we to get there?" "Wait, and you will see!" was the answer.

We touched at Castelnuovo, which was in the sixteenth

century the capital of the Herzegowina. It was taken by the Spaniards, the allies of Admiral Doria, who, after building the massive fortress which bears their name to this day, were in turn driven out by Khaireddin Barbarossa, the Turkish Admiral. Passing the warm, amphitheatric hills, rich with groves of olive, chestnut, and sycamore, we made for the southern end of the bay, which all at once opened laterally on the left, disclosing a new channel, at the head of which lay the little town of Perasto. Mountains, grey, naked, and impassably steep, hung over it. As we approached, a church and monastery, which seemed to float upon the water, rose to view. They were built upon rocks in the bay—quaint, curious structures, with bulging green domes upon their towers. After passing Perasto, where the captain joyfully pointed out his house (a white handkerchief was waving from the window), the bay curved eastward and then southward, actually cleaving the mountain range to the very foot of the central peak of snows. On all sides the bare steeps arose almost precipitously from the water to the height of 3,000 feet. We were on a mountain lake; the fiercest storms of the Adriatic could not disturb the serenity of these waters. They are barricaded against any wind that blows. At the extremity of the lake, under the steepest cliffs, lay Cattaro, with its sharp angled walls of defence climbing the mountain to a height of nearly a thousand feet above it. The sun had long since set on the town, although the mountains burned with a tawny lustre all along the eastern shore. We steamed up and cast anchor in front of the sea-wall.

We landed at once, in order to take advantage of the

vanishing daylight. A wild design for a moment came into my head—to take horses and a guard, ride up the mountain and over to Cettigne, the capital of Montenegro, and back again by sunrise—but unfortunately there was no moon, and I should have had the danger and the fatigue for nothing. Cattaro is a fortress, and the town, squeezed within the narrow limits of the walls, has the deepest and darkest streets. We discovered nothing of note in the course of our ramble. The place, I suspect, is much as it was when Venice defended and Khaireddin besieged it. We stood a moment in the public square to see the overhanging mountains burning with vermillion and orange in the last splendor of sunset, and then threaded the town to the further gate, where a powerful spring of the purest beryl-colored mountain water gushes out from under the walls.

A native Cattarese, who spoke some Italian, hung on to our skirts, in order to get a little money as a guide. "Find me some natives of Montenegro!" I said to him. "Oh, they wear the same dress as the Dalmatians," said he, "but you can tell them by the cross on their caps." Soon afterward we encountered an old man and his son, both of whom had a gilded Greek cross on the front of the red fez which they wore. "Here are two!" exclaimed the guide. He then stopped them, and without more ado, pulled off the old man's fez, showed us the cross, and opened the folds of the cap, where a second cross and a number of zwanzigers were hidden. "Here they keep their money," he explained. The old fellow took the whole proceeding very good-humoredly, and was delighted when I said to him

"*S bogo!*" (the Illyrian for "good-bye!") at parting. Soon afterwards we met some *pandours* or irregular soldiers, of the Vladika of Montenegro. They wore a spread-eagle on their caps, in addition to the cross. Our guide stopped them, and informed them (as I guessed) that we wanted to look at them. A proud straightening of the body, a haughty toss of the head, and a glance of mingled dignity and defiance was the only answer, as they held their way. I was delighted with this natural exhibition of their self esteem, though it had been called forth in so offensive a way.

I heard very contradictory accounts respecting the present Vladika (Prince) of Montenegro. Our captain spoke of him as a highly-accomplished man, with a marked taste for literature, and rather sneered at his wife, the daughter of a Trieste merchant, who pinched himself to give her a dowry of a million of zwanzigers (about $168,000) and thereby secure the hand of Prince Danilo. On the other hand, an English officer who visited Cettigne, informed me that the Vladika is a rough, boorish, and stupid fellow, and that his wife is handsome, accomplished, and fascinating. I should judge the latter report to be the correct one, as we are beginning to hear the most arbitrary and brutal acts charged against the Vladika. His predecessor was a Bishop, which did not prevent him from being a capital shot and a good horseman. It is easy to see that this little robber State will not be very long-lived, and that it will finally fall into the claws of Austria. But she will neither get it nor hold it without fighting.

We lay all night at Cattaro. So completely is the place

inclosed that the climate is different from that of Castel nuovo. The night was very cold, and as we steamed off in the morning we found the bay covered with a light sheet of ice from shore to shore. Outside, the air was mild and delightful. A short distance beyond the Bocca di Cattaro, we passed Budua, another Venetian colony, and the last Austrian port. Early in the afternoon we reached Antivari, in Albania, the seaport of the large city of Scutari, which is nearly a day's journey in the interior. The coast grew wilder and bolder; huge, tawny mountains soared from the sea to the clouds which rested on their snow-streaked summits, and the signs of habitation became less and less frequent. The next morning we were at Durazzo, a singularly picturesque town on a hillside defended by massive Venetian walls, above which shoots the slender shaft of a minaret. Thence we ran along under the Acroceraunian mountains, whose topmost peak, Mount Tschika, a shining wedge of snow, serves as a landmark for all this part of the Albanian coast. At Avlona, we saw the huge fortress built by Ali Pasha, the Turkish city in the rear, with its ten minarets, and the old Greek town and acropolis crowning the mountain ridge above. Acroceraunia is a wild and gloomily grand region, full of glorious subjects for the landscape painter.

Our deck now began to be covered with picturesque forms—Turkish soldiers, Albanians, with white kirtles and whole arsenals in their belts, Greek and Moslem merchants. Among them I noticed a Bosnian, whose white turban and green jacket denoted particular holiness. Accosting him in Arabic, which he spoke imperfectly, I found he was a *hadji*, having made the grand pilgrimage to all the holy places. We quite agreed upon the subject of Damascus, the mere mention of which brought the water into his mouth. He prayed with praiseworthy regularity, at the stated times, generally finding the direction of Mecca within four points. One evening, however, while we were at anchor, the ship drifted around with the tide, and the hadji, not noticing this, commenced praying with his face towards Rome. I at once perceived this scandalous mistake and interrupted the devotions of the holy man, to set him right. "In the name of God!" he exclaimed; "but you are right. This comes of trusting the Frank vessels."

CHAPTER III.

FIRST DAYS IN GREECE

Our steamer lay four days at Corfu, during which time we took up our quarters in a hotel on shore. The days were warm and sunny, and we had no need of fire except in the evenings. Corfu is one of the pleasantest of the Mediterranean islands. Particularly agreeable to me was the English order, cleanliness, and security which prevail here, as everywhere else under the shadow of the British flag. Many of the Ionians are dissatisfied with the English protectorate, and would willingly be incorporated into the Hellenic Kingdom. I venture to say that, if this were done, five years would not elapse before the islands would be as insecure, the internal improvements as much neglected, and the Government as corrupt, as that of Greece itself. There are two things without which the English cannot exist—civil order and good roads; and they are just the things which Greece most wants.

During a short excursion into the interior of the island, I was struck by the indolence and lack of enterprise of the inhabitants. We drove for miles through groves of splendid olive-trees, many of them upwards of five hundred years old, and bending under their weight of ungathered fruit. Thousands of barrels of oil were slowly wasting, for want of a little industry. I was told, to be sure, that the Albanians had been sent for to assist in gathering in the crop, and would come over as soon as their own work was completed; the Corfiotes appeared to be in the meantime resting on their oars. The currant crop had been much damaged by violent rains, and the people, therefore, complained of hard times; but there always will be hard times where thrift and forethought are so scarce. Col. Talbot, the Resident for Cephalonia, informed me that the natives of that island, on the contrary, are very industrious and economical.

We left Corfu at midnight, and by sunrise the next morning reached Prevesa, situated just inside the mouth of the Ambracian Gulf, and opposite to the low point on which stood Actium. Through the narrow strait by which we had entered, fled Cleopatra in her gilded galley, followed, ere long, by the ruined Antony. The ruins of Nicopolis (the City of Victory), which Cæsar built to commemorate the battle, are scattered over the isthmus between the sea and the gulf, about three miles north of Prevesa. Here we took on board His Excellency Abd-er-Rakhman Bey, military Governor of Candia, and his suite, consisting of an ugly adjutant, a stupid secretary, and two wicked-looking pipe-bearers. The latter encamped on the quarter-deck, but the Bey took a first-cabin passage. As he spoke no language but Turkish, our communication was rather limited, although he evinced a strong desire to be social with us. His supply of oranges was distributed without stint, and one day at dinner he surprised the lady-passenger by sending for a hard-boiled egg, which he carefully shelled, stuck upon the end of his knife, and handed across the table to her. He was particularly careful not to touch pork, but could not withstand the seductions of wine, which he drank in great quantities. In proportion as he drank, he breathed asthmatically, and became confidential. At such times, he would complain of the enormous expense of his household, occasioned by his having three wives. One he had married because he loved her, another because she wanted to marry him, and the third he had bought at Trebizond for twenty thousand piastres. He was obliged to keep thirty servants, ten for each wife, and the three dames, he gave us to understand, were not particularly harmonious in their mutual relations. Thereupon the Bey sighed, and, I have no doubt, wished he was a Frank.

We touched at Santa Maura, the capital of Leucadia. A single palm-tree and some chimneys rose above the heavy Venetian walls of the town, which frown defiance at the old Turkish fortress across the strait. The island appears to be well cultivated; we sailed for several hours under its western shore, which falls in steep masses of pale red rock to the sea. Sappho's Leap, of course, was the great point of interest. It is a precipice about two hundred feet in height, near the southern extremity of the island, and, I should judge, well adapted for the old lady's purpose. I must confess that, in spite of Sappho's genius—and I believe her to be the only genuine female poet for two thousand years before and after her time—her theatrical death does not move me now. It once did. At the age of seventeen, I wrote a poem, wildly thrilling and full of gushing pathos, on "The Death of Sappho." Of course, I represented her as a young and beautiful girl. But it makes a difference, when you know that she was old enough to be Phaon's mother, and that, although Alcæus sings of her as the "violet-haired and sweetly-smiling Sappho," the probability is that she was sallow, scraggy, and ill-favored, as are all Grecian women at the age of fifty.

The fact is, the mist of antiquity enlarges, glorifies, and transfigures everything. As it was in the days of Solon and Pisistratus, so it is now. The Heroic Age is far behind us; the race of demigods has disappeared from the earth. Perhaps it is as well that the Past is so doubtful, that we look upon its figures as on the procession of a marble frieze, not applying to them the littleness of our own everyday life. We should else lose somewhat of our veneration for them, and thereby, for what is noble in our own time. Plato in patent-leather boots—and yet, no doubt, Plato conformed to the petty fashions of his time—would not be for us the honey-lipped sage of the Academy. Every man of those old Greeks had his faults, his jealousies, his sins— not less than our own, but rather more. The historic interest attaching to a place, is one thing; the emotion which it inspires in the traveller's mind, is another. When the latter does not come unsought, it is a pitiful hypocrisy to counterfeit it, and I therefore promise the reader, that, as I do not consider the ancient Greeks a whit better than the Anglo-Saxons, although in specialities they obtained a higher development, I shall concern myself with them as little as possible.

Cephalonia now rose before us, with the steep, blue hills of Ithaca on the left, and at sunset we were at anchor in the spacious Gulf of Argostoli. The town is built along one side of a circular bay, and makes a very pretty appearance from the water. Here we landed Col. Talbot, the Resident of the island, a very agreeable and intelligent gentleman, who appears to be quite popular among the natives. During the night we touched at Zante, and by sunrise lay at anchor off Missolonghi, renowned through the names of Bozzaris and Byron. The bay is so shallow that large vessels cannot approach nearer than four or five miles, owing to which cause we were unable to go ashore. The town is built on level, marshy ground, at the foot of the Acarnanian Mountains, yet, in spite of its situation, it is said to be quite healthy. Among our passengers was a native of Missolonghi, a gigantic Greek, by the name of "George," the avant-courier of a Russian nobleman. He remembered Byron in his Greek costume, very well. His father was killed during the siege, himself, mother, and sisters taken by the Egyptians and sent as slaves to Cairo, whence they only escaped after seven years' servitude. After serving as courier for many years, he had come back to Missolonghi to settle, and had laid out his earnings in a currant plantation; which speculation, on account of the vine-sickness and heavy rains, turned out so badly that he was obliged to go back to his old business. He looked like an honest fellow, and in spite of his extreme obsequiousness and constant use of "*gnädiger herr*" (which came from having lived in Vienna), I agreed to employ him until we should get settled in Athens.

On the southern or Achaïan shore of the Gulf of Corinth, sixteen miles distant, is Patras, one of the most flourishing ports in Greece. The mediæval town, as well as the broad, rich plain behind it, were completely laid waste by the troops of Ibrahim Pasha, and only the fortress, which crowns a steep height, and from which the Greeks never were able to dislodge the Turkish garrison, even when all the rest of the Morea was in their own hands, has been spared. From its walls, on the warm, cloudless afternoon of our visit, we overlooked the beautiful Achaïan plain, whose olive orchards, barely old enough to give a faint, silvery gleam to the landscape, showed how complete the desolation had been. At our feet lay the white, bustling, new town, a very hive of industry; then the dark, dazzling purple of the Gulf, beyond which the stupendous headlands of Kakiscala and Arássova rose like colossal pyramids.

At Patras, I set foot, for the first time, on the mainland of Greece, and nowhere could a stranger receive a more favorable impression of Modèrn Hellas. The streets are broad, regular, and kept in very good order, the houses comfortable and substantial, the bazaars crowded, and the shops of the mechanics, open to the street, present a succession of busy pictures. Few idlers were to be seen; even the shoemaker was putting out a row of soles to dry, in the principal street, and some ropemakers were reeling in another. Meeting the Bey, who was walking about in state, followed at a respectful distance by his attendants, we invited him to accompany us to a garden outside the town, whither George proposed conducting us The unusual procession attracted a number of spectators, and we were followed by a large crowd of boys to the outskirts of Patras. The garden was of considerable extent, and filled with superb orange and lemon trees, boughs of which were broken and laid before us. The attendants brought a table, the Bey lit his pipe, and three of the delights of the Orient—shade, smoke, and verdure—were at once supplied. In an arbor near us were a party of Greeks, the gentlemen in crimson jackets and leggings and snowy fustanellas, and the ladies in the coquettish little fez, with its golden tassel, which gives such a charm to black eyes and black hair.

The next morning we passed between the fortresses of Morea and Roumelia, touched at Lepanto (the ancient Naupactus), and found ourselves fairly within that long, land-locked gulf, whose shores are mountains of immortal name. The day was of a crystalline clearness, and the long, rhythmical undulations, the grouped or scattered peaks of those interlinking mountain-chains, which seem to have arisen, like the walls of Thebes, to the sound of music, were as clearly and delicately cut upon the blue plane of the air as the figures of a frieze of Phidias. As we stood across towards Vostitza, the snowy hump of Parnassus rose above his tawny, barren buttresses, crowning the Dorian hills. Further eastward, the faintly-streaked summit or Helicon, whose base thrust a bold headland into the gulf; still further, floating in the dimmest distance, Cithæron, and on the southern shore, before us, the wild, dark masses of the Erymanthian hills, sloping away towards the white zone of Cyllene, whose forests sheltered the young Jupiter. Apart from the magic of these names, the Corinthian Gulf is a noble piece of water, deep, sheltered, and with few impediments to navigation. But how deserted! During the day we spent in traversing its whole length, crossing twice from shore to shore, we did not see three vessels. At Galaxidi, near the foot of Parnassus, however, shipbuilding is carried on to some extent, the wood being brought down from the Dorian forests. The Greek vessels are all very small, and the largest of those on the stocks at Galaxidi would not exceed two hundred tons.

By sunset, we were anchored at Lutraki, on the Isthmus of Corinth, at the foot of a spur of the Geranean Hills. Corinth and its grand acropolis lay to the south, eight or ten miles distant, guarding the entrance into the Peloponnesus; the Nemean Hills, the boundary of Argos, rose duskily in the rear. A chilly *tramontana*, or northwind, was blowing, and the barren, rocky, desolate shore suggested Norway rather than Greece. Notwithstanding Lutraki is the port of transit for the western side of the Isthmus, which is here only four or five miles in breadth, the place consists of just three houses. A warm mineral spring, with decided healing properties, gushes out of the earth, on the shore of the Gulf, but nobody can make use of it, because there is no house erected, and no possibility of getting a bed or a meal in the whole town. That evening, at dinner, the Greeks told us how the road across the isthmus is guarded with troops, because only two years previous sixty thousand drachmas ($10,000) belonging to the Government were taken by robbers. Also, that the same gentlemen had quite recently entered Corinth, plundered the house of a merchant and carried off his little son whom they retained in the mountains until the father raised an immense ransom. I began to find my respect for Modern Greece rapidly diminishing.

The next morning we were transported across the isthmus in shabby, second-hand carriages. The country is a wilderness, overgrown with mastic, sage, wild olive, and the pale green Isthmian pine. Companies of soldiers, in grey Bavarian uniforms, guarded the road. The highest part of the isthmus is not more than a hundred feet above the sea, and it is estimated that a ship canal could be cut through for about two millions of dollars. Kalamaki, on the eastern side, is a miserable little village, with this advantage over Lutraki, that it possesses a khan. The steamer from Piræus, which was to take us thither, had not arrived, and towards noon the pangs of hunger compelled us to visit this khan. We found the Greek passengers already assembled there, and regaling themselves on the various delicacies displayed at the door. There were fish of various kinds, swimming in basins of rancid oil, but they had been cooked two or three days previous, and were not to be eaten. We had more success with the bread, but the wine resembled a mixture of vinegar and tar, and griped the stomach with sharp claws. The appearance of the cheese, which was packed into the skin of a black hog, who lay on his back with his snout and four feet in the air, and a deep gash in his belly, in order to reach the doubtful composition, was quite sufficient. We at last procured a few eggs and some raw onions, both of which are protected by nature from the contact of filthy hands, and therefore cannot be so easily spoiled.

I went into some of the rooms of the khan, which offered simply bare walls, a dirty floor, and no window, for the accommodation of travellers. An Albanian Greek and his wife, who took their breakfast in one of these rooms, were obliged to pay half a dollar for the use thereof. The Albanian had been for some years settled in Athens, where he was doing business as a small shopkeeper. At length, he felt the need of a wife, and, true to the clannish spirit of the Greeks, went off to his native Janina to procure one. There were plenty of better educated and handsomer women in Athens, but he preferred the stout mass of health, stupidity, and pitiable ignorance which he was taking home, because she belonged to his own tribe. I do not suppose she ever before wore a Christian dress, or ate otherwise than with her fingers, and he was obliged to look after and assist her, as if she had been a three-years-old child. In the morning, he superintended her toilette, helping her to wash and dress herself; at table, he placed the food upon her plate and showed her how to eat it; and he never dared to leave her for a moment through the day, lest she should make some absurd mistake. I admired his unremitting care and patience, no less than her perfect reliance on his instructions. In fact, it was quite touching at times to see her questioning, half-frightened look say to him: "What must I do now?" If he sought a healthy mother for his children, he certainly found one, but I suspect that is about the only advantage he will derive from his union with her

It was noon before we embarked, and a violent north wind retarded our slow old steamer. We ran across the Saronic Gulf, between the islands of Salamis and Egina, catching a glimpse of Megara on the right, while the Acropolis of Corinth sank and grew dim behind us. But every body knows the letter of Sulpicius to Cicero, rhymed by Byron, and I shall not quote it again. On Egina I saw, in the last rays of the setting sun, the temple of Jupiter Panhellenius. Turning to one of the Greeks on board (an ex-member of the Legislature of the Ionian Islands), I pointed it out to him. "Ah," said he, "I did not know there was a temple there!"—and yet, thence came the Eginetan marbles. As we turned the corner of Salamis, the Acropolis of Athens detached itself from the shadows wrapping the base of Hymettus, and shone with a beckoning gleam. In half an hour more, it was dark. The wind blew fiercely, the moon shone cold, and we moved slowly into the harbor of the Piræus.

The competition of the boatmen was something frightful. George, however, shielded us, and in the course of time we landed with our baggage. Lumbering carriages were in waiting to take us to Athens. Nobody called for passports, and a huge official, with baggy island trowsers and a smiling, rotund face, turned his back when our trunks were brought ashore, in consideration of the moderate fee of sixteen cents.

Now we set off for Athens, shivering in the sharp wind, and looking out on either hand on bare, bleak fields, lighted by the full moon. After an hour, some olive-trees appeared, and we crossed the Cephissus; then bare fields again, bleaker and colder than ever. At last the ground became more uneven, broke into detached hills on our right, over which towered the Acropolis—there was no mistaking that —and we recognised without difficulty, the Hill of the Nymphs, the Areopagus, and the Muscion. Now commenced the town itself—low, shabby houses, streets lighted only by the moon. Here, thought I, is a terrible disenchantment. Can anything be more forlorn and desolate? The chill, grey hue of all things, the bareness and bleakness of our approach, the appearance of the modern town, the cold, piercing air, made, all together, the most disheartening impression upon me.

But when we got into Hermes street, and thence to our hotel (*de l' Orient*), things looked much more cheerful and promising. Once inside that edifice, we forgot our disappointment—forgot Athens, indeed—for a Christmas dinner awaited us, and there were **other places and other people to be remembered.**

CHAPTER IV.

ON THE ACROPOLIS.

Our first Athenian day was bright and fair, and what we saw during a walk to the temple of Jupiter Olympus was entirely sufficient to remove the chill impression of the previous night. There are few towns of its size in the world as lively as Athens. We saw almost the worst of it on entering from the Piræus. All the northern portion, which is newer, is very substantially built, and has a comfortable air of growth and improvement. As half the population may be said to live out of doors, the principal streets are always thronged, and the gorgeous raiment of the dandy palikars brightens and adorns them amazingly. It is not the Orient, by a great deal; yet it is far removed from the soberness of Europe. Indeed, the people speak of Europe as a continent outside of Greece. Neither is Athens particularly Greek, with its French fashions and German architecture. It is simply gay, bizarre, fantastic—a salad in which many heterogeneous substances combine to form a palatable whole.

I found one old friend—François, the false Janissary, the intrepid guide, the armed confronter of robbers, and the enthusiastic spouter of Homer, whose mingled wit, activity, intelligence, and ferocity, have been described at length by the Countess de Gasparin, the Rev. Dr. Strauss, and your humble servant. The day after our arrival, his Albanian nose and formidable moustache entered my room, followed by himself and his voice of surprise and welcome. As a natural consequence, he was booked as the future companion of our Hellenic journeys, and we took up our quarters in his house. Through him, I at once procured from Pittakys, the Conservator of Antiquities, a ticket of admission to the Acropolis, and we devoted the next day to our first visit.

Fortunately—as so much of one's satisfaction depends on the luck of his first impression—the day was a gift from heaven; not a wind blowing, not a cloud floating, and so warm that we threw open all our windows. Hymettus, Corydallus, and Parnes melted into vapory purple in the distance, but the nearer hills shone clear against the bluest of Grecian skies. François came at noon to accompany us. All Athens was in the streets, and the crimson jackets and clean white fustanellas of the palikars sparkled far and near through the dismal throng of Frank dresses. We passed down Hermes street to the outskirts of the city, in order first to visit the Temple of Theseus. This edifice, the best-preserved of all ancient temples, stands on a mound at the foot of the Areopagus, on its western side, overlooking part of the modern city. Its outer colonnade of Doric pillars, tinted with a rich golden stain, is entire; the cella is for the most part so, and little but the roof is wanting. It is small, but very beautiful, and with such a background!—the olive groves of the Academy, Colonos and Parnes.

Our way was through the depression between the Areopagus and the Pnyx, but François took us aside to show us the smooth, rocky slant on the Nympheon, down which the sterile dames of Athens were wont to slide, in order to remove their reproach. The pregnant women also performed the same ceremony, it is said, in order to ascertain the sex of the unborn child, through the inclination of the body to the right or left. It is an exposed steep plane of native rock, with a rough seat at the top, polished very thoroughly by the action of so much expectant maternity. F. seated himself and slid down, in order to show us how the act was performed, affirming that the belief still exists, and that many of the Athenian women of the present day continue the practice.

At last we had climbed the bare surface of the hill, and stood before the ancient entrance of the Acropolis—a sloping pylon, now closed by a wooden grating. An arched way through a Venetian wall on the right admitted us to a sort of ruinous terrace, overlooking the theatre of Herodes Atticus, which has recently been excavated down to the floor of the arena, and now shows its semicircular tiers of seats up to the topmost gallery. Here we stood directly under the south-western corner of the wall of the Acropolis, over the shoulder of which, like an ivory wedge in a field of lapis-lazuli, gleamed a corner of the pediment of the Parthenon. Who could stand looking down into a theatre of the time of Hadrian, when the Periclesian temple of Pallas Athene beckoned to him from the sky?

We turned back, climbed a little further, entered a gateway, exhibited our ticket (a month's permission to visit the Acropolis), and then passed through another wall to the broad marble staircase leading directly up to the Propylæa of the Acropolis. This staircase has been cleared of the rubbish of sixteen centuries, the dislodged stones have been partially replaced, and the work of restoration is gradually and carefully progressing, so that in the course of time the ancient entrance will be almost reconstructed. On the right hand, the steps for pedestrians remain in their original position, and in the centre are fragments of the inclined plane, roughened by parallel grooves, for the feet of horses and the wheels of chariots. Above us, tenderly enshrined in the blue air, rose the beautiful Doric pillars of the Propylæa, bereft of capital and architrave, but scarcely needing such a crown to perfect their exquisite symmetry.

"You are now going up the same steps where Pericles walked," said François. Not only Pericles, but the curled Alcibiades, the serene Plato, the unshaken Socrates, the divine Phidias, Sophocles and Æschylus, Herodotus and Themistocles, and—but why mention names, when the full sunshine of that immortal era streams upon our pathway? And what is it to me that they have walked where I now walk? Let me not be wheedled out of my comfortable indifference by the rhythmic ringing of such names. The traveller comes here expecting to be impressed by the associations of the spot, and by a strong effort he succeeds in impressing himself. Repeat the same names for him elsewhere, and he will produce the same effect. But for me, I am hardened against conventional sentiment; I have seen too much to be easily moved; I can resist the magic of ancient memories, no matter how classic. What is it to me that Pericles walked up these steps—that the gilded robes of Aspasia swept these Pentelican slabs—that Phidias saw the limbs of a god in the air, or Sophocles chanted a chorus as he walked? They were men, and I am a man, too—probably in many respects as good as they. Had I lived in their time, I should no doubt have looked upon them without the least awe—have slapped them on the back, and invited them to dinner. Now why should their ghosts shake me with weak emotion, and rob me of my cool judgment? No. I shall be indifferent.

So meditating, I walked up the steps. When we reached the first range of pillars stretched across the stairway, and came upon the level of the abutments which project on either hand, we stopped. On the end of the right terrace stands the little temple of *Nike Apteros*, or Wingless Victory, which has been recovered, piece by piece, and re-erected in its original form. Opposite to it is a massive square pedestal, twenty feet high, on which once stood, according to antiquarian surmise, equestrian statues of the sons of Xenophon. The little temple is a jewel of a structure not half so large as that of Vesta at Rome, and consists only of a cella with four Ionic columns at each end. Nevertheless, it lightens wonderfully the heavy masses of masonry against which it stands, and though neither in the lines of its erection, nor in any other important respect, harmonizing with the colonnades of the Propylæa, I defy any one to show wherein it does not harmonize with the general impression produced by this majestic front. I restrained my impatience awhile, to view it, and was well repaid by the sight of the bas-relief of Victory untying her sandals, the conjectured work of Phidias.

The pillared portal, one colonnade rising above another, as the rock ascends, now received us. Capitals and architraves are gone, except those of the last rank, and huge blocks of the superb marble lie heaped in the passages between the columns. Beautiful as these are, lightly as their tapering stems rise against the blue vault, the impression created by the Propylæa is cheerful and elevating. And when you turn, looking down through the fluted vista, over the Areopagus, over the long plain of the Cephissus, shimmering silverly with the olive groves of the Academy, to the pass of Daphne and the blue hills of Salamis, you feel no longer the desolation of ruin, but inhale, with quiet enjoyment, the perfect harmony of the picture.

The Propylæa still form a portal which divides two worlds. You leave modern and mediæval associations behind you, and are alone with the Past. Over the ramparts of the Acropolis, you see no more of the mountains or the distant Ægean islands than the oldest Greek—large outlines, simple tints, and no object distinct enough to tell whether it be modern or ancient. The last of the portals is passed: you are on the summit alone with the Parthenon. You need no pointing finger: your eye turns, instinctively, to where it stands. Over heaps of ruin, over a plain buried under huge fragments of hewn and sculptured marble—drums of pillars, pedestals, capitals, cornices, friezes, triglyphs, and sunken panel-work—a wilderness of mutilated Art—it rises between you and the sky, which forms its only background, and against which every scar left by the infidel generations shows its gash. Broken down to the earth in the middle, like a ship which has struck and parted, with the roof, cornices, and friezes mostly gone, and not a column unmutilated; and yet with the tawny gold of two thousand years staining its once spotless marble, sparkling with snow-white marks of shot and shell, and with its soaring pillars imbedded in the dark-blue ether (and here the sky seems blue only because they need such a background), you doubt for a moment whether the melancholy of its ruin, or the perfect and majestic loveliness which shines through that ruin, is most powerful.

I did not stop to solve this doubt. Once having looked upon the Parthenon, it was impossible to look elsewhere, and I drew nearer and nearer, finding a narrow lane through the chaos of fragments piled almost as high as my head, until I stood below the western front. I looked up at the Doric shafts, colossal as befitted the shrine of a goddess, yet tender and graceful as flower-stems, upholding without effort the massive entablature and the shattered pediment, in one corner of which two torsos alone remain of all the children of Phidias, and—to my confusion I must confess it—all my fine resolves were forgotten. I was seized with an overpowering mixture of that purest and loftiest admiration which is almost the same thing as love, and of unmitigated grief and indignation. Well—consider me a fool if you like—but, had I been alone, I should have cast myself prone upon the marble pavement, and exhausted, in some hysterical way, the violence of this unexpected passion. As it was, I remained grimly silent, not venturing to speak, except when François, pointing to the despoiled pediment, said: "All the other statues were carried away by Lord Elgin." The strong Anglo-Saxon expression I then made use of, in connexion with Lord Elgin's name, was not profane, under such provocation, and was immediately pardoned by the woman at my side.

We ascended the steps to the floor of the temple, walked over its barren pavement past the spot where stood the statue of ivory and gold, past the traces of hideous Byzantine frescoes, to the centre, where the walls and colonnades on either hand are levelled to the very floor, and sat down in the marble chairs of the ancient priests, to contemplate the wreck in silence. Oh, unutterable sorrow!—for all the ages to come can never restore the glory which has here been destroyed. Ye may smile, ye yet unshaken columns, secure in your immortality of beauty, but ye cannot take away the weight of that reproach uttered by your fallen brethren. Man built them, man ruined them, but he can no more recreate them than he can rebeget the child which he has lost. In their perfect symmetry was solved the enigma of that harmony which is the very being of God and the operation of His laws. These blocks of sunny marble were piled upon each other to the chorus of the same song which the seasons sing in their ordered round, and the planets in their balanced orbits. The cheerful gods are dethroned; the rhythmic pulsations of the jubilant religion which inspired this immortal work have died away, and Earth will never see another Parthenon.

The air was perfectly still, the sky calm as Summer overhead, and, as we sat in the marble chairs, we looked out over the ruins and the parapet of the Acropolis, to the purple hills of Pentelicus and Parnes in the north and west, and to the Ægean Sea, flashing in the sunshine like a pavement of silver between the shores of Attica and Ægina Poros and Hydra, in the distance. The glorious landscape, bathed in all beautiful tints, and filling the horizon with swelling curves and long, vanishing outlines, wore that soothed and tranquil air which a day of Summer, falling suddenly in the lap of Winter, always brings with it. But there was no solace for me in the sunny repose of the Grecian world below. I sat in a temple dedicated to Eternal Sorrow—

"So beautiful, if Sorrow had not made
Sorrow more beautiful than Beauty's self"—

and a grief, in which there was no particle of selfishness, overcame me. Is it egotism to mention these things? Or can I tell you what the Parthenon still is, better than by confessing how it impressed me? If you want feet and yards, cubic measure, history and architectural technicalities, you shall have them—but not to-day. Let me indulge my sacred fury!

After awhile, Braisted desperately lit a cigar, saying: "I must have something between my teeth, or I shall grind them to pieces. I would destroy all the later architecture of Europe, except the Duomo at Milan, to restore this." So, almost, would I. For this is the true temple of Divinity. Its perfect beauty is the expression of love and joy, such as never yet dwelt in the groined arches of Gothic aisles, or the painted domes of Roman worship

But Ruskin says that Grecian architecture is atheistic," whispers a neophyte of the fashionable school. Then tell Ruskin, who is so sagacious in some things, so capricious in others, that, in endeavoring to be terse and original, he has simply been absurd. I will not say a word against the solemnities of Gothic Art, which he declares to be the only religious form of architecture; but I ask, is there no joy, no cheerfulness, no comfort, no hopeful inspiration, in our religion? If there is, God has no better temple on earth than the Parthenon.

Atheistic? Prove it, and you glorify Atheism. You may take models of the Parthenon, at home, you may take drawings and photographs, and build up any super-transcendental theory out of such materials. Then come here, stand in the midst of its ruin, listen to the august voice which yet speaks from these sunburnt marbles, and unless you be one of those narrow souls who would botanize upon his mother's grave, you will fall down upon your knees and repent of your sins.

I thought all these thoughts, and a thousand more, while sitting in the marble chair, fronting the vacant pavement of the sanctuary of Pallas Athene. I did not care for the dethroned Pallas, nor her dead worshippers; I thought not of myself nor my race, of Greeks or Americans, of 400 B.C. or 1857 A.D. I was possessed with the spirit of the glorious temple around and above me. And the reflection came, involuntarily: Are not the triumphs of human art the sublimest praises of Him who created the human mind? What conceptions of a Deity guided the hand which daubed yonder barbarous frescoes, and that which raised these perfect pillars? What ancient or modern Saint dares to sneer at *Heathen* Greece, where Socrates spake, and Phidias chiselled, and Ictinus built, glorifying God through the glory of Man for all time to come?

We walked slowly away, and looked down from the northern rampart upon modern Athens, the whole of which lay spread out beneath our feet. It was a depressing—I had almost said disgusting—sight. A company of dirty Greeks were gambling in the street at the foot of the Acropolis; the bells were ringing in the churches, and some bearded priests, with candles in their hands, were chanting nasally and dismally, in slow procession; still further, shabby fiacres moving to and fro, slovenly soldiers in German uniforms, country people with laden asses, and beggars by the wayside. The King's Palace shone bald and broad at the foot of Mount Lycabettus, and the new portion of the city, with its square German houses, stretched scatteringly away over the brown swells, until the eye passed it to rest, relieved, on the olive orchards of Colonos and the fair blue gorges of Mount Parnes.

We went through and around the Erechtheion, and then slowly picked our way through the wilderness of ruin to the Propylæa again. But, as I descended the steps of the Acropolis, I remembered who had walked there—not Pericles, nor Plato, nor Æschylus, nor Demosthenes—but Ictinus, the builder, and Phidias, the sculptor of the Parthenon.

CHAPTER V.

WINTER LIFE IN ATHENS.

Our first week in Athens was spent at the Hotel d'Orient, whose large, dreary, uncomfortable apartments we were glad to leave. The nominal cost of living at this establishment is ten francs a day, for which, however, one only receives a bed and two meals, the latter neither choice nor plentiful. Everything else is an extra charge, at the highest possible rates. Our little fire was kept alive with bits of ancient olive-tree roots, at the rate of a franc and a half the basketful. The landlord and servants endeavored to make up for their awkwardness and neglect by a cringing obsequiousness, which only rendered them more disagreeable. The other **Athenian** hotels, I understand, are conducted on the same principle. Like all other establishments of the kind in the Orient, they are probably good enough in Summer, when fresh air is the traveller's greatest luxury.

At the end of eight days we migrated to the *pandocheion* of François, in a pleasant situation near the University

Here we found less pretentious and more comfortable apartments, and equally good meals, at a reasonable price. The doors and windows were shaky and admitted the wind, it is true, but our sitting-room fronted the south (with a view of the Acropolis and the Areopagus), and could be kept warm without more labor or expense than would be required for an entire dwelling at home. Our principal anxiety was, that the supply of fuel, at any price, might become exhausted. We burned the olive and the vine, the cypress and the pine, twigs of rose-trees and dead cabbage-stalks, for aught I know, to feed our one little sheet-iron stove. For full two months we were obliged to keep up our fire from morning until night. Know ye the land of the cypress and myrtle, where the flowers ever blossom, the beams ever shine? Here it is, with almost snow enough in the streets for a sleighing party, with the Ilissus frozen, and with a tolerable idea of Lapland, when you face the gusts which drive across the Cephissian plain.

As the other guests were Greek, our mode of living was similar to that of most Greek families. We had coffee in the morning, a substantial breakfast about noon, and dinner at six in the evening. The dishes were constructed after French and Italian models, but the meat is mostly goat's flesh. Beef, when it appears, is a phenomenon of toughness. Vegetables are rather scarce. Cow's milk, and butter or cheese therefrom, are substances unknown in Greece. The milk is from goats or sheep, and the butter generally from the latter. It is a white, cheesy material, with a slight flavor of tallow. The wine, when you get it unmixed with resin, is very palatable. We drank that of

Santorin, with the addition of a little water, and found it
an excellent beverage. There are also three German breweries
in Athens, which produce Bavarian beer. Last and
not least, the water, especially that of the fountain of
Callirhoë, is delicious.

The other inmates of our house consisted of a Servian
Greek, with his family, from Thessalonica, and three Greek
ladies from Constantinople. They were all wealthy persons
and probably good specimens of the Greeks of their class.
Two of the ladies received their education in Mrs. Hill's
school, and spoke French passably well. The Servian was
an amiable fellow, devoted to his wife, whom he had
brought to Athens for her health, but who lay for weeks at
the point of death. She had her bedroom scrubbed soon
after our arrival, and slept in it immediately afterward.
Besides spending the coldest of the winter nights in prayer
in a church, her husband brought a couple of priests every
day to help her by the chanting of nasal liturgies. Once
they came in the middle of the night to administer the
sacrament to her. As the poor woman survived her
spiritual treatment, the material remedies administered to
her must have been of remarkable efficacy. Although her
complaint was simply an inflammation of the lungs, the
three Fanariote ladies finally left the house, through dread
of an infection. During their stay, they never appeared at
breakfast, their custom being to remain in a loose undress
until evening. They generally lay in bed until noon,
and Theodori, the chamber-man, carried in the dishes to
them. The afternoon was devoted to dress, and the evening
to cards. Their faces were daily brightened by a new coat

of paint (an almost universal practice among the Greek ladies), and one of them, who was a widow for the second time, was confined to her room two days every fortnight, by an illness, from which she always recovered with an astonishingly jet-black head of hair.

Our intercourse, however, was mainly with the foreign residents, and our Greek acquaintances were made, for the most part, at their houses. The latter have the reputation of being rather clannish, and do not open their doors readily to strangers, though Mr. Hill, Dr. King, and others who have resided in Athens for many years, are on intimate social terms with many Greek families. Whatever the cause may be, there is certainly more reserve exhibited towards foreigners than in most other countries in Europe. The contrast with Sweden and Norway, in this respect, is very great. I made the acquaintance of a number of Greek gentlemen, but very few of them asked me to visit them at their houses.

There is nothing particularly Greek in the physiognomy of Athens. The houses of the better sort are German in outward appearance, while the poorer dwellings resemble those of the Italian villages. A few squat, ancient churches, which have a mellow flavor of the Lower Empire, remain here and there, and the new ones are likewise Byzantine, but of a plainer and less picturesque stamp. The only modern building which has any pretensions to architectural beauty is the University. It is a low structure, well-proportioned, and with an inclosed portico of Pentelican marble, the pillars of which are finely relieved against the soft neutral-orange stain of the inner wall. The old Turkish town was built close against the foot of the Acropolis, on the northern side. Scarcely a single building was left standing at the close of the Revolution, and only a mosque or two (now appropriated to other uses) remain in anything like their former state. The new town has stretched itself northward to the foot of Mount Lycabettus, and northwestward across the plain toward Colonos. For some years, apparently, nothing was done toward regulating and improving the streets, and they present the same tangled labyrinth as in most Oriental towns. The newer portions of the city, however, are well laid out, with broad, handsome streets, and spacious main avenues, converging to the palace as a centre. The city is intersected by two principal thoroughfares—Eolus street, which starts from the Temple of the Winds, at the foot of the Acropolis, and takes a straight course through the city to the plain of the Cephissus, and Hermes street, commencing in the middle of the square in front of the palace, and running south-westward to the foot of the hill on which the Temple of Theseus stands. The course of the latter street is broken in one place by an ancient church, around which it diverges in two arms, leaving the old, brown, charmingly-picturesque little building standing like an island in the midst. Above this interruption, its appearance, with the long white front of the king's palace closing the ascending vista, is astonishingly like that of the *Carl-Johansgade*, in Christiania. Athens is a little smaller than the latter capital, having at present about 30,000 inhabitants. It would be interesting to institute a series of comparisons between Norway and Greece, both new nations of nearly equal age, population, and resources, but peopled with races of very different blood and character.

Except during the severely cold weather, Athens is as lively a town as may be. One-fourth of the inhabitants, I should say, are always in the streets, and many of the mechanics work, as is common in the Orient, in open shops. The coffee-houses of Beautiful Greece, the Orient, Olympus, Mars, &c., are always thronged, and every afternoon crowds may be seen on the Patissia Road—a continuation of Eolus street—where the King and Queen take their daily exercise on horseback. The national costume, both male and female, is gradually falling into disuse in the cities, although it is still universal in the country. The islanders adhere to their hideous dress with the greatest persistence. With sunrise the country people begin to appear in the streets with laden donkeys and donkey-carts, bringing wood, grain, vegetables, and milk, which they sell from house to house. Every morning you are awakened by the short, quick cry of "*gala! gala!*" (milk) followed, in an hour or two, by the droning announcement of "*anthomiró kai masti-i-i-iku!*" (mastic and orange-flower water). Venders of bread and coffee-rolls go about with circular trays on their heads, calling attention to their wares by loud and long-drawn cries. Later in the day, peddlers make their appearance, with packages of cheap cotton stuffs, cloth, handkerchiefs, and the like, or baskets of pins, needles, buttons, and tape. They proclaim loudly the character and price of their articles, the latter, of course, subject to negotiation. The same custom prevails as in Turkey, of demanding much more than the seller expects to get. Foreigners are generally fleeced a little in the beginning, though much less so, I believe, than in Italy. Nevertheless, I cannot quite endorse the opinion expressed by Lord Carlisle and Professor Felton with regard to Grecian honesty.

I do not know why travellers should have said that there are few beggars in Athens. In reality, there are a great many, both stationary and itinerant. The former, of both sexes and all ages, sit at street corners and on the sunny side of walls, where they keep up an incessant exhortation to the passers-by, to give an alms for the sake of their souls, and those of all their relatives. I noticed that the Greeks very frequently give them a few *lepta*, sometimes with the remark that it is for their souls' sake. One of the beggars, a blind old man, who sits in Hermes street, was formerly a noted captain of pirates in the Archipelago. He lost his sight by the explosion of a package of cartridges, and now subsists on charity, while many of his comrades are rich and move in respectable society. The beggars who go from house to house are still more numerous, but equally successful in their business. The Greeks have this prominent virtue, that they care for their relatives who are in want, without considering it any particular merit.

The municipal government of Athens is perhaps a little more imperfect than that of New York. The Demarch is appointed by the King, out of three candidates chosen by electors, never with regard to his fitness for the office, but from his capacity to make a pliant tool of the Court. There are courts of justice, a police system, and regulations for houses, streets, &c.; but the main object of the government, as with our own city—until recently, at least—has been the good of its members rather than that of the public. The streets are supposed to be lighted, but it is not safe to go beyond either of the two principal thoroughfares without carrying a lantern. There was a lamp opposite to our residence, which was usually lighted about midnight, after everybody had gone to bed. In our street, which was one of the broadest and finest in Athens, various excavations and levellings were carried on for two months, and at night there was neither a lamp nor a bar to prevent persons from falling into the pits. The Queen's Mistress of Ceremonies, Baroness Pluskow, while on her way to a ball at the Turkish Minister's, was precipitated, in her carriage, down a perpendicular bank three feet high, running across the road. The French Secretary of Legation, who, for safety, took the opposite side of the street, went down a still higher bank, broke his carriage, bruised his limbs, and lost all his decorations in the mud. This state of things favors the thieves who still abound in the city. Athens is no longer besieged by banditti, as it was about four years ago, but burglaries and highway robberies are frequent.

The Winter of 1857–8 was the severest in the memory of any inhabitant. For nearly eight weeks, we had an alternation of icy north-winds and snow-storms. The thermometer went down to 20° of Fahrenheit—a degree of cold which seriously affected the orange if not the olive trees. Winter is never so dreary as in those southern lands, where you see the palm-tree rocking despairingly in the biting gale, and the snow lying thick on the sunny fruit of the orange groves. As for the pepper trees, with their hanging tresses and their loose, misty foliage, which line the broad avenues radiating from the palace, they were touched beyond recovery. The people, who could not afford to purchase wood or charcoal, at treble the usual price, even though they had hearths, which they have not, suffered greatly. They crouched at home, in cellars and basements, wrapped in rough capotes, or hovering around a *mangal*, or brazier of coals—the usual substitute for a stove. From Constantinople we had still worse accounts. The snow lay deep everywhere; charcoal sold at twelve piastres the *oka* (twenty cents a pound), and the famished wolves, descending from the hills, devoured people almost at the gates of the city. In Smyrna, Beyrout, and Alexandria, the Winter was equally severe, while in Odessa it was mild and agreeable, and in St. Petersburg there was scarcely snow enough for sleighing. All Northern Europe enjoyed a Winter as remarkable for warmth as that of the South for its cold. The line of division seemed to be about the parallel of latitude 45°. Whether this singular climatic phenomenon extended further eastward, into Asia, I was not able to ascertain. I was actually less sensitive to the cold in Lapland, during the previous winter, with the mercury frozen, than in Attica, within the belt of semi-tropical productions. It would be an interesting task for some one to collect and compare the meteorological records of that Winter, with a view of ascertaining the causes of these singular fluctuations of temperature.

CHAPTER VI.

A GREEK BAPTISM.

During my residence in Athens, I neglected no opportunities of witnessing the ceremonials of the Greek Church, especially those which are associated with the domestic life of the people. In the East, the sacraments of the Church have still their ancient significance. The people have made little or no spiritual progress in a thousand years, and many forms, which, elsewhere, are retained by the force of habit—their original meaning having long since been lost sight of—are still imbued with vital principle. They have, therefore, a special interest, as illustrations of the character nd peculiar phases of the popular belief.

The Rev. John H. Hill—whose missionary labors in Greece, during the last thirty years, have made his name so well known to the Christian world—befriended me in every possible way, and I was indebted to him for the means of observing some features of Grecian life, not generally accessible to the curious traveller. So when, one windy morning in January, I received a note from him, inviting us to attend the baptism of a child in a Greek family, I cast aside Grote, my Romaic grammar, and the unfinished letters for home, and set out for the Mission School. Æolus street, down which we walked, deserved its name. Icy blasts blew from the heights of Parnes and filled the city with clouds of dust. I should like to know whether Socrates and Alcibiades walked, bare-legged and bareheaded, wrapped only in the graceful folds of the chlamys, in such weather. The winter-wind of Athens bites through the thickest overcoat; and you look at the naked figures on the temple-friezes with a shudder. Those noble youths in the Panathenaic procession of the Parthenon, who bestride their broad-necked Thessalian horses, are very fine to behold; but give me pantaloons and thick stockings, rather than such unprotected anatomy.

Mr. and Mrs. Hill accompanied us to the residence of the happy parents, which was in the older part of the city, near the Temple of the Winds, and just under the Acropolis. The mother was a former pupil of the Mission School. She and a younger sister had been left orphans at an early age, and were taken and educated by Mrs. Hill. They inherited some property, which was in the charge of an uncle, who had succeeded in making away with the greater part of it, leaving the girls destitute. About a year and a half previous, a rich Athenian bachelor, of good character, applied to Mr. Hill for a wife, desiring to marry a girl who had been educated in his house. The elder of the sisters attracted him by her intelligence and her skill as a housekeeper, though she was far from beautiful, being deeply pitted with the small-pox. The result was that he married her, took her sister also to live with him, and, through law suits which he instituted, recovered nearly all the property, out of which the two had been defrauded. This was a pleasant history in a world, and particularly in a land, where justice is not the rule; and we were glad of the chance to be present at the baptism of the first child.

The parents received us at the door. We were kindly welcomed, as friends of Mr. Hill, and ushered into a room where the other guests—all Greeks, and some thirty or forty in number—were already assembled. It was an Athenian room, without stove or fire-place, and warmed only with a brazier of coals. I therefore retained my overcoat, and found it still cold enough. Everything was in readiness for the ceremony, and the family had evidently been waiting for our arrival.

The priest, a tall, vigorous Macedonian—a married man, who had come to Athens to educate his sons—and the deacon, a very handsome young fellow, with dark olive complexion, and large languishing eyes, now prepared themselves by putting long embroidered collars over their gowns. They then made an altar of the chest of drawers, by placing upon it a picture of the Virgin, with lighted tapers on either side. Then a small table was brought into the centre of the room, as a pedestal for a tall, tri-forked wax-candle, representing the Trinity. A large brazen urn (the baptismal font) was next carried in, the priest's son, a boy of twelve, put coals and incense into the censer—and the ceremony began. The godfather, who was a venerable old gentleman, took his station in front of the font. Beside him stood the nurse, holding the babe, a lively boy of six weeks old. Neither of the parents is allowed to be present during the ceremony.

After some preliminary chants and crossings—in the latter of which the whole company joined—the priest made the sign of the cross three times over the infant, blowing in its face each time. The object of this was to exorcise and banish from its body the evil spirits, which are supposed to be in possession of it up to the moment of baptism. The godfather then took it in his arms, and the Nicene Creed was thrice repeated—once by the deacon, once by the priest's son, and once by the godfather. A short liturgy followed; after which, the latter pronounced the child's name—"*Apostolos*"—which he had himself chosen. It is very important that the name should be mentioned to no one, not even the parents, until the moment of baptism: it must then be spoken for the first time.

The position of godfather, in Greece, also carries with it a great responsibility. In the two Protestant sects which still retain this beautiful custom, it is hardly more than a form, complimentary to the person who receives the office, but no longer carrying with it any real obligation. Among the Greeks, however, it is a relation to which belong legally acknowledged rights and duties, still further protected by all the sanction which the Church can confer. The god father has not only the privilege of paying the baptisma expenses, and presenting the accustomed mug and spoon, but he stands thenceforth in a spiritual relationship to the family, which has all the force of a connexion by blood. For instance, he is not permitted to marry into the family within the limits of consanguinity prohibited by the Church

—which extend as far as the *ninth* degree, whatever that may be. He also watches over the child with paternal care, and in certain cases, his authority transcends even that of the parents.

The priest and deacon put on embroidered stoles (rather the worse for wear), and the former rolled up his sleeves. Basins of hot and cold water were poured into the font, and stirred together until a proper temperature was obtained. The water was then consecrated by holding the Bible over it, blowing upon it to expel the demons, dividing it with the hand in the form of a cross nine times (three apiece for each person of the Trinity), and various other mystical ceremonies, accompanied with nasal chanting. The censer—now puffing a thick cloud of incense, was swung toward the Virgin, then toward us, and then the other guests in succession—each one acknowledging the compliment by an inclination of the head.

A bottle of oil was next produced, and underwent the same process of consecration as the water. The priest first poured some of it three times into the font, in the form of a cross, and then filled the godfather's hollow hand, which was extended to receive it. The infant, having been, meanwhile, laid upon the floor and stripped, was taken up like a poor, unconscious, wriggling worm as it was, and anointed by the priest upon the forehead, breast, elbows, knees, palms of the hands, and soles of the feet. Each lubrication was accompanied by an appropriate blessing, until every important part of the body had been redeemed from the evil powers. The godfather then used the child as a towel, wiping his oily hands upon it, after which the priest placed it in the font.

A GREEK BAPTISM.

The little fellow had been yelling lustily up to this time, but the bath soothed and quieted him. With one hand the priest poured water plentifully upon his head, then lifted him out and dipped him a second time. But instead of effusion it was this time complete immersion. Placing his hand over the child's mouth and nose, he plunged it completely under, three times in sucession. The Greek Christians skilfully avoid the vexed question of "sprinkling or immersion," on which so much breath has been vainly spent, by combining both methods. If a child three times sprinkled and three times dipped, is not sufficiently baptized, the ordinance had better be set aside.

The screaming and half-strangled babe was laid on a warm cloth; and while the nurse dried the body, the priest cut four bits of hair from the top of his head (in the form of a cross, of course), and threw them into the font. A gaudy dress of blue and white, with a lace cap—the godfather's gift—was then produced, and the priest proceeded to clothe the child. It was an act of great solemnity, accompanied by a short service, wherein each article assumed a spiritual significance. Thus: "I endow thee with the coat of righteousness," and on went the coat; "I crown thee with the cap of grace," and he put it on; "I clothe thee with the shirt of faith," etc. This terminated the ceremony, so far as the little Christian was concerned. He was now quiet enough; and in a few minutes afterwards, I saw him sleeping the sleep of peace in the next room.

A hymn of praise and thanksgiving, interspersed with the reading of chapters from the Bible, was still necessary, and lasted some fifteen or twenty minutes longer In order to save time, the priest commenced washing his hands in the baptismal font, with a huge piece of brown soap, chanting lustily all the while. He was so little embarrassed by the solemnity of the occasion, that he cried out: "Oh, you fool!" in the middle of a prayer, to the boy who offered him a towel. This mixture of sacred and profane things is not unusual in the convenient Christianity of the East. I once heard something very similar to it on board an ocean steamer, during the prevalence of the cholera. The captain, who officiated at the burial of a poor fireman, read the service with one eye, while he looked after the men with the other, and the sacred text was interpolated with his orders and remarks, in this wise: "And now (Steady there!) we commit the body of our deceased shipmate to the deep. (Let go!) Our Father, who art in Heaven (Lubberly done!), hallowed be Thy name," etc.

At last the ceremonies were over, much to our satisfaction—for we began to be heartily tired. The font was carried out, after the godfather had washed his hands in it; the bureau, the image of the Virgin being removed, became a bureau again; the Trinitarian candle was extinguished, and the old Bibles, stoles, and collars tied up in a sheet. The parents were now allowed to enter the room, and receive the congratulations of the guests. They looked proud and happy, with the knowledge that their little Apostolos was cleansed of the hereditary taint of sin, and rescued from the power of the devil. The father produced a dish containing a quantity of the smallest Greek silver coins, each pierced and tied with a bit of blue ribbon, and presented one to each guest, as a souvenir of the occasion. Then followed the usual course of refreshments—first, a jar of jelly, accompanied with glasses of water; then, cakes and almond-milk. In the old families, the jelly is often served with a single spoon, which each guest is obliged to use in turn—rather an ordeal to a stranger, until he becomes accustomed to it. We, however, were furnished with separate spoons and glasses, much to our satisfaction.

By this time the heavy canopy which stretched from Hymettus across to Parnes, spanning the plain of Attica, had broken into a storm of mingled snow and rain, and the solitary palm beside the Temple of the Winds wrestled despairingly with the wintry gusts. Snow upon palm-trees makes the same impression upon you as gray hair upon the head of a child. We returned home in a carriage, piled the roots of olives, and the shaggy, faun-like arms of grape-vines upon our expensive fire, and sat down again to **Grote, Leake, Mure, and Modern Greek.**

CHAPTER VII.

THE COURT OF KING OTHO.

The Grecian Court, though rigidly hedged about with the stiffest German etiquette, is nevertheless easily accessible to strangers. I therefore asked for a presentation, in order that I might attend the Winter balls at the Palace, which furnish much the best opportunity of seeing the Greeks of the present day. The preliminary formalities were easily arranged. Our Consul, the Rev. Dr. King, called on the Grand Marshal of the Palace, Notaras, one morning, and the same afternoon I received an invitation to the New Year's ball.

As, according to the etiquette of larger Courts, which is strictly copied in this little one, a Consul cannot present strangers, this duty is performed by the Grand Marshal, whom, therefore, it was necessary that I should previously know. A company of Americans, some four or five years ago, made themselves ridiculous, by asking for a presentation, and then staying away at the appointed hour, on the childish plea that this regulation was intended as a national insult. Dr. King was kind enough to accompany me to the Palace, where we were ushered into the Grand Marshal's chamber—a large, bare room, with a table, sofa, and half-a-dozen chairs, scarcely warmed by a fire of olive-roots. Notaras is a large, heavy man, of about sixty, with prominent eyes, a broad face, and thick lips. He wore the fustanella, and a jacket covered with silver embroidery. Singularly enough, for a person holding his office, he does not understand any language but Greek. He explained to me, through the medium of Dr. King, what was necessary for me to do. "Come to the Palace," said he, "go where you see the others go, and when the King and Queen come in, get into the circle around them. Then, when the time for presentation arrives, I will do so, (making a sign with his hand), and you will step forward." All this was clear and satisfactory, and we departed.

Dr. King had stated in his note that I had travelled extensively and was the author of some books. It was intimated by the Marshal that he would do well to send a list of the same to the Palace. At his request, therefore, I furnished such a list, in French, the purpose of which I ascertained when the time for presentation arrived. I could not but wonder how much of the reputation which an author fancies he has achieved is made up in this way. You meet with Dr. Pitkins at a party, on a steamboat, or anywhere else. Somebody whispers to you: "He is the author of a work on the dramatic poetry of the Tartars." By-and-by you are introduced to him: you start a literary topic, and soon take occasion to say, "Your Tartar studies, Dr. Pitkins, make you an authority on the subject." Of course, the Dr. is delighted to find that his fame has gone before him, and, if he accepts your invitation to call upon you, will find a copy of his work, three pages of which you have read, conspicuously displayed upon your parlor-table. Now, I was perfectly aware that King Otho knew no more of me or my books than of the Cherokee language, and when he said, "We have heard of you as a great traveller," etc., was neither surprised nor flattered, and was polite enough not to suggest whence his information had been derived.

As the ordinary full dress of European society is sufficient for admittance into the Palace, there was no further difficulty. The company were directed to assemble at a quarter before nine, but as all Athens was invited, and the city furnished but one carriage to every ten guests, I was obliged to go early, so that the same vehicle might be used to carry others. It was one of the coldest and windiest nights of the Winter, and, when the north wind blows, Attica is as dreary as Lapland. The vestibule of the Palace is too depressed to answer even the promise of its mediocre exterior, and the staircase, narrow, and with grades of inconvenient height—a single one being too little, and two taken together too much for the foot—is so clumsy, that one suspects that the original plans of the architect, who was no less than Leo von Klenze, cannot have been carried out. It is pitiful to see bad taste embodied in Pentelican marble.

I was therefore surprised and delighted on entering the ball-rooms, which are large, nobly planned and decorated with excellent taste. I have not seen, in any of the palaces of Europe—not even in the famous *Neue Residenz*, ir

Munich—apartments at the same time so imposing and so cheerful as these. There are three in all, connected by lofty Ionic doorways of white marble, the fillets and volutes of the capitals relieved by gilding. The length and breadth of the halls is proportionate to their height, which is full sixty feet. The walls are of scagliola, with an ornamental frieze at half their height, above which they are painted in the Pompeiian style. Chromatic decoration is also introduced in the sunken panel-work of the ceiling, the predominant colors being red and dead-golden. The general effect is wonderfully rich and harmonious, without being in the least glaring. Add to this the immense bronze chandeliers and candelabra, which pour a flood of soft light upon the walls and inlaid floors, and you have a picture of a festive hall, the equal of which can scarcely be found outside of St. Petersburg. The Greeks are proud of it; but I could not keep back the reflection, What avails this single flash of imperial splendor, in a land which has not a single road, where there is no permanent security for life and property, and whose treasury is hopelessly bankrupt?

There were not more than a dozen guests when I arrived, and their scattered figures were quite lost in the vast, brilliant space, so that I had a quarter of an hour of comparative solitude, which is a thing to be enjoyed in such places. One is thus familiarized to the unaccustomed pomp, is toned up to it (so to speak), and ere long finds himself comfortably at home and self-possessed. Presently, however, a full stream poured into the main hall—a tide of flashing, glittering, picturesque life, a mingling of the heroic and the common-place, of the semi-barbaric and the super-civilized, which is the most striking feature of Grecian society, and of course is exhibited in the broadest light at a Court Ball. There were Greeks in the simple national costume, a sober-colored jacket and leggings, of cloth or velvet, embroidered with silk, red fez, and white fustanella; gaudy palikars, in the same dress, but of crimson, blazing with gold; diplomatic gentlemen, in the uniforms of their various courts, glaring but inelegant, with the exception of the English and French; ministers with blue ribbons and a multitude of orders; military and naval officers, Greek, English, and French; old captains of the war of independence, with wild hair streaming down their backs; beautiful Greek girls, national upwards from the waist, and French downwards; Hydriote and Spetziote women with their heads bound up in spangled handkerchiefs; islanders in their hideous dark-blue or green baggy trowsers; fine European ladies in the latest Parisian toilet; and lastly, some individuals, like myself, in the ordinary black and white, who all look as if they had just dropped the napkins from their arms.

I saw at once that modern conventionalities would not be able to frigify such a mass as was here thrown together, and that consequently, the ball would be more interesting and enjoyable than those of most Courts. The old palikars brought a refreshing mountain air with them. They walked the inlaid floors and lounged on the damask divans in as careless and unconstrained a way as if these had been rock and heather. Even the Grand Marshal, who now made his appearance in a jacket so covered with embroidery that he resembled a golden armadillo, failed to person ify the idea of rigid ceremony. I espied an acquaintance at last, a gentleman attached to the Royal service, who began to point out a few of the noted persons present. "Do you see those two talking yonder," he asked. "The tall one, in blue uniform, is the son of Marco Bozzaris, at present one of the King's adjutants." He was a graceful, well-made, strikingly handsome man of forty-five, with dark hair and moustache, large dark eyes, and features in whose regularly and clearly cut lines I fancied there was something of the old Hellenic type. "The other," he continued, "is the Prime Minister, Miaulis, son of the celebrated Hydriote admiral." Two such names to begin with! Miaulis is a little man, with straight hair, prematurely gray, clear, intelligent brown eyes, a prominent nose, and pale olive complexion. "Do you see the other small man yonder?" asked my cicerone. "What, the one with a little, sloping head, and monstrous nose, who looks so much like a monkey?" "Yes," said he; "that is the son of Colocotronis, and, in spite of his looks, he is not deficient in cunning and natural ability."

By this time, at least six or seven hundred persons were assembled, and the hall was crowded. The masses of rich color and the gleam of gold and jewels harmonized natually with the painted walls, which formed a proper frame o this gay, tumultuous picture. About nine o'clock, there was a stir in the halls beyond; the crowd parted, and the King and Queen, accompanied by the officers of the court and the ladies of honor, walked into the centre of the ballroom. The guests fell back, the foreign ministers and high officers of state pressed forwards, and a highly dignified circle of some size was thus formed. The King looked remarkably well in his Greek dress of blue and silver; in fact- I saw no other costume so rich and tasteful as his. The Queen wore a Parisian dress, white tulle over white satin, trimmed with roses, a coronet of pearls, a superb diamond necklace, and a crinoline of extravagant diameter. She turned towards the ladies, who, seated in three rows, occupied one side of the ball-room, while the King addressed himself first to Sir Thomas Wyse, and afterward to the other foreign ministers in succession. After he had gone around the circle, he went off to the ladies, and the Queen, who had meanwhile formed the centre of a large periphery of crinolines, came forward and saluted the ambassadors. I was standing beside some English naval officers, who were waiting for presentation, and I believe the same reflection suggested itself to all of us—that there can be no greater bore than to be obliged to address some mechanical remarks to scores of persons in succession. To make a witty, or even a sensible remark, to every one of such a number, requires either immense practice or an astonishing flexibility of intellect. The wonder is, that an hereditary monarch, educated in the life of a court, should retain any portion of his natural sense. There is nothing so paralysing to the mind as the being obliged to talk continually for the mere sake of saying something.

The English officers were at last summoned by Sir Thomas Wyse, who stood by as interpreter, neither of them knowing any language but their own. The conversation did not last long, and, as the officers informed me, consisted of inquiries as to what part of England they came from, and how they liked Greece. The Turkish Minister presented an Effendi, the Prussian Minister a naval officer, and, the golden armadillo then making the preconcerted signal, I stepped forward out of the ring. The Marshal had probably stated that I spoke German, as the King at once addressed me in that language. He is quite near-sighted, and thrust his head forward close to my face, as he spoke. He is of medium height, forty-two years old, and has some general resemblance to Jules Benedict, the composer. His head is bald on the crown, but he wears a large brown moustache, which almost conceals his upper lip. His nose is prominent, his chin pointed, and his large, hazel eyes rather deeply set. The prominent expression of his face is amiability, mixed with a certain degree of irresolution. His complexion is pale, owing to long-continued ill-health, and he has an air of weariness and sadness when his features are in repose. The throne of Hellas is evidently not an easy-chair. As a young man, he must have been handsome.

He commenced with a compliment, which—not knowing exactly how to reply to it—I acknowledged with a bow As he seemed at a loss to know what to say next, I took the liberty of making a remark, although this was rather an infringement of court etiquette. The conversation once started, he spoke very fluently and sensibly, questioning me particularly about the influence of climate, and the method I took in order to acquire different languages. He detained me some eight or ten minutes, after which I withdrew into the circle, to await the Queen's pleasure. Presently she sailed along, sparkling with her diamonds and roses, and the presentations were repeated to her, in the same order. When my turn came, she addressed me in German, in almost the same words as the King. Her remarks related principally to the beauty of Greece, and to the weather, which gave her occasion to state that during th twenty-one years of her residence in Athens, she had never known so cold a winter. She is near forty years of age, rather under the medium height, and inclining to corpulency. She is said to have been quite handsome, even so late as five years ago, but retains very little beauty now except such as belongs to robust health. Her face is large and heavy, her mouth long, thin and hard, and her eyes, of that fine clear gray which is so beautiful in a gentle face, express a coldly gracious condescension. She evidently never forgets that she is a Queen. Her movements and manners are certainly remarkably graceful and self-possessed, and she is withal a woman of will, energy, and ambition. I watched the two narrowly during a part of the evening, and a hundred indescribable little traits showed me that the amiability and kindness are all on the King's side, the pride, ambition, and energy on the Queen's. Neither one is the ruler required by Greece.

The ball opened with a somewhat stiff promenade around the room, in which Sir Thomas Wyse led off with the Queen, the King following with the lady of one of the Ministers, and after them the other Ambassadors and high Government officials, each changing his partner at every completion of the circle. The Mistress of Ceremonies, Baroness von Pluskow, also figured in this initiatory procession. It was odd enough to see, among the gauzy expansive phenomena of modern female costume, the figure of a Hydriote lady, in her island dress—an embroidered handkerchief tied over the head and hanging upon the shoulders, a dark, close-fitting vest, without ornament, and a straight, narrow skirt, falling directly from the hips to the ankles. At first glance, one half suspected that a kitchen-maid had slipped into the ball-room, resolved to have a little dancing before the supper-hour came. In itself, the costume is very picturesque and becoming, but the rocks of Hydra suit it better than these Pompeiian frescoes. One of the Queen's maids of honor belongs to a noted Spetziote family, and wore the same costume; but her handkerchief was of yellow silk, richly embroidered with gold, and the skirt of her dress, of somewhat more ample dimensions, was of the same material. She was young and handsome, with a remarkably straight, classical profile, and was to me one of the most striking figures in the company.

The ball having now been formally opened, cotillions commenced, succeeded by waltzes and mazourkas, but no polkas. Nearly all the Greek ladies danced, and most of the young officers, all with much elegance and correctness, but the only fustanella to be seen on the floor was the King's. A good many of the young palikars looked on curiously: the old captains withdrew, along with the Senators, Deputies, and many officers and ministers, to the central hall, which was well studded with card tables. The third hall had a comfortable divan around its walls, whereon groups, principally of old men, gathered to talk scandal or politics, or to get a good chance at the refreshments as they came in through the further doors. The space was so ample that the company, large as it was, did not seem in the least crowded.

While wandering through the throng, I came upon Sir Richard Church, the noble old Philhellene, now Commander-in-Chief of the Grecian army. He kindly took me in charge, and for two hours thenceforth sought out all the distinguished Greeks who were present, that I might see and speak to them. In this way I made the acquaintance of the brothers Miaulis, of Colocotronis, of Psyllas, the President of the Senate, of the sons of Admiral Tombazi, and a number of the old revolutionary heroes. The Minister Miaulis speaks English very well. He made particular inquiries concerning the latest American improvements in dock-yards and floating docks, as he was about refitting the navy-yard at Poros. I ventured to ask whether he thought it advisable to build up a Greek navy, seeing that the country cannot possibly maintain one large enough for even defensive operations. "The only enemies we are likely to meet," he answered, "are Turkey and Egypt, and in either case, you must acknowledge, the result will not depend on the number of vessels. The Greeks are born sailors, but the Turks never can be made so. We ought at least to be in a position to defend our islands." Even in this case, however, the main reliance of Greece ought, like our own, to be upon her mercantile navy. Her commerce has grown up amazingly, and, were it not for the miserable neglect of everything like internal improvement, her forests would furnish shipping to any extent required by the needs or the enterprise of her people.

What impressed me most, perhaps, in this survey of

Grecian notabilities, was the striking contrast which I found between the heroes of the Revolution and some of their immediate descendants, and the later generation which has crept into power since Greece became free. I was glad to be able to believe, after all, that the corruption and misrule which have gone so far to turn away the sympathies of the world from the young nation, are not justly chargeable to the former—that honor and honesty existed, and still exist, among the Greeks. One may be deceived in the impression created by a single individual, but hardly in that of a whole class, and the distinction was here too broadly marked not to be real. It was a refreshing thing to turn from the false, sneaking, plotting faces of some of the present hangers-on of the Court, to the brave, determined heads, keen, straightforward glances, and native nobility of bearing of the old chieftains. I said as much to Gen. Church. "I am glad to hear it," said he, "and you are right. These are good and true men. I have known some of them for thirty years, and have had every opportunity of testing their characters." This evidence, coming from a man whom to see is to trust, should be a sufficient answer to those who brand all Greeks with on sweeping sentence of condemnation.

Among others to whom the General introduced me was an old Suliote chief, who, having lived in Corfu some years, spoke English very well. He was a tall, strongly-made man, with short, gray hair, a face deeply pitted and sun burnt, and eyes of splendid clearness and steadiness. We sat down together and conversed about the Revolution. "Did you know Bozzaris?" I asked. "Certainly," said he, " we were companions in arms, fellow Suliotes." As General Church also knew Bozzaris well, I inquired whether he was a man of more than ordinary capacity, or simply an example of reckless courage. " He was entirely uneducated," replied the General, " but nevertheless his abilities were certainly above the average of men of his class." In front of us stood an old palikar from the Morea, with his gray hair hanging to his waist. He was one of the deputation sent to Munich in 1832 to accompany the young King Otho to Greece. As he stood in the circle of spectators, looking grimly at the waltz in which the King took part, I could not but wonder whether he contrasted Greece then, in her season of hope, with Greece now, twenty-five years further from the realization of that hope. Perhaps he did not think at all.

By one o'clock, I was sufficiently tired, but it is here considered a serious violation of etiquette to leave before three, the hour when their Majesties withdraw. So I left the ball-room, and wandering about the long, cold corridors of the palace, was attracted by the smell of smoke to a dark, bare room, in which some twenty or thirty of the Greek guests were puffing at their paper cigars. Two candles, which stood upon a table, were almost invisible through the thick, blue cloud. The table was covered with stumps, and the smokers, seated on some hard chairs along the wall, were absorbed and silent. I lit a cigar and so smoked away another half-hour, when, after having walked in the corridor long enough to air my clothes, I returned to the ball-room. The final cotillion, which lasts about an hour, had commenced, and the Queen, who is passionately fond of dancing, now had an opportunity of gratifying her taste. She was taken out every set, and I believe every gentleman on the floor had the satisfaction of dancing with her in turn. The Prussian Minister, Baron von G——, the ugliest person in the room, and wearing the ugliest costume, continually hovered around her, and, in fact, seemed to be on the most familiar terms with both their Majesties. This seemed to confirm what I had previously heard, that, since England, France and Russia have mutually decided not to exercise their influence any longer in controlling the affairs of Greece, Prussia, seeing the coast clear, has stepped in, for what reason no one can imagine (since she has no interest whatever in the Grecian question), and endeavors to fill the place of counsellor.

At three o'clock the dancing ceased, and some of the guests made a rush for their overcoats, while others hastened to get a bowl of the *bouillon* which is distributed at the close of the ball. Refreshments had been frequently handed around in the course of the evening—plentiful, but cheap. First, tea; then lemonade and almond-milk; then small portions of ices, with little sugared cakes; and finally hot rum-punch. The servants were mostly in Greek costume, though a few, who were Germans, wore the Royal Bavarian livery. I returned home on foot, in the face of a biting wind, which blew down from the snowy summits of Pentelicus and Parnes.

CHAPTER VIII.

GREEK FESTIVALS, RELIGIOUS AND CIVIC.

The festivals of the Greek Church are fully as numerous, if not even more so, than those of the Latin. About every third day is an *corti*, or holy-day of some venerable unwashed saint, or company of saints, whose memory is duly honored by a general loafing-spell of the inhabitants. The greatest benefit that could happen to Greece, and to all Southern Europe, would be the discanonization of nine-tenths of those holy drones, who do enough harm by sanctifying indolence, to outweigh a thousand times the good they may have accomplished during their lives. God's Sabbath is enough for man's needs, and both St. George, the Swindler, and St. Polycarp, the Martyr, have sufficient honor done them in the way of chapels, shrines, candles and incense, to forego the appropriation of certain days, on which no one thinks particularly about them. Not only are the laborers idle and the shops generally shut, on every one of these festival days, but the University, schools and public offices are closed also. The Greeks are very zealous professors, and would exhibit much more progress as a people, if they did not make a mill-stone of their religion, and wear it around their necks.

My Greek teacher, who was a student of law, insisted on being paid by the month, and turned his agreement to profit by rigidly observing every saint's-day. He was indebted to the lessons he gave me for the means of buying an overcoat, and always came into my room half frozen from his fireless chambers; yet, with that inordinate vanity which characterizes the Greeks of all classes, he declared that he was not obliged and did not wish to teach, but condescended to do so for the pleasure of visiting me! Next door to us there was a small, one-story house, inhabited by a poor family. The daughter, a girl of twelve or thirteen, attended the *Arsakeion*, or Seminary for Girls, a gift of Arsakis to the Greek people, just across the street. The ridiculous little chit must have a servant to carry her two books those thirty paces, and we sometimes saw her, when the school was over, waiting behind the door, not daring to appear in the street with books in her hand. Nearly all the girls who came to the Arsakeion (some two hundred day-scholars) were similarly attended, yet they were mostly from families of moderate means.

New-Year's Day (Jan. 13, New Style) was celebrated very much as it is with us, by a mutual interchange of visits. In the morning, however, there was a *Te Deum* at the Church of St. Irene, which was attended by the King, Queen, and all the principal personages connected with the Government. This is one of the four or five occasions when their Majesties—one of whom is a Catholic, and the other a Protestant—are obliged to attend Greek service. The King keeps a Jesuit priest and the Queen a Lutheran clergyman from Holstein, both of whom perform service in the Royal Chapel, but at different hours. I went to hear the latter, and found a small congregation, composed exclusively of Germans. The English Church, of which Mr. Hill is minister—the only instance, I believe, in which an American clergyman has been appointed Chaplain to an English Legation—is a solid building, of the plainest kind of Gothic, which looks as if it had strayed away from some new railroad town in England. The Russians also have a very neat Byzantine chapel, with detached belfry. The fine singing of the choristers, who are mostly boys, attracts many persons. The Russians have had taste enough to harmonize and thoroughly reform the chants of their Church, yet without destroying their solemn and antique quaintness. The elements of the music are retained, but reduced to order and made effective; whereas, in the Greek Church, the chanting is of a character acceptable neither to men nor angels. An attempt has recently been made here, also, to substitute harmony for chaotic discord; but the Patriarch, knowing how much of the power of the Church depends on its strict adherence to superannuated forms, refuses to sanction any such innovation.

To return to the Te Deum, the tedium of which I endured for half an hour. The King and Queen, who arrived in their state coach and six, were received at the door of the church by the Metropolitan, or Archbishop of Athens, a venerable old man with flowing gray beard, wearing a magnificent stole of crimson embroidered with gold, and a cap shaped like a pumpkin with one end sliced off. Behind him were a retinue of priests, who, with their mild faces, long beards, and flowing hair, resembled the Apostles somewhat, though their robes were of decidedly gayer color and finer texture. After the Royal pair, came a mass of Ministers, Generals, Judges, the Senate and Assembly, and others, in uniforms, ribbons and orders, or palikar costume, filling up the main aisle, which had been kept clear for them. The King and Queen were conducted to a daïs in front of the altar, where they remained standing during the ceremony. On this occasion, the latter wore the Greek dress, which, though she had slightly outgrown it, became her very well. The red cap set off to advantage her rich, dark-brown hair, and her handsome shoulders showed yet fairer above the jacket of crimson velvet, embroidered with gold. I noticed that the King crossed himself at the proper times, while the expression of the Queen's face was rather that of repressed mirth. Indeed, with all proper reverence for the feeling of reverence in others—with no disposition to make light of sincere religious feeling, however expressed—it was almost impossible for me not to smile, or stop my ears, at the tremendous nasal brayings which now and then shook the church. The bulls of Bashan, bellowing in concert, would have made music, compared to it. Again I say, Ictinus worshipped God better, when he built the Parthenon.

The festival of Epiphany is celebrated in a peculiar manner. The Archbishop repairs to the Piræus, and, after appropriate services in the church, walks with the priests in solemn procession to the harbor, where, with certain nasal exclamations, he casts a cross into the sea. This is called the Blessing of the Waters, and is supposed to be of great advantage to vessels, in preventing storms and ship wrecks. A number of sailors, who are at hand watching the moment, plunge after the cross. The lucky finder takes it to the Palace, where he receives a present from the King. At Volo, in Thessaly, the same ceremony is performed with the addition, that, by a special miracle, the waters of the sea become perfectly sweet, and are only restored to saltness when the cross touches them. Of course, no one is heretic enough to disclose a doubting spirit, by tasting the water. The Greeks also fast during three days at this time. At other periods, besides Lent, there are partial fasts: some days, they can eat fowl, but not flesh; others, oil and olives, but not fowl. In fact, the kitchen occupies as important a place as the Church, in the observance of the Greek Faith. The stomach and the soul have a singular sympathy, and salvation is attained not more by prayers than by an orthodox diet.

After Epiphany came the festival of the Three Hierarchs—St. Gregory, St. Basil, and St. Chrysostom. This is also celebrated by loafing, as well as by homilies in the Churches. I did not attend any of these, as I was not sufficiently advanced in the language to profit by them. The Greek Church, however, unlike the Roman, is better in its creed than in its forms, and its clergy, notwithstanding their ignorance, have a much higher moral character than the priests of Spain and Italy. As they are allowed to marry, they are saved from the scandalous excesses common to the latter. The absence of the doctrine of Purga tory also takes away from them an opportunity of much pious extortion. The Church, shorn of the monstrous excrescences of its *forms*, would differ very little from that of England. A proposal, on the part of the latter, to enter into Christian fellowship with it, in the seventeenth century, was only prevented by the difference of doctrine on the subject of the Eucharist.

Towards the close of January, the King and Queen visited Chalcis, in Euboea, whither they went to celebrate the completion of a channel for vessels, with a drawbridge, through the Evripean Strait. This is a work which should have been done twenty years ago, but—better late than never. A furious storm came on, the snow fell two feet deep, the house in which they were lodged took fire, the Queen was obliged to sleep in her robes of state, and the King came back with a fever. Nothing less than being blown up by an exploding powder-mill could shake the Queen's constitution. She is capable of heading an expedition to the North Pole.

In February there was an extra festival week, to celebrate the King's *Jubilæum*, or twenty-fifth anniversary of his landing in Greece. The first suggestion of this celebration came, it is generally understood, from the Court, and the Legislative Assembly, which has become merely an instrument in the hands of the Crown, immediately voted the requisite funds. Two hundred thousand drachmas ($33,333) were thus appropriated from an impoverished treasury in a land where the commonest means of communication fail. A member of the House of Deputies said to me that, to his certain knowledge, every member of the

House was opposed to such a grant—and yet there was a unanimous vote in its favor. In the Senate there was undoubtedly a large majority against it, but no member opened his mouth except to vote for it. "How is it," I asked a gentleman who has been living in Athens for some years, "that no one dares to oppose the Crown?" "It is interest," he replied, "and the fact that every appointment is actually in the King's hands. If the Opposition member holds no office himself, he has relatives or friends who do, and all such would immediately lose their places." The spirit of office-seeking is quite as prevalent in Greece as in the United States. With us, it manifests itself in sufficiently mean and grovelling forms, but in that little country it has undermined everything like independence of political action.

The festival was to have been held at Nauplia, where the King first landed, and, for a fortnight before the day, the little town was astir with preparations. Snow lay nearly two feet deep upon the plain of Argos, the wind blew uninterruptedly from the north, and there was no prospect of comfortable quarters in the fireless Greek houses; nevertheless, as deputations were expected from all parts of the Morea, it was a great chance to see the different Greek clans assembled together, and we made arrangements to go with the crowd. The fever, however, which the King caught at Chalcis, finally changed the programme. The physicians dissuaded him from going; the Queen, who did not relish the idea of sleeping again in her state robes, sided with them, and five days before the appointed time he gave way under the combined pressure. All the money spent at Nauplia was therefore thrown away, except such as had been employed in making the streets practicable for carriages. The Royal household and equipages, which had all been forwarded in steamers, had to be brought back in haste. Preparations were commenced anew in Athens, giving us an idea of the artistic talents of the Greeks, and the manner in which the previous appropriations had been employed at Nauplia.

First of all, the intersection of Hermes and Eolus streets, the very busiest spot in the city, was barred against the public. By employing carpenters day and night, an arch of triumph, with four faces, was at length raised, covered with white muslin and painted in imitation of marble. It was a little out of line, and when the sun shone the interior scaffolding showed through the thin covering; but by night, when it was decorated with banners and lamps, the effect was not so bad. Next, the sidewalks were broken up in Hermes street, holes dug on both sides and a range of wooden frames about twelve feet high, planted all the way to the palace. These frames, being circular, and covered with white muslin, puckered a little to represent flutings, were called Doric columns. Some of them were bound with blue ribbons; some were upright, and some leaned to one side or the other, while the spaces between them, though sufficiently irregular, failed to produce the harmonious effect of the studied irregularities of the Parthenon. When this grotesque colonnade was completed, a shield, containing the portrait of some revolutionary hero or distinguished Philhellene, was placed upon each column, all of which were then bound one to another by garlands more withered than green. The portraits were curiously painted in snuff-color on a blue ground. Byron and Cochrane would not have been recognised by their nearest friends. The effect of this colonnade was in the highest degree tawdry and shabby, especially when the wind got under the muslin and bulged out the Doric columns in the most absurd way. On each side of the Church of St. Irene stood three arches of scaffolding, covered in like manner, the piers between them being of blue muslin, over which were drawn strings of white tape, to represent flutings. Ancient and Modern Greece! was my involuntary thought, as I looked on these flapping calicoes, and then up to the majestic remnant of the Parthenon, visible over the wall of the Acropolis.

By Saturday morning, all the preparations, which, having been ordered by the Court and paid for by the Government, were supposed to represent an indefinite amount of popular joy, were completed. They reminded me of a little circumstance which occurred on Jenny Lind's first landing in New York; and, as Mr. Barnum has told many worse things of himself, I may tell this. I was standing on the paddle-box of the Atlantic, near the great showman, as we approached Canal-street wharf, on which was erected a large triumphal arch of evergreens, with the Swedish flag floating over it. "Mr. Barnum," I asked, "who put that up?" "An enthusiastic public, Sir," he replied with great gravity, and a peculiar twinkle of his left eye. Here, however, I noticed three or four private decorations, but of the rudest kind. The public was evidently pleased, for the Greeks have a childish delight in flags, music, fireworks, and the like. As the Carnival Week was to commence the next day, masks already began to appear in the street, and the hilarity of the religious festival lent its character to the political one. A few days before, the King's brother Prince Adalbert of Bavaria, arrived on a visit of congratulation, accompanied by Maurer, one of the Bavarian Regents who managed Greece during the King's minority. Austria also sent a deputation, consisting of Lieut. Field-Marshal Farr, and the sons of Prince Metternich and Baron Prokesch-Osten, to congratulate the King. These visits, together with the arrival of English, French, Russian and Dutch vessels-of-war at the Piræus, gave an unusual dash and brilliancy to Athenian life.

The ceremonies consisted of a Te Deum at the church in the morning, official visits of congratulation afterwards at the palace, and a grand state ball in the evening. As we had already heard one Te Deum on New-Year's Day, and had no wish to endure the crowd and the chanting a second time, we betook ourselves to Hermes street, and found a convenient place to see the cortège, in a gap between two companies of soldiers. At ten o'clock, the firing of cannon and the blast of trumpets announced that the King had left the palace. Presently, a mounted officer appeared, cantering lightly down the street, and followed by half-a-dozen wild-looking mountaineers, in their coarse white woollen dresses, bare-headed, and with long hair streaming in the wind. As they ran and leaped along, turning back now and then, they were picturesque enough to pass for a company of satyrs dancing before the chariot of Bacchus. After them came another company nearly as wild, but bearing large blue and white silken banners, with various inscriptions and devices, and running at full speed. These, I was told, were the representatives of the various trades, bearing the banners of their guilds. The Royal Carriage, which now appeared, was surrounded by a dozen more of them—rough, stalwart, bare-headed fellows, with flashing eyes, and hair that tossed in the wind as they sprang. They gave life and character to the spectacle, which would have been a frigid affair without them.

The King's appearance was the signal for a general cry of "*Zito!*" (*vive*, or *hurrah!*) He looked happy and excited, and his pale face was pleasantly flushed as he acknowledged the greetings. The Queen was all condescension, as usual. On the front seat sat Prince Adalbert, a burly, red-faced fellow, with the air and expression of a prosperous brewer. He contrasted unfavorably with the King, and the Greeks already disliked him. If he had any pretensions to the crown of Greece, his visit at that time was unfortunate. The Ministers, Generals, Foreign Ambassadors, and other dignitaries, followed in a long procession, which was about a quarter of an hour in passing. We afterwards went to the Palace, and witnessed the return, in which the countrymen and the tradesmen with their banners were the most conspicuous objects. There was, however, very spontaneous and hearty cheering from the thousands assembled, when the King came out on the balcony. Various official personages were cheered as they arrived to pay their respects, and it was perhaps a significant sign that the loudest *zitos* were for the Russian Minister.

I attended the ball in the evening, which was but a

repetition of the one I have already described. The next day, there was a great gathering at the Temple of Theseus, where the multitude were regaled with a hundred and fifty roasted sheep, several hogsheads of wine, and cart-loads of bread and onions. As we had not been informed of the hour, the dinner was over before we reached the spot, and I am indebted for a description of it to the King himself, who described it to me with evident pleasure, at a ball two days later. Among other incidents, a peasant, more than a hundred years old, appeared before the King and Queen, drank their healths out of a big bottle of wine, and danced the Romaïka before them with a good deal of spirit. While we were there, the barrels were on tap, and the tradesmen were dancing around their banners; but, out of five thousand people, I did not see ten who were intoxicated. I believe the Greeks to be the soberest Christians in the world.

Three days afterwards there was a select ball at the Palace, but here the Grecian element was less conspicuous, the foreign guests receiving the preference. Then the Demarch of Athens gave a grand ball to the King and Queen, in the Theatre. It was a frightful jam, more than a thousand persons being crammed into the little building. I endured it for about an hour, and then left, to save my ribs and lungs. Finally, on the evening of the seventh day, there was a brilliant display of fireworks from the open space in front of the palace, winding up with a wild Romaïc dance by soldiers holding burning blue-lights in their hands. In appearance, in sound, and in smell, the spectacle was absolutely infernal.

On the 25th of January, Sir Thomas Wyse, the English Minister, gave a grand ball, in honor of the Princess Royal's marriage. All the high dignitaries, short of royalty, were there, with more female beauty than I have seen gathered together for many a day. There were no Phidian faces, no pure antique profiles, nothing even so sweet and so stately as the caryatides of the Erechtheion, but superb hair, glorious dark eyes, fringed by long lashes ripely-curved Southern mouths, and complexions varying from the clear tint of sun-stained marble to the perfect white and red of Circassia. Conspicuous among the Greek girls were Photine Mavromikhali, grand-daughter of old Petron Bey, a Spartan beauty, tall, proud and stately, and Miss Black, daughter of the Maid of Athens. I was talking, as I supposed, to a young Hydriote girl, with the sweetest Madonna face tied up in her embroidered handkerchief, but afterwards learned that she had been a widow for five years past. Her mother, who was almost equally beautiful, did not appear to be ten years older.

CHAPTER IX.

AN EXCURSION TO CRETE.

AFTER waiting a month for a cessation of the cold and stormy weather, there seemed to be at last some promise of a change for the better, and I made preparations to cave Athens for a few weeks. The festivities connected with the King's Jubilæum closed on the evening of the 12th of February; the frolics of the Carnival had become worn out and spiritless, and but two more days intervened before the commencement of Lent, during which time the Greeks do real penance, and are melancholy from bodily, not from spiritual causes. Lent in Athens is inaugurated by a universal gathering of the people before the columns of the temple of Jupiter Olympus, where they consume their first *lean* meal in public, and dance for the last time before Easter. An immense quantity of onions, leeks and garlic is consumed on this occasion, and the spectacle is therefore calculated to draw tears from the contemplative observer I did not, however, consider it worth while to lose a week of good weather for the purpose of attending this festival

Our destination was Crete, the least visited yet most interesting of all the Grecian islands. (I use "Grecian" in the ancient, not the modern sense. Crete has been, since 1669, subject to Turkey.) Braisted and I, accompanied by François as dragoman and purveyor, with his kit, camp beds, and a multitude of Arabic saddle-bags, left our joint mansion in Athens, and descended to the Piræus. The steamer which was to take us to Crete was just coming into the harbor, with the Lord High Commissioner of the Ionian Islands and his suite on board, which circumstance obliged us to wait until long after dark, before we could get under way for Syra. We awoke next morning in the island-harbor, opposite the white pyramidal town, in the aspect of which I could not notice the slightest difference since I first saw it, more than six years ago. Our steamer lay there all day—a very tedious detention—and started in the evening for Khania, about 150 miles distant in a southern direction. Crete lies between the parallels of 35° and 36°, not much further removed from Africa than from Europe, and its climate, consequently, is intermediate between that of Greece and that of Alexandria.

In the morning, the island was already visible, although some thirty miles distant, the magnificent snowy mass of the White Mountains gleaming before us, under a bank of clouds. By ten o'clock, the long blue line of the coast broke into irregular points, the Dictynnæan promontory and that of Akroteri thrusting themselves out toward us so as to give an amphitheatric character to that part of the island we were approaching, while the broad, snowy dome of the Cretan Ida, standing alone, far to the east, floated in a sea of soft, golden light. The White Mountains were completely enveloped in snow to a distance of 4,000 feet below their summits, and scarcely a rock pierced the luminous covering. The shores of the Gulf of Khania, retaining their amphitheatric form, rose gradually from the water, a rich panorama of wheat-fields, vineyards and olive groves, crowded with sparkling villages, while Khania, in the centre, grew into distinctness—a picturesque jumble of mosques, old Venetian arches and walls, pink and yellow buildings, and palm trees. The character of the scene was Syrian rather than Greek, being altogether richer and warmer than anything in Greece.

We entered the little port, which is protected by a mole, but is too shallow and confined to contain more than a dozen vessels of average size. In fact, it is partly filled up, and needs digging out again. The Seraï, or Government Palace, resting on lofty arches, which spring from the remains of some old Venetian defences, fronts the entrance; a little yellow mosque nestles under it, close upon the water, and an irregular mass of rickety houses, with overhanging balconies, incloses the port. On the right, as we enter, is a battery, the walls of which are crowded with idle Turkish. soldiers. The narrow stone quay around the port is thronged with Oriental costumes, among which the white turban of the Moslem is frequent. Everything has a mellow tint of age, indolence, and remoteness from Progress.

After a time, we obtained pratique, and were put ashore at a little yellow custom-house beside the mosque. While the people were crowding around us with great curiosity, I was accosted with the question: "Are you from the States?"

The speaker was an Englishman, who probably belonged to a coaler in the harbor. "Because," he continued, "the dragoman of the American Consul lives close by, and he can help you get your things through." At this moment, the dragoman—an Ionian Greek—made his appearance, and conducted us at once to the Consulate. We found the Consul, Mr. Mountfort, in a rickety little house, overlooking the harbor. The American flag was profusely displayed on the walls: I counted no less than five specimens. "There is no khan in the place," said the dragoman, "you must stop here." After some deliberation, we took possession of the servant's room, which was dry and well ventilated, by means of holes in the floor. The preliminary arrangements made, the Consul entertained us with some excellent old Cretan wine, and a full account of his doings since he came to the island. He claimed to have been the first to introduce rum, soda-ash and soap-bags into Crete. "I intend to build up quite a trade in American rum," said he. "Your failure would be a better thing for the Cretans than your success," I could not help remarking.

Khania occupies the site of the ancient Cydonia, by which name the Greek bishopric is still called. The Venetian city was founded in 1252, and any remnants of the older town which may have then remained, were quite obliterated by it. The only ruins now are those of Venetian churches, some of which have been converted into mosques, and a number of immense arched vaults, opening on the harbor, built to shelter the galleys of the Republic. Just beyond the point on which stands the Seraï, I counted fifteen of these, side by side, eleven of which are still entire

A little further, there are three more, but all are choked up with sand, and of no present use. The modern town is an exact picture of a Syrian sea-port, with its narrow, crooked streets, shaded bazaars, and turbaned merchants. Its population is 9,500, including the garrison, according to a census just completed at the time of our visit. It is walled, and the gates are closed during the night.

In the evening, we paid a visit to Mademoiselle Kon taxaky, better known throughout the East as "Elizabeth of Crete." I had a letter of introduction to her from Mr. Hill, in whose family she was educated. Her profound scholarship, wit, enthusiasm and energy are characteristics of the rarest kind among the Greek women of the present day, and have therefore given her a wide celebrity. Of course, her position is not entirely a pleasant one. While some of the Greeks are justly proud of her, others dislike and some fear her. Her will, talent and a certain diplomatic aptness give her considerable power and influence, the possession of which always excites jealousy and enmity in a Greek community. Consequently, she has many enemies, and is assailed at times by the meanest slanders and intrigues. She is about thirty years of age, of a medium stature and, with the exception of her lambent black eyes, there is nothing very striking in her appearance. She speaks English, Greek and French with almost equal fluency, and has the ancient Greek authors at her fingers' ends. She talks with great rapidity, ease, and with a rare clearness and sequence of ideas, in narration. I was interested at finding in her the same quickness and acuteness of mental perception for which the old Greeks were famous. She is not a Hypatia, yet there is no doubt that both her achievements and her influence would be greater were the sphere of woman in those countries less circumscribed. She has been mentioned as an evidence of what the race is still capable of, but I think unfairly. She would be an exceptional woman in any country.

The following morning, the Consul sent his dragoman to request for us an interview with Vely Pasha, the Governor of Crete. Shortly afterwards, the dragoman of the latter called upon us and gave notice of the hour when we would be received. We found the Pasha in the Seraï, in a handsomely furnished room, which was decorated with busts and pictures. Conspicuous among the latter was a large tinted lithograph of Stuart's head of Washington. The Pasha came forward to receive us, shook hands, and conducted us to the divan, where, instead of dropping cross-legged on the cushions, we all took our rest on comfortable Boston rocking-chairs. He spoke French very well, having been, as the reader may remember, Turkish Ambassador at Paris for three years, during the whole period of the war, when his post was more than ordinarily important. Previous to this, he had been Governor of Bosnia. He has, besides, served in Egypt, and speaks, as he informed me, seven languages. He is a very handsome man, above the average size of the Turks, and not more than thirty-five years of age. His costume, except the fez, was entirely European, and he is the first Oriental I have seen who wears it naturally and gracefully.

If I was pleased with Vely Pasha at first sight, his kindness during this interview certainly gave me no reason to change my opinion. Learning that we intended visiting the monasteries of Akroteri next day, he immediately offered us horses from his own stable, and an officer as guide and attendant. Besides promising to have a firman written for our journey into the interior, he ordered his secretary to prepare letters of recommendation for me, to the Governors of Rhithymnos and Candia, and the Greek Bishop and Archbishop, and concluded by offering to send an attendant with us during the whole journey. I hesitated to accept so many generous offers, but he declared it to be his earnest desire that the island should be seen by strangers, that it may become better known and more frequently visited, and therefore he considered it his duty to furnish me with all the facilities at his command. While we were discussing this matter, in combination with some pipes of delicious Latakia, his carriage was brought to the door, and we set out, under the secretary's escort, to visit the Pasha's country palace and gardens at Seviglia, about four miles distant.

Passing through the large Turkish cemetery, which was covered with an early crop of blue anemones, we came upon the rich plain of Khania, lying broad and fair, like a superb garden, at the foot of the White Mountains, whose vast masses of shining snow filled up the entire southern heaven. Eastward, the plain slopes to the deep bay of Suda, whose surface shone blue above the silvery line of the olive groves; while, sixty miles away, rising high above the intermediate headlands, the solitary peak of Mount Ida, bathed in a warm afternoon glow, gleamed like an Olympian mount, not only the birthplace, but the throne of immortal Jove. Immense olive trees sprang from the dark-red, fertile earth; cypresses and the canopied Italian pine interrupted their gray monotony, and every garden hung the golden lamps of its oranges over the wall. The plain is a paradise of fruitfulness, and alas! of fever. The moist soil, the dense shade, with lack of proper drainage and ventilation, breed miasma which make it dangerous, durin a part of the year, to pass a single night in any of the villages. We found the Pasha's house dismantled, and the furniture—mostly carpets and cushions—heaped up in two or three rooms; but the garden, with its tanks and water-pipes, its hedges of blooming roses, its thickets of rhododendron and bowers of jasmine, was a refreshment to the soul. The gardener gathered us oranges and bouquets, while I sat upon the highest terrace and made a sketch of the splendid plain.

In the morning, the horses were brought to us at an early hour, in charge of Hadji Bey, a jolly old officer of gendarmes, who was to accompany us. As far as the village of Kalepa, where the Pasha was then residing, there is a carriage-road; afterwards, only a stony mountain path. From the spinal ridge of the promontory, which we crossed, we overlooked all the plain of Khania, and beyond the Dictynnæan peninsula, to the western extremity of Crete. The White Mountains, though less than seven thousand feet in height, deceive the eye by the contrast between their spotless snows and the summer at their base, and seem to rival the Alps. The day was cloudless and balmy; birds sang on every tree, and the grassy hollows were starred with anemones, white, pink, violet and crimson. It was the first breath of the southern spring, after a winter which had been as terrible for Crete as for Greece.

After a ride of three hours, we reached a broad valley, at the foot of that barren mountain mass in which the promontory terminates. To the eastward we saw the large monastery of *Agia Triada* (the Holy Trinity), overlooking its fat sweep of vine and olive land; but as I wished to visit the glen of Katholikó, among the mountains, we crossed the valley to a large farm-house, in order to procure a guide. The sun shone hot into the stony and dirty court-yard, surrounded by one-story huts, and not a soul was to be seen. There was a little chapel at hand, and a carved piece of iron suspended to an orange tree beside it, in lieu of a bell. Hadji Bey shouted, and François beat the sacred metal with a stone, until a gray-bearded native and two young fellows, with hair hanging in a long braid down their backs, made their appearance. What was our surprise, then, to see the doors open and a number of women and children, who had previously concealed themselves, issue forth! We were now regaled with wine, and Diakos, one of the long-haired youths, mounted his mule to guide us. In the deep, dry mountain glen which we entered, I found numbers of carob-trees. Rocks of dark-blue limestone, stained with bright orange oxydations, overhung us as we followed the track of a torrent upward into the heart of this bleak region, where, surrounded by the hot, arid peaks, is the monastery of Governato.

A very dirty old monk and two servants were the only inmates. We were hungry, and had counted on as good a dinner as might be had in Lent, but some black bread, cheese, and an unlimited supply of water were all that we obtained. The monk informed us that the monastery was dedicated to St. John, and was celebrated for the abundance of its honey; but neither honey nor locusts could he give us. Behind the chapel was a vault in which they put the dead monks. When the vault gets full, they take out the bones and skulls and throw them into an open chamber adjoining, where their daily sight and smell furnish wholesome lessons of mortality to the survivors. François was so indignant at the monk's venerable filthiness and the Lenten fare he gave us, that he refused to pay anything "to the Church," as is delicately customary.

We descended on foot to the monastery of Katholikó, which we reached in half an hour. Its situation is like that of San Saba in Palestine, at the bottom of a split in the stony hills, and the sun rarely shines upon it. Steps cut in the rock lead down the face of the precipice to the deserted monastery, near which is a cavern 500 feet long, leading into the rock. The ravine is spanned by an arch, nearly 50 feet high, at one end of which is a deep, dark well, wherein refractory monks were imprisoned. The only living thing we saw was a shepherd-boy, who shouted to us from the top of the opposite cliffs. Of St. John the Hermit, whom the monastery commemorates, I know no more than I do of St. John the Hunter, who has a similar establishment near Athens.

At Agia Triada, we found things different indeed. As we rode up the stately avenue of cypresses, between vineyards and almond trees in blossom, servants advanced to take our horses, and the *hegoumenos*, or abbot, shouted

'*Kalos orizete!*" (welcome) from the top of the steps
With his long gown and rotund person, he resembled a
good-natured grandmother, but the volumes of his beard
expressed redundant masculinity. We were ushered into
a clean room, furnished with a tolerable library of orthodox
volumes. A boy of fifteen, with a face like the young
Raphael, brought us glasses of a rich, dark wine, something
like Port, jelly and coffee. The size and substantial character of this monastery attest its wealth, no less than the
flourishing appearance of the lands belonging to it. Its
large court-yard is shaded with vine-bowers and orange
trees, and the chapel in the centre has a façade supported
by Doric columns.

It was sunset when we reached Kalepa, where we stopped
to dine with the Pasha, according to previous arrangement.
He has a country-house handsomely furnished in the most
luxurious European style, the walls hung with portraits of
prominent living sovereigns and statesmen. On the dinner-
table was an *epergne* of pure gold, two feet long and
eighteen inches high; the knives, forks and spoons were
also of the same metal. He had an accomplished French
cook, and offered us, beside the wine of Crete, Burgundy,
Rhenish and Champagne. He drank but sparingly, however, and of a single kind. After dinner, I had a long
conversation with him on the state of the Orient, and was
delighted to find a Turk in his position imbued with such
enlightened and progressive ideas. If there were nine
men like him, the regeneration of the East would not
be so difficult. One man, however—unless he fills the
very highest administrative position—is almost powerless,

when the combined influence of the European Powers is brought to bear against him. Before the close of 1858 Vely Pasha was recalled from Crete, and the good works he had begun completely neutralized. The real condition of affairs was so thoroughly misrepresented that in all the newspapers of Europe but a single voice (the correspondent of the *London Times*) was raised to do him justice.

CHAPTER X.

A CRETAN JOURNEY.

My plan of travel, on leaving Khania, was to visit the wild mountain region of Sfakia, which lies beyond the White Mountains, in the southwestern corner of the island. This district bears a similar relation to the rest of Crete, as that of Maïna does to Greece, being inhabited by a savage remnant of the ancient race, who, until within a very few years, have maintained a virtual independence. It is in such out-of-the-way corners that the physical characteristics of the original stock must now be looked for. I have long believed that some rills of Hellenic blood must still continue to flow on the ancient soil, untouched by those Slavonic and Ottoman inundations which have well nigh washed it out of the modern race. I was quite sure that in Sfakia, where a dialect, conjectured to be the old Cretan-Doric, is still spoken, I should find the legitimate stock—the common, not the heroic type, preserved almost intact. The passes of the White Mountains are difficult at all seasons, and I ascertained that the *xyloscala*, or " wooden ladder," by which I had intended to descend into Sfakia, was not to be reached on account of the snow; but there is another road around the eastern base of the mountains, and I determined to try it.

The Pasha endeavored to dissuade me from the attempt. The roads in Crete," said he, "are absolutely frightful and though, as a traveller, you must be prepared for any experience, yet, when the season is bad, they become quite impassable, even to the natives. I have had a carriage-road surveyed and located from here to Heracleon, and a small portion of it is already finished, near Rhithymnos; but the people oppose it with all their might, and at least five or six years must elapse before enough is done to demonstrate to them the use and value of such improvements.* I am satisfied that Turkey will never advance until she has means of communication sufficient to make her internal resources available. This is the first step towards the regeneration of the Orient—and the *only* first step in the path of true progress. The power and civilization of Europe rest on this foundation." There is great truth in these remarks, as, indeed, there was in the Pasha's views on the Oriental question. They disclosed an enlightened and practical mind, the rarest apparition among the Governors of the East.

At last, on the morning of our departure, the Pasha sent me Captain Nikephoro, a dashing Sfakiote chieftain, who was ordered to accompany us through the territory, as guide and guard. He was a tall, handsome fellow, with

---

* The building of this road was the main cause of the rebellion in Crete, a few months later!

fiery black eyes, raven hair and moustache, and an eagle's beak of a nose. A pair of long, silver-mounted pistols, and a yataghan, with a silver hilt and scabbard, adorned his belt. Hadji Bey wore his blue uniform and sabre, and was mounted on a sturdy gray horse. The chief muleteer, Anagnosti, who was chosen for us by the Consul's dragoman, as an honest and skilful man (and whom we afterwards discharged as the very opposite), was also mounted, so that, with our two baggage-mules, we made quite a respectable caravan. The Consul, who had hospitably entertained us during our stay, accompanied us to the gates of Khania, and we set off on our first Cretan journey, in the midst of a soft, thick rain.

The road to Suda, four miles, is a broad, carriageable way, leading through the rich plain of Khania. Peasants were busy plowing the mellow, dark-red loam. Vineyards, olive orchards and wheat-fields succeeded each other, and the flourishing villages on the lower slopes of the mountains on our right, glimmered through the gray veil of the falling showers. Suda is a deep, beautiful bay, open only toward the north-east, where an old Venetian fortress, on a rocky island, commands its mouth. The ground at it head is marshy, and near the shore there are salt pans. Vely Pasha, however, had the intention of draining these marshes and building up a town on the spot. A better situation, in fact, could scarcely be found on the island.

Our road followed the shore for a short distance, and then began to climb the base of Mount Malaxa, which towered far above us, its summit wrapped in clouds. This is probably the ancient Berecynthus, the scene of the Idæan

Dactyls, where fire was first brought down from heaven, and metal forged. Antiquaries are divided in opinion, some affirming that the mountain is of calcareous rock (which it certainly is)—others that it is schistose, and may therefore contain veins of metal. I do not see that this question is of much importance. All myths had a location, of course, and in the days when they formed a part of the prevalent religion, men were not in the habit of testing them by inquiry and research. Malaxa corresponds, geographically, with the position of Berecynthus, and we need not trouble our heads about the rest.

Clumps of myrtle and oleander filled the glens, and the mastic shrub, sage and wild thyme covered the stony shoulders of the hills. We still plodded on in the rain, passing here and there a ruined keep, climbing rocky ladders, or slipping on the polished surface of an old road, where the stones had been laid together in some sort of order. After three hours, when we were all tolerably wet, cold and hungry, we crossed the crest of the shore hills and came upon the broad table-land of Apokorona, at the eastern base of the White Mountains. Cheered by the hope of soon reaching our destination—a monastery at Paleokastron, on the site of Aptera—we hurried on to a little village. The people crowded to the doors to see us and give us directions. "Good day, palikar!" said a woman whom I greeted. The men, all of whom had very cheerful and friendly faces, accompanied us a little distance to point out the road, and tore down the stone fences for our mules, that we might find a shorter way across their fields.

The plain of Apokorona presented a pleasant picture of

fertility and cultivation. Wheat-fields, divided by stone fences, and dotted with clumps of olive-trees, stretched as far as the eye could reach. In half an hour we reached some of the ruins of Aptera. Hewn blocks, among them fragments of small Doric pillars, were scattered over the soil, and along the highest part of the hill ran a low wall of square stones. A little further was the monastery, a massive square stone building, standing in the midst of some ruins of the Roman time. The place is a *Metókhi*, or branch, of the Monastery of St. John, on Patmos. It is occupied only by one priest, a married man, who rents from the Government a large tract of the land lying round about it, for 12,000 piastres ($500) a year. He received us in the court, ushered us into a small leaky room, and in due time we procured a meal of eggs fried in oil, fresh cheese-curds, and coarse but good bread. Notwithstanding Lent had commenced, the priest was willing to furnish heretics with the means to break it, for a consideration. We tried to dry our soaked garments over a brazier of coals, and gave up all hopes of proceeding further that day.

Aptera (*Wingless*) derives its name from the combat between the Sirens and the Muses, wherein the former were stripped of their wings, and plunging into the sea, became the rocks of Leucæ, which lie in the mouth of the Bay of Suda. The ruins near the convent are those of cisterns, undoubtedly of Roman construction. One of them is nearly one hundred and fifty feet long, with a branch at right angles. Another is a triple vault, in a nearly perfect state, its walls of division resting on four arches of cut stone On inquiring for the Cyclopean walls, the priest said they were further to the eastward. Captain Nikephoro put on his thick capote to keep off the rain, and accompanied us Along the brow of the mountain, for the distance of nearly half a mile (which was as far as we traced it), runs a polygonal wall, composed of huge undressed masses of rock. Its breadth is seven feet, and its greatest height twelve, the upper portion having been either thrown down or carried off. The masonry, though massive, is rude, and evidently belongs to the earliest period.

In the evening a number of peasants came in with coins, Greek, Roman and Venetian, some of which I bought. Among them were some autonomous coins of Aptera, with a bee on the obverse. The most of them, however, were illegible, and held by their finders at prices far above their real value. We occupied the priest's bed for the night, which was a raised platform across the dry end of the room. The sacerdotal fleas were as voracious as Capuchin friars, and though they were distributed over four persons instead of two, they murdered sleep none the less. Next morning the rain continued, but after a long consultation and much delay, we set out for Rhithymnos. Riding over the plain for an hour or more, through fine old orchards, we reached a new khan about the breakfast hour. A priest and some wayfarers were within, smoking their narghilehs and drinking the pale-red Cretan wine. In Crete the wine is not resined, as in Greece, and we can therefore get at its natural flavor, which is fully equal to that of the ordinary wines of Spain. I much prefer it to the renowned wine of Cyprus, notwithstanding Mrs. Browning's Bacchic pæan to the latter. In Greece the wine was no doubt resinous in ancient times. The pine-cone topping the staff of Bacchus is probably one symbol of the fact. By adding the raw resin—which is collected by tapping the pine trees—it is not only more easily preserved, but may be increased by the addition of water. It is a most wholesome beverage, but the flavor, to an unaccustomed palate, is horrible.

In front of the khan a silvery waterfall gleamed through the olive trees, and Braisted and I walked thither, accompanied by the faithful Sfakiote, who never allowed us to get out of his sight. The place reminded me of the sources of the Jordan, at Banias. A stream large enough to drive a cotton factory gushed out of the earth at the foot of a pile of rocks, fell over a mossy dam, and rushed away through the meadows towards the sea. Nikephoro informed me, however, that it dries up in summer. Our road, for some distance after leaving the khan, was a mere scrambling track over stony ridges, impassable for anything except the sure-footed Cretan mules. Our course was a remarkably tortuous one, winding hither and thither without any regard to the direction we should go. We at last discovered that Anagnosti was as ignorant as he was lazy, and did not know the road. François thereupon took fire with his usual readiness, and we had a storm of Greek epithets. "I have always heard," said he, "that the Cretan Turks were scamps, but now I see that it is the Cretan Christians who are so. St. Paul told the truth about this lying race."

After a while we reached an old monastery, near a village called *Karidi* (The Nut), on a hill overlooking the interior valleys. The houses were ruinous and half deserted, but the orange, olive, and carob trees were of fine growth, and the barley fields of unusual richness. In another hour we came upon a village called Exopolis, on the brow of a steep hill overlooking the valley of Armyro. A dreary rain was setting in, and Hadji Bey declared that it was impossible to reach the next place before dark; so we took up our quarters in the house of an old fellow who called himself the chief of the village. It was a hut of stones and mud, without a window, and with a roof through which the rain leaked in little streams; but it was at least slightly better than out of doors. There were much better houses in the village, but all were roofless and in ruins. Captain Nikephoro accompanied us to a Turkish tower of hewn stone, whence we had a striking view of the wild valley below. Hadji Bey lodged in the café, a dark, windowless hut, where they gave us cups of burnt barley for coffee. Some Musselmans and Christians were within, disputing violently, in loud, screaming voices. The Cretans are the most argumentative people in the world. We cannot ask the simplest question without getting a different opinion from every bystander, and thereupon ensues a discussion, in which everybody is edified except ourselves. The people informed us that they had had snow and rain for a hundred days previous—a thing unheard of in the island. Many of the oldest olive trees, as we had occasion to notice, had been broken down by the weight of the snow upon their limbs, and a great number of sheep and goats had perished.

The captain was probably the richest man in the village. His wealth consisted of a field of barley, four sheep, five goats, four pigs, and an ass. He was about seventy years old, had a gray beard, but his youngest child was only five. Both he and his wife exhibited a laudable curiosity to learn the customs of the *eklambrotati* (Their Brilliancies!) the *basilikoi anthropoi* (Royal Men), who had honored his hut with their presence. They took care to be on hand when we undressed, and they came and went so frequently during the night as to disturb our rest materially, but I discovered an evidence of their attention in the morning, on finding that I was covered with various dirty garments, placed under the holes in the roof, to intercept the droppings. In the morning the woman came up to me, suddenly fell upon her knees, kissed my muddy boots, and then arose and kissed my hand, before I fairly noticed what she was about. I gave little Levteri, who sat in the chimney-corner, a piece of money, whereupon he did the same thing, and his mother said: "May God permit you to enjoy your sovereignty many years!"

When we arose it was still raining, slowly, steadily, dismally. It was evident that we must renounce all hope of visiting Sfakia, for in such weather the single road into that region was already impassable. We therefore discharged Captain Nikephoro, who had been detailed for this special service, parting with the splendid fellow with genuine regret. Hadji Bey, also, was disinclined to set out. It was quite natural that he should wish to make things as easy as possible; he was travelling for our pleasure, not his own. However, I determined to get into good quarters at Rhithymnos, and as soon as the rain held up a little, the mules were packed in spite of Anagnosti's curses, and we set out. Descending the hill by a frightful path, alternate rock and quagmire, we reached the river of Armyro. The remains of an old Venetian fortress are upon its banks, and a short distance further a Turkish castle, mosque and khan, dismantled and deserted. Even here, on the sea-level, the snow had made great havoc among the olive trees. Finally we emerged upon the sea-shore, where the sand and pebbles made better footing for our mules, but the north-east wind, laden with rain, swept upon us with full force. Hadji Bey and the muleteers were in constant alarm during this part of our journey, assuring us that the Sfakiotes, who live during the winter in the neighboring village of Dramia, frequently pounce upon and plunder travellers. "But you need not be afraid of them on such a day as this," I suggested. "Oh, this is just the weather they choose for their attacks," said the Bey. By the shore large timbers had been collected, for the purpose, we were told, of building a mud machine for the port of Khania. At last we struck the hills again, which here thrust out a bold, rocky promontory, the base of which the sea has gnawed into a thousand fantastic forms.

After scrambling for some time over the insteps of the hills, we reached a tremendous gorge, cleft into their very heart, down the bottom of which rushed a rapid stream. Near the sea were the abutments of a massive sloping bridge, the arch of which was entirely gone. It had the appearance of having been overthrown by an earthquake, and Hadji Bey informed me that it was entire only sixty years ago. We were now upon the track of an ancient road, fragments of the pavement of which we saw in places. The gorge was inclosed by precipices of blue limestone rock, whose fronts were stained with bright orange-colored oxydations. In color and outline the picture was superb. The geological formation of Crete is a continuation of that of the mainland of Greece, the rock being principally the same *palombino*, or dove-colored limestone.

Our road beyond this was the next thing to impracticable. The rock, channeled and honeycombed everywhere by the action of water, was worn into a series of deep holes, filled with soft mud, in and out of which our mules plunged. On every headland stood a ruined watch-tower, of the Venetian or Turkish times. After more than two hours of this travel, we caught sight of the fortress of Rhithymnos, crowning a projecting cape some distance ahead. Two minarets and a palm-tree, rising above the gray houses of the town, relieved the view a little, but had it been ten times more dismal, the sight would have been a welcome one to us, in our cold, sore, and hungry condition. Soon afterwards we came to a very wild and deep ravine, spanned by a bridge of a double row of arches, one above the other—undoubtedly a Roman work. We now struck upon the new road, which fully justified Vely Pasha's description. It was a broad, solid, substantial, *English* highway, even better than the wants of the island demand. Two or three hundred men were at work, hauling the broken stone in hand-cars, or breaking them in the shelter of natural caves in the side of the hill. We pressed on, passed the village of lepers, whose houses are stuck like swallows' nests in the interstices of a solitary mass of rock, and at length entered the town by a long, low, gloomy gate.

CHAPTER XI.

OUR IMPRISONMENT AT RHITHYMNOS.

WE looked upon Rhithymnos as a port of refuge after our stormy journey, and it was therefore a matter of some importance to decide where we should go. The Pasha had given me letters to the Turkish Governor and the Greek Bishop. As a Protestant, I was equally an infidel in the eyes of both, but the Turk is more hospitable than the Greek, everywhere, and the Bishop, besides, was famishing in the leanness of his Lent; so I directed Hadji Bey to conduct us to the Governor. We passed through a street of bazaars, wholly Moslem in appearance, and soon reached the residence of the *Kaïmakan*, Khalim Bey, near the port. He was absent at the Council, but a servant—at a hint from our Hadji—conducted us to a large, unfurnished room, one-half of which was a daïs, covered with straw matting, and had our baggage brought up.

Soon afterwards the Governor arrived. He was a stout man of about fifty, with an open, pleasant countenance. He was a native of Monastir, in Macedonia, but had served in Syria and Egypt, and even spent some months in Paris. He shook hands cordially, ushered us into his divan, a low, barely-furnished room, and then read the Pasha's letter. I begged him to assist us in obtaining lodgings in the town, but he declared at once that he would be greatly mortified if we thought of leaving his house. He considered us his guests, and would feel highly honored if we would accept such poor quarters as he could give, so long as we might choose to stay. After making all allowance for Oriental exaggeration, there was still enough left to justify us in accepting the Governor's hospitable offer. François managed to hint delicately to him that we were almost famished, and an early dinner would be very acceptable. Coffee and pipes were at once ordered, and repeated again, with many apologies for the delay, for a long time elapsed before dinner was announced. The table was set in our room, in quite the European style, with two large bottles of red Cretan wine. The meal was plentiful and good, although the dishes were mostly Turkish. We had soup, pillau, wild fennel, stewed in oil, a salad of spinach, kid with a sauce of eggs and lemon juice, and *yaourt*, which I had not seen since my pilgrimage through Asia Minor.

We retired to chibouks and coffee in the divan, and then ensued a long conversation between the Governor and François, in alternate Turkish and Greek. I understood enough of the latter language to see that F.'s remarks were dexterously turned to our advantage. He spoke of us as *Beyzadehs*, or hereditary Beys. After giving an account of our visit to Khania and the very hospitable reception of the Pasha, he related our former travels in the East, and added something about my journeys in various parts of the world. The Governor was much pleased to learn that I was more interested in the country, its productions and people, than in its antiquities, concerning which he seemed to entertain no very high opinion. "But is that the Beyzadeh's only object in travelling?" he asked. "Does he not get tired of going about the world so much?" "Tell his Excellency," said I, "that there is nothing better than to know, from personal experience, the different nations of the earth; to learn their languages, to observe their character, habits, and laws, and thus to find out what is good in each." "Mashallah, but that is true enough," was the answer.

"And then," added François, "whatever the Beyzadeh sees, or hears, or experiences, during the day, he writes down at night. Every day he writes, and takes all the papers home with him. You should just see him write! It would take three men to keep pace with him—his pen goes so fast. He has made more than sixty thousand books, all about his travels." "Stop!" said I, "explain to the Governor that I have written six books only, but that perhaps ten or fifteen thousand copies of each have been printed and sold." "*Polá prágmata!*" (great things! ejaculated the Governor. "But," inquired the Secretary, "what does he make these books for? why are so many of them sold?" "Don't you see," said François, "that there are many millions of persons in America who cannot go over the world as the Beyzadeh does, but they want to know about other countries. Now, when they buy one of these books, they find in it all the papers which the Bey zadeh writes every night, and they know just as much as he does." The Governor exhibited much more than the ordinary Turkish intelligence, and was exceedingly curious to hear all the news of the world. Fortunately, he had consideration enough to retire early to his harem, and leave us to our beds.

On the morrow, it still rained, in the same dreary, hopeless manner. The first thing we did was to discharge our lazy, ignorant, insolent Anagnosti, and his mules. He was rogue enough to demand more than the price agreed upon in Khania, which was double what I had paid in Syria for horses. We counted out the proper sum, which he scornfully left lying upon the table, went out and got drunk, and then came back and took it. During a pause in the rain, the Governor sent a serjeant with us to show us the fortress, one of those massive, irregular Venetian affairs, for the construction of which lands were ruined and people robbed and starved. Over the gate, and in panels on every bastion, was the proud lion of St. Mark, his head in every instance knocked off by the Turks. Splendid bronze guns lay dismounted on the ramparts, and even the neglected walls were cracking and falling in pieces. The amount of labor and treasure expended by Venice on fortifications is almost incredible. No wonder that the oppressed Cretans joyfully hailed the Turks as deliverers from her iron rule. We shed poetic tears over her fall— we prate of Turkish barbarism, Turkish oppression, Turkish vandalism, when it is really Venice that has despoiled and impoverished the Levant. Thank God that she has fallen!

say I. Behead the winged lion—let the harlot, not the bride of the sea, sit in her ruined palaces, and lament, like Tyre, for the galleys that come no more, bringing tribute to her lust!

The Governor issued from his harem at an early hour and came to join us at coffee. He had a China service, and gave us Turkish zerfs of delicate silver filagree work, as egg-cups. We had also hot milk with our coffee, and crisp rolls, covered with grains of sesamé. I was a little surprised to find that his habits were so much Europeanized, but the truth leaked out that he was only imitating French customs temporarily, on our account, the cups, plates, spoons, &c., being borrowed for the occasion, some of one person and some of another. Two lieutenants of gend'armes, in their uniform, acted as waiters, getting free board in the Governor's house, in consideration of their services. Their wages were 150 and 300 piastres ($6 and $12) a month. At midday we had a breakfast, consisting of as many courses as the dinner, and composed of the same dishes.

I sent my letter of introduction to the Bishop, or *Despot*, as he is termed. He was ill with rheumatism or gout, but sent word that he would receive us in the afternoon. The Governor politely accompanied us to his residence. He was a stout, plethoric fellow of sixty, with large gray eyes, a venerable gray beard, and a countenance which expressed intelligence, shrewdness, and coldness. We were entertained with preserved quinces and water, followed by pipes and coffee. The conversation related principally to his ailment, and is not worth repeating. François was rather scandalized because I ignorantly used the ordinary Greek form of address, "*e eugeneia sas*" (your nobility) instead of "your holiness," in speaking to him. The attendants were young priests in apostolic hair and blue velvet jackets. The Despot was evidently suffering, and we made but a hort stay, congratulating ourselves, as we left, that we had made choice of the Governor for our host.

Towards evening, we received a visit from Mr. Woodward, the English engineer who had charge of the new road. He had been a year and a half in Crete, and seemed very glad to get a chance of speaking his own language again. His account of the people went very far to confirm my own impressions. They are violently opposed to improvement of any kind, and the road, especially, excited their bitterest hostility. They stole his flag-poles, tried to break his instruments, and even went so far as to attack his person. He was obliged to carry on the work under the protection of a company of Albanian soldiers. The Cretans, he stated, are conceited and disputatious in their character, to an astonishing degree. His greatest difficulty with the laborers on the road was their unwillingness to be taught anything, as it wounds their vanity to confess that they do not know it already. They even advised him how to use his instruments. If a stone was to be lifted, every man gave his advice as to the method, and the day would have been spent in discussing the different proposals, if he had not cut them short by threatening to fine every man who uttered another word. Their pockets are the most sensitive portion of their bodies, and even vanity gives way to preserve them. The law obliged the population of each district, in turn, to work nine days annually upon the road, or commute at the rate of six piastres a day This was by no means an oppressive measure, yet men worth their hundreds of thousands were found in the ranks of the laborers, in order to save the slight tax. Some of the villages were just beginning to see the advantage of the road, and, had a few miles been completed, the engineer thought the opposition would be greatly diminished. Nothing but an enlightened despotism can accomplish any good with such a population.

In the evening, the British Consular Agent, an Ionian Greek, paid us a visit, and there was a long *fumarium* in the Governor's divan. The Agent, waxing confidential, began explaining to the Governor, how it was possible to cheat in selling oil. "When you buy your oil," said he, "get the largest cask you can find—the very largest that is made—and fill it. You must have it standing on end, with the cock quite at the bottom. When you sell an oka of it, the pressure forces it out in a very strong stream; it becomes inflated with air, and the measure is filled with a less quantity of oil. You can make a gain of three per cent. in this way." He then went on to describe other methods by which, all together, the gain might be increased to fifteen or twenty per cent. François becoming impatient, cried out: "Now I see that the ancient Greeks were perfectly right, in having the same god for merchants and thieves!" The Governor laughed heartily, but the Agent, considerably nettled, exclaimed: "Do you mean to speak of me as a thief?" "No," answered François, with the greatest coolness; "I speak of you as a merchant." At this the Governor laughed still more loudly, and the discomfited Agent was obliged, by Oriental politeness, to laugh too.

The same person attacked François violently for his disbelief in the annual Easter miracle at Jerusalem, proclaiming that the fire actually came down from Heaven, and none but an infidel could doubt it. The belief in this blasphemous imposture, I may here remark, is almost universal among the Greeks. F., who has a hearty detestation of all Christian paganism, broke out with, "A miracle, indeed! I can perform as great a miracle with a lucifer match. Ask the patriarch of Jerusalem if he knows what phosphorus is! If he can turn Mount Ida into a lump of cheese, so that we can all cut from it as long as we like, I should call that a miracle worth something—but you go to Jerusalem and pay five hundred dollars to save your soul, by lighting a candle at his lying bit of wax!" The Governor, who had been at Jerusalem, enjoyed the dispute, until he found the parties were getting too much excited, when he adroitly changed the subject.

On Monday morning the weather changed, but for the worse. A violent storm of wind and rain set in, which continued the whole day and night, and the greater part of the next day, making us compulsory guests of the Governor. I was at first rather embarrassed at this long trespass upon his hospitality, but finding he was quite wealthy, and judging that our visit was rather a pleasant interruption to the monotony of his life, than otherwise, resigned myself to our fate. His kindness and courtesy, in fact, never flagged, and we should have been much more comfortable had he been less anxious to show us attention. After coffee, we must sit in his divan until the nour for Council arrived. On his return therefrom, he sent to let us know, and ask if we would not take a pipe with him. The afternoon was passed in the same manner and the evening devoted entirely to pipes and conversation. Our room was so cold and leaky, that our only alternative was the divan and its restraints. Seeing, on Tuesday, that there was no hope of change in the weather, I proposed to engage mules for Megalokastron, or Candia, but the Governor refused to send for them. "What would the Pasha say," said he, "if I should let you depart now? No, you are here, and here you shall stay until the weather is better." On the fifth morning, finally, when the storm had somewhat abated, although a heavy sea thundered on the beach, I prevailed upon him to order mules for us.

With the aid of François, I managed to give the Governor a tolerably clear idea of our country and its form of government, and to obtain from him, in return, some information concerning the administration of Crete. The only tax, it appears, is that paid in kind, by the agricultural population—one-tenth of the produce. Not only is there no direct tax on real estate, but trade of all kinds is entirely exempt, and pays nothing. In Greece, the burdens are much heavier, for the agricultural tax is the same, and in addition, all sorts of trades and occupations are made to pay heavily for their license. The revenue of Crete is about half a million of dollars annually, which is just about sufficient to pay the expenses of its Government. Were a just and equal system of taxation introduced, the revenue might be doubled without oppressing the people The direct tendency of the present system is to discourage the most important branch of industry. Crete is one of the richest islands in the Mediterranean, and there is no reason why it should not support now, as it once did, a population of a million.

We often hear it stated that the reforms which the Sultan has sanctioned, are only so many paper proclamations, which are never actually put in force. This has been very much the case in European Turkey and Asia-Minor, heretofore, but a new order of things is commencing. The *Hattihumayoon*, or bill of Religious Liberty, promulgated just two years previous, was in full force in Crete at the time of my visit. Singularly enough, the greatest opposition to it arose from the Christian, not the Turkish, population. A conspiracy was already on foot to procure the removal of Vely Pasha, because while he had allowed *two hundred and forty families* of Cretan Turks to embrace Christianity, he had protected some five or six Christians who voluntarily became Moslems, from the fanaticism of the Greek mob. "In Europe," said he to me, "we are called fanatical and intolerant, but I sincerely think we are less so than the Oriental Christians. I consider the Hattihumayoon a just and necessary measure, and am determined to keep it in force, and it is discouraging to find that the very people who are the most benefited by it, conspire to thwart me." He had given, under the Sultan's direction, 100,000 piastres towards the building of the new Greek Cathedral in Khania. What Christian government ever helped to build a mosque? What Catholic country ever gave funds to a Protestant Church? Let us, hereditary Pharisees that we are, learn a lesson of Christian tolerance from the infidel!

On the sixth morning we broke away from Rhithymnos against the good Governor's will. But five days had exhausted our patience, and some gleams of sunshine, touching with gold the solitary snowy cone of the Cretan Ida, set us in motion. Our destination was the Grotto of Melidoni, then the ruins of Gortynna, and the conjectured site of the famous **Labyrinth.**

CHAPTER XII.

THE CAVERNS, MOUNTAINS, AND LABYRINTHS
OF CRETE.

THE village of Melidoni, where we stopped on the afternoon of our departure from Rhithymnos, lies in the midst of a very beautiful and fertile valley, between Mount Ida and a group of barren hills on the coast. It was a very flourishing place before the Revolution, but is now for the most part a heap of ruins. The houses are built on a flat foundation of solid rock. We threaded the narrow lanes to a sort of café, where a group of lazy villagers were collected, and waited while Hadji Bey went off to summon the Governor. The latter came after a while, looking flushed and bewildered; he had been drunk, and was trying to appear as if he had not been. He was quite a young man and a brother of one of the Pasha's secretaries. He immediately treated us to coffee of burnt barley, and then conducted us to his house, which had an upper room, dry and tolerably decent. It was too late to visit the celebrated grotto of Melidoni, which is in the side of a mountain tc the westward, so I went upon the house-top, and succeeded in getting a sketch of Mount Ida, between the showers of rain. It rose in one splendid, sweeping peak of unbroken snow, from a base of lower summits, girdling the central cone. Under these, again, were bare and bleak masses, glooming blue and purple in the shadows of heavy clouds, while Ida shone with an angry lustre in the streaks of sunset light which came and went, as we gazed. This was our only near view of the glorious mountain, though we afterwards scaled many of its rugged buttresses.

Ismail Bey, the Governor, gave us a good dinner in the evening, with many apologies that he could not entertain us more worthily. The Greek priest and some subordinate officials came to pay their respects, and the former very courteously assisted the servants in waiting upon the table. His own fare was confined to olives and some of our caviar, but he drank his share of the wine, and heaped our plates with the forbidden flesh. We had already given up eating ham, except in a raw state, out of consideration for Hadji Bey, who was nearly starved whenever we had any of it cooked. Noticing that he looked with a longing eye at the wine, François offered him a glass. He had previously declined, like a good Mussulman, but this time he said, "If you will not report it at Khania," and swallowed the beverage with great satisfaction. The most genial and fraternal spirit pervaded the party, and there was every evidence of the truth of what I had heard—that the Christians and Turks of Crete, in the villages, live together in the most amicable manner. It is not always easy to distinguish them, outwardly. Many of the Turks have Christian names, and even have their children baptized by the Christian priests. There is little of that bitterness of feeling between them which exists in other parts of the Ottoman Empire. In the course of the evening, the priest asked me: "Did Your Brilliancies come to Crete in your own steamer, or did you hire one of the Austrians?" The Governor gave us his own bed, and retired to lodge in a friend's house.

He was very anxious that I should take his portrait, and I could do no less than comply, in the morning. The likeness was admitted by all the villagers to be very good, but he was greatly disappointed because I did not represent his light-blue undercoat, which was covered by another of a darker color! His secretary, a Christian, stood near me, and very kindly suggested what colors I should use. Some drawings of seaports which he had made were pasted on the walls, and, thinking that he might have some little talent that way, I explained to him that his houses should be made with upright lines, or they would appear to be tumbling down; but no, he knew better, the houses were right. He knew all about drawing, and nobody could teach him anything.

We walked up to the cave in the rain, accompanied by three or four of the villagers. Notwithstanding the entrance is in full view from the valley, they lost their way in climbing the mountain. The grotto of Melidoni is said to be almost equal, in extent and beauty, to that of Antiparos. It was dedicated of old to the Tallæan Hermes, in an inscription which is said still to exist, near the entrance, although I looked in vain for it. In modern times, it has obtained a melancholy notoriety from the fate of the inhabitants of Melidoni, who took refuge in it during the rebellion against the Turks. In 1822, when Hussein Bey marched upon the village, the inhabitants, to the number of three hundred, took refuge in the cave, taking with them their valuables, and provisions sufficient for six months. The entrance is so narrow and steep that they were perfectly secured against an attack, and the Turks, in their first attempt, lost twenty-five men. Finding that they refused submission on any terms, Hussein Bey ordered a quantity of combustibles to be brought to the entrance and set on fire. The smoke, rolling into the cavern in immense volumes, drove the miserable fugitives into the remoter chambers, where they lingered a little while longer, but were all eventually suffocated. The Turks waited some days, but still did not dare to enter, and a Greek captive was finally sent down, on the promise of his life being spared. The Turks then descended and plundered the bodies. A week afterwards, three natives of the village stole into the cavern to see what had become of their friends and relatives. It is said that they were so overcome by the terrible spectacle, that two of them died within a few days. Years afterwards, when the last vestiges of the insurrection had been suppressed, the Archbishop of Crete blessed the cavern, making it consecrated ground, and the bones of the victims were gathered together and partially covered up, in the outer chamber.

After crawling under the low arch of the entrance, we found ourselves at the top of a very steep and slippery plane, about fifty yards in depth. The descent was a matter requiring precaution, especially as the vaulted roof kept the same level, and our wax tapers were more and more feeble in the yawning gloom. At last, we reached a level floor, and found ourselves in a vast elliptical hall, about eighty feet in height, and propped in the centre by an enormous stalactitic pillar. On all sides, the stalactites hung like fluted curtains from the very roof, here in broad, sheeted masses, there dropping into single sharp folds, but all on a scale of Titanic grandeur. As our eyes became accustomed to the gloom, the roof expanded into loftier arches, and through the Gothic portals opening on our left gleamed spectrally the pillars of deeper halls. Rounded bases of stalagmite arose on all sides, some almost within reach of the giant icicles which grew downward to meet them, while a few others had already touched, and resembled a water-spout, the column of which is about to part in the middle. Under these grand and silent arches, under the black banners of eternal Night, lay heaped the mouldering skulls and bones of the poor Christians. They could not have had a more appropriate sepulchre.

Following our guides, we entered a smaller hall, superbly hung with drapery of gleaming alabaster, and then, crawling along a low passage and down an almost perpendicular descent of about fifteen feet, found ourselves in the great hall of the cavern, which is 150 feet long and about 100 feet high. The rock is almost entirely hidden under the immense masses of stalactite, which here take the wildest and most startling forms. Indeed, as a specimen of stalactitic formation, the cavern surpasses anything which I have ever seen. The floor of the last hall is composed of large masses of rock which have fallen from above, and descends rapidly to the further end, where there are three small chambers. Here the last of the victims perished, reached even there by the stifling fumes of sulphur and resin kindled at the mouth of the cave. Skulls rolled away under our feet, and on one of the stalagmites lay a long, thick braid of woman's hair. The atmosphere was heavy and stifling, and a sickening odor of mortality still exhaled from the ghastly remains. We returned to the entrance hall, and then explored another branch, which terminates in a deep pit, down which you see the fluted white curtains, fold falling behind fold—the roof, apparently, of still deeper halls, which have never yet been explored. Many of the largest stalactites were broken off by the earthquake which desolated Crete in October, 1856. Another beautiful appearance in this part of the cavern was that of a series of frozen cascades, falling in broad, thin sheets from the horizontal shelves of rock. Greatly as we were impressed by these wonders, however, we were not sorry when our exploration was at an end, and we could climb the slippery plane to daylight again.

Ismaïl Bey had in the meantime killed a fine turkey for us, and we were obliged to postpone our departure until it was cooked. The priest again ate with us, and complacently munched his olives while we attacked the succulent quarters of the fowl which the Governor laid before us. At noon, we started in the rain for Axos, the distance whereof from Melidoni it was impossible to ascertain, some saying it was two, some three, and some six hours. A violent discussion at once arose, and I became convinced that if the Cretans are not liars, according to Epimenides and St

Paul, they at least call themselves so. Our road, for some distance, led through a wild, broken, but remarkably fertile region, through orchards of immense olive, interspersed with clumps of plane and crab-trees, the former completely overgrown with gigantic grape-vines. Some of the olive-trunks were full six feet in diameter, showing an age of from ten to fifteen centuries. The ground was strewed with limbs broken off by the snow. This forcible pruning, however, will rather benefit the trees than otherwise, as the people are in the habit of leaving them entirely to nature, when, by judicious pruning, their yield might be greatly increased. Seven years ago, the olive-trees in Attica were so much injured by a cold winter, that it was necessary to cut off all the tops. For two or three years, the people lost their crops, but now the trees produce as they have never done before. In the district of Melidoni, during the winter, upwards of 12,000 sheep and goats had perished from the cold.

We at last came upon the large, rapid river of Axos, the "*rapidum Cretæ veniemus Oaxen*" of Virgil, which we were obliged to ford twice. Passing a picturesque fountain, shaded by plane-trees, we climbed up a steep, rocky hill to the village of Gharazo. This place, which is celebrated for the beauty of its women, contains many fine old ruined buildings, apparently of the Venetian time. The three women we saw were hideous creatures, greatly to our disappointment. We stopped at the house of the captain of the village, where Hadji Bey wished us to halt for the night, as the rain was increasing, but the captain cruelly said to him: "I wish you would pay me for the last time you were here." I determined to push on to Axos, but as everybody gave us a different direction, we were obliged to hire a villager as guide. Hadji Bey was rather disconsolate at the prospect, and sang no more of his doleful songs of love that day. We now commenced ascending the northern spurs of Ida, and the scenery was of the wildest and grandest kind, though dreary enough in the pelting rain, which increased every hour. All the steep mountain slopes, far and near, were covered with vineyards, which produce the excellent red Cretan wine. There are fortunes to be made by some one who has enterprise and skill enough to undertake the business of properly preparing and exporting the wines of Crete.

The vines, I learned, are much more exempt from disease than in Greece and the Ionian Islands. They are subject, however, to the ravages of a caterpillar, for the expulsion of which, when all other means have failed, a singular superstition is employed. The insects are formally summoned to appear before the judicial tribunal of the district, in order to be tried for their trespasses, and the fear of a legal prosecution, it is believed, will cause them to cease at once from their ravages! If this be true, caterpillars are the most sagacious of vermin. In some parts of Crete, a not less singular remedy is applied. It is one of those peculiar customs which most travellers, like th historian Gibbon, express "in the decent obscurity of a learned language;" but I do not know why I should not say that the remedy consists in an immodest exposure on the part of the women, whereat the worms are so shocked that they drop from the vines, wriggle themselves into the

After riding for nearly two hours along a lofty con b, we approached the wild gorge once crowned by the ancient Axos, through scattering groves of fine oak-trees. The only ruins in the modern village are a Byzantine chapel and some Roman brick-work, but there is a small fragment of Cyclopean wall on the summit above. We rode at once to the captain of the village, who invited us into his house, or rather den, for it was a long, low pile of stones, heaped against a rock, without window or chimney. The interior was divided into several compartments, some for beasts and some for men—the former being more comfortable than the latter. We crept into the dark hovel, where we were at least secure against the rain, except such as came through two holes in the roof, out of which a portion of the smoke escaped. The captain, an old Christian, dirty enough to be a saint of the Greek Church, and with a long, venerable white beard, kindled a fire to dry our wet clothes, giving us the alternative of either being blinded by the smoke or returning into the rain. Finally, the wet wood burned into coals, François fried some eggs, the village supplied excellent wine, and we made our hermitage as endurable as possible. The captain, whom we were obliged to invite to dinner, made inroads upon our stock of caviar, the only thing he dared eat. He had a spacious bedroom, which we hoped to occupy; but he had not yet learned Turkish hospitality, and we were obliged to sleep in the kitchen, with the rain trickling through the roof upon our heads. A number of the villagers came during the evening, to stare at us, and ask questions. We endeavored to get some information from them respecting the road to Heracleon, but finally gave up the attempt in despair. François completely lost his patience, and protested that in the whole course of his life he had never lodged in such holes, or been brought into contact with such a rascally set of people. St. Paul, referring to the Cretan poet Epimenides, says: "One of themselves, even a prophet of their own said, The Cretans are always liars, evil beasts, slow bellies. This witness is true." It is just as true at the present day, as applied to the Cretan Christians, and to many, but not all, of the Turks. I scarcely know which disgusted me more, during the journey—the beastly manner of life of the Cretans and their filthy bodily habits, or their brazen falsehood and egregious vanity.

In the morning, it rained as before, but I was determined to leave Axos, even if we had to take refuge in a similar den. The muleteers, nevertheless, refused to stir. "Kill us, if you like," they said, "but we will not move in such weather." I gave them until noon to decide, declaring that I should then take a mule, ride to Heracleon, and return for them with half-a-dozen Albanian soldiers. François, however, employed the more potent argument of a jug of wine, and, in proportion as they grew wet within, they became indifferent to the wet without. At noon, they were ready. The villagers brought us a great number of coins, Greek, Roman, Arabic and Venetian; they were mostly obliterated, but I succeeded in finding some copper pieces with the symbols of ancient Axos upon them. The captain demanded an exorbitant price for the use of his house, and the quarrel which ensued made us regret again that we were not among the Turks. We had engaged a man as guide to the next village of Kamariotes, and when we were about to start, he coolly turned to the villagers and asked: "Which way must I go? I never was there but once, and that was in the night!" He had previously told us that he knew every step of the road.

We passed through the gap behind Axos, and then turned eastward into the heart of the wild, barren mountains. It was no road, but a stony ladder, which we traversed, and any animal but a Cretan mule would have broken his neck in the first half mile. We kept along one of the spurs of Ida, near the line of snow, through a dreary wilderness, for two hours, when we reached the next village. It was a miserable forlorn place, and the lanes between the houses were so deep in snow that it was impossible to pass through them. We learned, however, that there was another place, called Asterakia, three or four miles further, and determined to push on. Upon hearing this announcement, Hadji Bey, whose whining love-plaints had already been soaked out of him, became desperate. "I forbid you," he shouted to François; "*I* have charge of the Beyzadehs, and they shall stop here!" We laughed, turned our mules' heads, and went on, whistling. Looking back, after we had gone half a mile, we saw the Hadji and the baggage mules following us in sad, funereal procession. After crossing another ridge, a long cheerful valley, sprinkled with groves of noble oaks, brought us to Asterakia—"The Little Star," but a more appropriate name would be "The Little Dunghill."

We went into the captain's house. The first room was

a stable, containing two asses and four pigs. Through this we reached a small windowless den, where two of the ancient Muses were baking bread, while a sick man lay upon a floor, under a heap of thorny furze. The women seemed angry at our intrusion, and I sent François to seek other lodgings, but he soon returned, saying that this was a palace compared to the other dwellings. The captain, who was very anxious that we should stay, gave his commands, and the tragic Muses immediately became comic, in their cheerfulness. We gave some advice to the sick man, who had a violent cold, with some fever, but the women said: "It is no use giving him anything; if he don't get well, he will die." They baked their bread in a small oven, heated with dry broom and furze. The neighbors came in to witness our dinner, and partake of our caviar, which was an unheard-of delicacy in those parts. They were a lively, good-humored set, but had the same fatal inability to answer a question. I asked one how far it was to Heracleon, but he answered that he had never been there in all his life.

We were now, fortunately, within an easy day's journey of the town, and when the morning dawned with a lowering sky, but without rain, we encountered no opposition from our guard and attendants. The road led over wild mountain ridges for some miles, when we struck upon the *basiliko dromos*, or Royal Road, from Rhithymnos to Heracleon. It is an old Venetian way, roughly paved in parts, so that the rugged mountain side is preferred by the mules. At last, from a ridge at the foot of Stromboli, a conspicuous conical peak, we saw the sea again, and the warm, green plain of Candia, lying far below us. To the south-east, out of the plain, rose the dark, isolated mass of Mount Juktas, the sepulchre of Jupiter. Behind us, under the eaves of the clouds, glimmered the snows of Ida, his birthplace. The remains of the tomb of the " Father of gods and men," who was worshipped in Crete as late as the eighth century, are still to be seen on the summit of Juktas—a parallelogram of hewn stones, eighty feet in length.

Eleven days of continuous rain had given us a surfeit of Cretan travel, besides which the mountain roads were becoming impassable, and the streams too high to be forded. I therefore renounced my project of visiting the ruins of Gortyna, on the southern side of Mount Ida. In themselves, the remains of the ancient city are insignificant, but in the adjacent mountain there is an excavation, known all over Crete as "The Labyrinth." We know that the famous labyrinth constructed by Dædalus was in the vicinity of Cnossus, the site of which is about three miles from Heracleon, and plainly visible from its walls. There are numerous caves in the neighboring hills, which may have given rise to the tradition; but the labyrinth of Gortyna is undoubtedly a work of art. It is of great extent, and the exploration of it is a work of some danger, owing to the number and intricacy of the various passages. The English engineer at Rhithymnos, who explored it by means of a bag of chaff, which he scattered as he went, considers it to have been a quarry. The natives are frequently bewildered and lost in it, and hence they never enter it without fear. This place exhibits certainly all the characteristics of the fabulous labyrinth except its location. On the latter ground, I believe antiquaries reject it entirely. The symbol on the coins of Gortyna is Europa and the bull, while those of Cnossus have a ground-plan of the labyrinth on the obverse. I procured one of the latter at Axos.

I learned that a splendid sarcophagus had been recently exhumed near Hierapetra (the ancient Hieraptyna), on the southern shore of the island. The sides contain bas-reliefs representing the combat for the shield of Achilles. It was at Arvi, near the same place that the sarcophagus with the triumphal procession of Bacchus, now in the Museum at Oxford, was found. It would be a very easy matter, said my informant, to get possession of this interesting relic, and smuggle it out of the island. I mention this fact for the benefit of those especially interested in such matters.

CHAPTER XIII.

TWO DAYS WITH AN ARCHBISHOP.

The chief city of Crete is known in Europe by its Venetian name of Candia, which during the Middle Ages was applied to the whole island. The country people, however, invariably speak of it as Megálo-kastron, or the Great Fortress, while the educated Greeks, both in Crete and elsewhere, have restored the ancient name of Heracleion, which was a small seaport, near Cnossus. Of these names, the latter is preferable, and I therefore employ it. Both among Greeks and Turks, the island has always retained the name of "Crete," instead of the bastard Venetian name of "Candia," which is only just beginning to be relinquished in Europe. The latter word is never heard in the Orient, and we have no longer any right to use it. I have given the classic name as the only correct one.

At Heracleion, as at Rhithymnos, I was provided with a double recommendation, through the kindness of Vely Pasha, and the choice of taking up my abode either with the Turkish Governor, or the venerable *Metropolitan* (Archbishop) of Crete. The hate manifested towards the latter by the bigoted Greek party in the island, and their intrigues to have him removed by the Patriarch of the Church, at Constantinople, convinced me that he must be a good man, and I therefore determined to claim his hospitality. We reached the city early in the afternoon, in a very battered and rusty condition, splashed with mud from head to foot, and, as we threaded the streets on our jaded mules, were the objects of general curiosity. Travellers are yet so scarce in Crete as to be personages of some importance. Hadji Bey guided us to the Metropolitan's residence, a large, rambling building, with three separate court-yards, a chapel and large garden. His Holiness was not at home, but we were courteously received by several priests and a secretary who spoke Italian. They at once appropriated a room to our use, entertained us with pipes and coffee in the large audience room, and then considerately allowed us to withdraw and change our clothes.

Presently the arrival of the Metropolitan was announced, and we found him waiting for us at the foot of the steps. His age was sixty-three; he was a little under the medium height, but erect and commanding in his appearance, with large, intelligent, benevolent gray eyes, a strong, straight, Albanian nose, and a majestic silver beard, which fell to his girdle. He wore a long, cinnamon-colored robe, over which was a dark-green pelisse, trimmed with fur, and the usual round black cap of the Greek priesthood, which somewhat resembles an inverted sauce-kettle. There was no fear of mistranslating the look of welcome upon that reverend face, or the cordial grasp of his extended hand. The extent of his hospitality will be better understood when I state (what we only learned on leaving) that he had made preparations for his departure into the interior on the morrow, and immediately postponed the journey on our account. Still holding my hand, he led us up-stairs to the divan, called for *glyko* (sweets)—a delicious jelly of strawberries prepared at Constantinople—pipes of the finest Rumeli tobacco, and coffee. I then gave him the Pasha's letter and a few lines of greeting from Elizabeth of Crete.

With François' help—as it was rather a delicate subject—I said to him that we would not trespass upon his hospitality further than to make use of the room allotted to us, as we were provided with every other requisite. He apparently acquiesced, to our great satisfaction, and I dispatched François to give into the charge of some Turkish baker, for cooking, a brace of hares which we had picked up at Asterakia. Shortly afterwards, however, when we had retired from the audience, two priests came to bring us back again, stating that we were to occupy the divan. I protested, but in vain. The Metropolitan would hear of nothing else, and as the evenings were still cool, he ordered a huge *mangal*, or brazier of coals, upon which were laid strips of lemon peel, to neutralize the gas and perfume the apartment. It was a lofty, spacious room, with a raised seat covered with damask at the further end, and a thick straw matting on the floor. The only ornaments were some Byzantine pictures of the Sacrifice of Abraham, the

Murder of Abel, and Joseph's adventure with Potiphar's wife—singular ornaments for an ecclesiastical residence As I was resigning myself to this hospitality and its consequent restraints, the Metropolitan stated that dinner would soon be ready. So it appeared that we were doomed to eat at his table, also. Dinner with an Archbishop, in the midst of Lent! We were desperately hungry, and the hares, I thought, must be nearly done by this time. Farewell, visions of the savory roast, and the odoriferous stew! Garlic and pulse are our portion.

It was after dark when we were summoned, and descended together to a lower room, where the Metropolitan sat down to the table with us, while two priests stood by to wait upon us. There were two salads, a plate of olives, and some bread. We groaned in spirit, as we thought of the flesh-pots of Egypt—as the officials of a European Court groaned, when they beheld an American Minister's temperance breakfast. Enforced holiness is even worse than enforced teetotalism. The priests handed us plates of soup. Hot gruel, I thought; but no, it had a flavor of chicken, and before the plates were emptied, a heretical boiled fowl was placed under my very nose. Then, O miracle! marched in our hares, dripping with balmy sauce —cooked as never hares were cooked before. Meanwhile the ruby blood of Ida gushed in our glasses, and we realized in its fullest sense the unreasonableness of Lent—how much more contented, grateful, and recognizant one feels when feasting than when fasting. I could not help ejaculating, in all sincerity, "*Doxasi 'o theos!*"

All this time, the good old man was contentedly eating

his salad *w* l olives. "This is liberal and truly Christian,' I said to François. "Oh," replied that worthy, "his Holiness has sense enough to know that we are no better than atheists." In fact I do not doubt that, in the eyes of the two attendant priests, we were utterly lost.

During the whole of our stay, we fared sumptuously The table groaned twice a day under its weight of fish, flesh, and fowl, and, so far from being shocked, the Metropolitan benevolently smiled upon our mountain appetites. I explained to him that the Protestants eschewed outward observances of this kind, considering that the fast should be spiritual and not bodily. In order to make the matter clearer to him, I referred to St. Paul's remarks on the subject of circumcision. "I understand it very well," he replied, "but we cannot do otherwise at present. My health suffers under the observance, but if I were to violate it, I should be chased from my place at once." I must confess I have a higher reverence for the virtue of hospitality than we seem to set upon it at present. When a Turk regales a Christian with ham (as it happened at Athens the same winter), when a lenten priest roasts his turkey for you, when an advocate of the Maine Law gives his German friend a glass of wine, when some of my own anti-tobacco friends at home allow me to smoke a cigar in the back-kitchen with the windows open, there is a sacrifice of self on the altar of common humanity. True hospitality involves a consideration for each other's habits—not our *excesses*, mind you, but our usual habits of life—even when they differ on such serious grounds as I have mentioned. But I have **dined** with Vegetarians who said, "Meat is unwhole some, so my conscience will not let me give it to you," or with the Ventilators, who proclaimed that "fires in bed rooms are deleterious"—and I have been starved and frozen.

The Metropolitan, finding that I spoke a very little Greek, insisted on dispensing with the aid of an interpreter. The purity of his accent, after the harsh Cretan dialect, in fact, made it comparatively easy for me to understand him, but it kept my brain constantly on the stretch to follow the course of his conversation, and to find suitable replies. He was a native of Epirus, of which province he was Bishop for ten years, before coming to Crete. He was therefore, of Slavonic, not Hellenic blood. It is well known that Bishoprics and Archbishoprics in the Greek Church are marketable commodities in the hands of the Patriarch, and François says, with how much truth I know not, that our host's place cost him 300,000 piastres ($12,000). It seemed certain, however, that he would not be allowed to keep it long—he was far too enlightened and progressive for the owls and bats who haunt the darkness of Eastern Christianity. His first act was to establish a school at Heracleion, and already sixteen hundred children of both sexes were receiving instruction in it. All his influence had been exerted in persuading the monasteries of Crete, which are the very hives of indolence and rapacity, to establish schools for the peasantry with a portion of their ample revenues; but only three or four of them consented to do so. In his endeavors, also, to assist Vely Pasha in carrying into force the *Hattihumayoun*, he incurred the hostility of the ultra-Greek party, who called him, in derision, the "Turko-polite." It was very cheering to light upon an evidence of true progress, in the midst of the disheartening experiences which constantly meet the traveller in Greece and the Orient. But what availed all his efforts? In six months after our visit, he was dead, Vely Pasha was dismissed, and Europe was satisfied.

The day after our arrival, the Metropolitan accompanied us on a walk through the city. The place was totally destroyed by an earthquake in the year 1856, between five and six hundred people perishing in the ruins. Advantage of this has been taken, in rebuilding, to widen the streets and improve the general plan of the town, though not to such an extent as the Government designed, on account of the violent opposition of the people. One sees everywhere heaps of ruins. As we walked through the streets, followed by the two secretaries, the tradesmen and mechanics in the bazaars saluted the Metropolitan by rising to their feet, and in return he gave them his benediction by lifting two fingers. We first called upon the Turkish Governor, a young man, whom I should have set down anywhere as an American, from his face. He offered us house, horses, and everything else in his power, but we only accepted an officer as guide to the fortifications and the old Venetian arsenal. The former are of immense strength and solidity, and the bronze guns of St. Mark still grin through the embrasures of the sea-wall. The port is quite small, and partly choked up with sand. It is protected by a mole, which is tumbling down, with a deserted fort at the extremity. Considerable commerce is carried on with other ports of the Levant, and even with England, the principal exports being soap, oil, wine, silk, and wool.

The arsenal is one of the most curious relics of the Middle Ages which I have ever seen. It is a massive stone building in the Palladian style. One side was thrown down by the earthquake, and the other walls cracked in many places from top to bottom, but fortunately not beyond the possibility of repair. It is completely stored with arms of all kinds, heaped together in great piles and covered with rust. Scores of cannon, with their carriages, lean against the walls; great haystacks of swords rise above one's head; heavy flails, studded with spikes, lances, arquebusses and morning-stars are heaped in dusty confusion along the length of the dark hall. In the upper story is a space evidently devoted to trophies taken in war. To every pillar is affixed a wooden shield with a Latin motto, around which are hung helmets, pikes, rapiers, and two-handed swords. There are also a multitude of tents, cordage, and kettles of balsam, which was used in making plasters for the wounded. Everything appears to be very much in the same condition as it was left by the Venetians, two centuries ago. The officers gave me leave to select an arrow from the sheaves of those weapons, cautioning me, however, not to scratch myself with the point, as many of them were poisoned. The Metropolitan's secretary, who longed for a Christian relic, secretly slipped one of them up his sleeve and carried it off.

We then visited the Venetian cathedral, afterwards a mosque, and now, owing to the earthquake, a beautiful ruin. While I sketched it, the two secretaries who stood near, conversed about us. "How is it," asked one, "that the Americans have Hellenic faces? The officers of the frigate

Congress all looked like ancient Greeks, and so do these two!" The remark was evidently intended to be overheard, for nothing could be further from the truth. We had at last sunshine again, and the twenty palms of Heracleion waved in the balmy air, which brought them greeting from the near Libyan shore. Ida rose unclouded in the west, its superb pinnacle just visible above its buttresses of gilded snow, while over the warm wheat-plains and the low hill of Cnossus towered Juktas in lonely grandeur, as if proud to be the sepulchre of Jove. I projected a ride thither, but the Thunderer's tomb was not to be trodden by profane feet: the snow still lay deep on the summit, and the monks of the monastery of Arkhanic, at its base, reported that the mountain was inaccessible.

We went the round of the schools in company with the Metropolitan, who introduced us both to teachers and scholars, making a short address to each class. The more advanced boys were reading Xenophon, which they parsed and explained with great glibness. I was delighted to see such a number of bright, intelligent faces, especially among the younger boys. Their eager, earnest expression was an evidence that their attendance was not compulsory. The Metropolitan was kind enough to translate a few words to them, for me, and I really felt, as I told him, that such a sight was better than a ruined temple. He informed me that Vely Pasha intended establishing a school in the city, in which both Greek and Turkish children were to be taught together, and I was very glad to find that he was himself strongly in favor of the measure. But if this plan ever succeeds, it will be in spite of the *Greek* population.

Outside the walls, there is a separate village for the lepers, as at Rhithymnos. These unhappy creatures are obliged to leave their native villages as soon as the disease makes its appearance, and consort with those who are cut off from intercourse with the healthy population by the same fate. The disease, in Crete, although presenting nearly the same features as in Norway, is slower in its operation and less hideous in its appearance. It is not considered contagious, as there are many instances on the island of a leprous man being married to a sound woman, and the reverse, without communicating the disease. The children of such unions are sometimes healthy, even. The number of lepers in Crete is upward of 1,200, and is at present on the increase, the disease invading even Sfakia, where it has hitherto been unknown. It has been ascribed, as in Norway, to the use of salt fish, together with excessive quantities of oil, and especially new oil, which has a fiery, acrid quality, which it loses after a few months. The filthy habits of life of the Cretans no doubt assist in developing the disease. The Medical Inspector of Heracleion, a French physician, informed me that all his endeavors to cure or check it had been in vain. He was very decided in the opinion that it was not contagious. He mentioned to me, as a very curious fact, that venereal diseases are unknown on the island.

The same gentleman was well acquainted with Sfakia, and his enthusiastic description of the people made me more than ever regret that I could not have visited them. He considers them Cretans of unmixed blood—the legitimate descendants of the ancient stock, asserting that they still retain all the physical marks of the old Hellenic race, both in face and form. In fact, one sees more Greek faces in a day in Crete than during a year in Athens. But in the greater part of the island the type has been modified by additions of Saracenic, Venetian, and Turkish blood: only in the mountain fastnesses of Sfakia does the true race of Minos exist.

We left Heracleion in the Austrian steamer after a sojourn of sixteen days in Crete, and returned to Athens by way of Syra. Our parting with the noble old Metropolitan was the parting from a revered friend, and François, who acknowledged that he had at last found one priest worthy of his office, kissed devoutly the hand stretched out to take his own.

CHAPTER XIV.

THE EARTHQUAKE AT CORINTH.

A WEEK after my return from Crete, I again left Athens for a tour through the Peloponnesus, which I could not enter upon sooner on account of the severity of the weather. The party consisted of Braisted and myself, accompanied by the indispensable François, all three mounted on sturdy, plodding horses, and two baggage animals under the charge of our *agoyats*, Pericles and Aristides. We had the necessary store of provisions, with two beds, a camp-table and stools, without which it is still impossible to travel with any comfort in Greece. Athens is semi-civilized, but the greater part of the country remains in a state of comparative barbarism.

The day of our departure augured a fortunate journey. It had stormed on the previous day, but now the azure pavement of heaven shone new-washed in the beams of the rising sun, and all the sounds and colors of Spring were doubly fresh in the crystalline air. A cool wind blew from the west, and every tint of the landscape was retouched and restored with the loveliest effect. The elder-trees in the gardens had already put on their summer dress; the tall Grecian poplars stood in a green mist of blossoms; the willows dropped their first tresses of milky emerald, and the pink petals of the almond flowers showered upon the earth. The plain of Attica, over which we rode, through the olive grove of the Academy, was like a paradise. The wheat was already high enough to ripple and shift its color in the wind, and the vines, among which the peasants were busily working, pruning the last year's shoots and heaping the earth between the rows, were beginning to put forth their leaves. As we turned, at the pass of Daphne, to take a farewell look at Athens, I was more than ever struck with the unrivalled position of the immortal city. The Acropolis is the prominent object in every view, and the rock-crested Lycabettus, with its pyramidal front, harmoniously balances it on the north, both being exquisitely relieved against the blue background of Hymettus.

I never saw a more superb sea-color than that of the Gulf of Salamis, as it shone in the distance, between the pale pinkish-gray walls of the pass. It was a dazzling, velvety blue-green, covered with a purple bloom, and shone with a semi-transparent lustre, like that of a dark sapphire. Neither brush nor pen could represent it. The scarlet anemones just opened, burned like coals of fire by the road-side, wild almonds and hawthorns hid their crooked boughs in a veil of blossoms, and the lily and asphodel shot forth new leaves. It was a day loaned from the treasury of heaven, and we shouted, as we rode, from an overplus of animal joy. We breakfasted at the tomb of

Straton, rode over the rich plain of Eleusis, passed the horned Mount Kerata (Cuckold), the eastern headland of Cithæron, and reached Megara in the afternoon. I noticed the ease with which good roads may be made in Greece. The soil abounds with broken limestone fragments, which only need shovelling together and rolling, to make an excellent macadam, not exposed to the chance of being injured by frosts or heavy rains. On the plain of Megara no road at all had been made, and yet there was a very good carriage track. In spite of this, however, the means of internal communication in Greece are inferior to what they were in the days of Homer.

Soon after leaving Eleusis, a few clouds gathered, the wind fell, and the sky darkened in such a manner that we feared a most unfavorable change in the weather. The landscape became singularly cold and dreary, and our spirits were unaccountably depressed. The foliage lost its bright color, the distant hills became dark and dull, the lively sounds of bird and beast ceased—in short, some gloomy spell seemed to have fallen upon the world. I tried in vain to shake off the uncomfortable weight, but it clung to me like a nightmare, and the fact that I could not account for it worried me still the more. On reaching Megara, however, we saw boys with bits of smoked glass, and the whole thing was explained. Our testimony, therefore, to the moral effect of a solar eclipse may be taken as perfectly impartial, and it may serve to explain the alarm felt by savage races on the occurrence of such a phenomenon.

The town of Megara is built in a dip between two hills

which rise out of the middle of the plain. It has a lively, bustling air, and shows some signs of progress. Large and handsome houses are springing up in the midst of the one-storied heaps of rough masonry which usually constitute a Greek town, and although about every fourth building is a church, the population must be considerably above a thousand. The plain on one side was a vast green floor of wheat, rye, and barley; on the other it was simply plowed, and would be partially planted with maize or beans. Next year the order of crops will be reversed, and so from year to year, in regular rotation. Manuring, or any improvement of the soil, is never thought of, and the plow is the same kind used by Ceres, when she planted the first grain. I was glad to see, however, by the orchards of young olives, and the encroachments of fields upon the bases of the mountains, that the area of this rude cultivation is extending. The city museum of antiquities is a dark, dirty hut, in which are three headless statues, one of them presenting its back to the visitor. During the evening the streets rang with the voice of a crier, who went around calling upon all those who were not at work, to attend church. This custom is probably borrowed from the Moslem call to prayer, but the cry is by no means so musical and impressive.

The next day we crossed the Geranean Mountains by the pass of the Skyronian Rocks. The breakneck bridle-path follows the chariot-road constructed by Hadrian, of which the massive supporting walls remain in many places. The Greek Government has at last commenced the task of constructing a new road, which will probably be finished in the course of twenty years, although it might be done in twelve months, thereby completing the communication between Athens and Corinth. The haunt of the robber Skyron, destroyed by Theseus, was near the southern limit of the mountains, where they tower high overhead, gaping with caverns, and showing white breaks in their tawny orange fronts, where huge fragments have fallen off. Near the sea, the marble rock, smoothed and polished by the rains of thousands of years, rises like a hewn wall to the height of more than a hundred feet. Whether Skyron was a strong wind which blew travellers off the cliff, or whether he was a real, live robber, is a question over which scholars may break their heads. A more important fact is that there are bands of robbers in the Isthmus now, and no chariot roads.

Thence to Kalamaki was a ride of four hours, over a plain almost entirely covered with mastic, wild olive, and the Isthmian pine—unplowed and uninhabited. In one spot, heaps of rough sulphur were piled on the seashore, and we saw, in the face of the mountains on our right, the quarries whence they came. As we approached Kalamaki, the ruin wrought by the earthquake which visited the Isthmus on Sunday, February 21, became evident. In the whole town but two houses appeared to be uninjured, and those of which the walls yet stood were so damaged as to be entirely uninhabitable. The town was a mass of hideous ruin—a mere heap of stones and broken tiles, out of which the rafters and roof-trees rose like the shattered spars of shipwrecked vessels. The khan where we had breakfasted on our way to Athens, was level with the earth; a large house opposite was so riddled and cracked that it resembled a basket, and great gaps, still yawning in the earth, showed how terrific had been the upheaval. The quay had sunk perceptibly, and a barrack at its extremity, split clean into two equal parts, leaned outward, threatening to fall at any moment. The people told us that the whole thing was the work of a second. It came like a thunderbolt, out of a clear sky, with no previous sign of warning. The sound and the shock were simultaneous; houses fell, the earth heaved up and down, cracked open as it rose, and when the cracks closed again as it sank, streams of water spouted up from them like fountains, high into the air. Four persons were killed, and but two wounded.

We could learn very little as to the probability of getting quarters for the night nearer Corinth, but determined to push on. A mile from Kalamaki our road passed over the site of the renowned Isthmian games. The inclosure of the stadium is still distinctly marked by the heaps of hewn stones, but of the temple of Neptune there are only shapeless fragments. As we rode over the deserted stadium, Braisted broke a branch of Isthmian pine as a souvenir and I repeated Schiller's "Gods of Greece:"

> "Then like palaces arose your temples,
> Lived for you each old, heroic game;
> At the Isthmus, rich with crowns and garlands,
> Chariots thundered to the goal of fame."

Two miles more brought us to the quarries whence Corinth and the Isthmian temples were built—vast hollows, walled by the hewn rock, their extent denoting the amount of material drawn from them. The plain was partially cultivated, its rich, mellow loam, more moist than that of Attica, producing admirable crops of wheat.

We stopped at the village of Hexamilia, about an hour's ride from Corinth, as there was no habitable house in the latter town, and the tents furnished by government barely sufficed for the destitute inhabitants. Hexamilia, though so near Corinth, suffered less than Kalamaki, which appears to have been directly on the line of the greatest vibration. Lutraki, only five miles distant, on the western shore of the Isthmus, escaped with comparatively trifling damage. We found quarters for the night in the house of the Demarch—a handsome two-story building of hewn stone, one end of which had been thrown down. Nevertheless, enough was left to shelter us from the rain, which began to fall heavily. A few of the houses in the village were levelled to the earth, but the most of them escaped with cracked walls, broken roofs, or the loss of a gable. Nobody was injured, but among the hills to the south four peasants and about thirty goats were killed by the falling of a mass of rock, in the grotto where they were lying.

The Demarch, who was a good-humored, communicative fellow, with rather more than the ordinary intelligence, informed me that he was in Corinth when the earthquake occurred. In a moment, he says, came the thunder and the shock. The houses all fell together, and there was such a dust that one man could not see another, standing near him. Many of the citizens were at the office of the Demarch, intending to elect new candidates. The walls

fell, but fortunately fell outwards, and nobody was injured
In another house a number of children were dancing, while
their mothers were gathered together to talk scandal. The
latter succeeded in holding up the falling roof until the
children escaped, and were then, in turn, rescued by some
men. Twenty-five persons were killed on the spot, or
afterwards died of their wounds, and the number wounded
was estimated at over fifty. This slight loss of life, when
compared with the extent of the catastrophe, is explained
by the fact that the earthquake took place between ten and
eleven o'clock in the forenoon, when the inhabitants are
mostly out of doors.

While the Demarch was relating to me these particulars,
there was suddenly a sound like distant artillery, and the
house trembled slightly. "There it is again!" said he;
"we have heard it every hour or two since the beginning."
In the evening there was another shock; two during the
night; and at six in the morning, while we yet lay in bed,
one so violent that some stones were dislodged from the
wall, and rattled on the floor over our heads. This latter
was accompanied by a deep, hollow, rumbling sound, which
seemed at the same time to be under and around us. It
was probably my imagination which gave me the impression
that it came from the west and rolled towards the east
Although we were convinced that the worst was past, and
that we were no longer in any danger from these shocks,
their uncertain recurrence and mysterious threatening
character gave us a vague feeling of alarm. The Demarch,
his brother, their wives and children, our *agoyats* and ourselves all slept on the unpaved floor of the house, but the

family were so accustomed to the shocks that they no longer paid any attention to them.

As it was raining next morning, we waited until nearly eleven o'clock, when, finding no signs of a change, we set out in the storm. A ride of half an hour brought us to Corinth—or rather what *had been* Corinth—for, although a few houses were standing, they were cracked from top to bottom, and had been abandoned. The greater part of the city was a shapeless heap of ruins, and most of the inhabitants seemed to have deserted it. Some tents had been pitched, and a few rough wooden barracks erected, which, at least, sheltered them from the weather. The force of the shock appeared to have been of about the same violence as at Kalamaki. All accounts concurred in representing it as a sudden, vertical upheaval, not accompanied with horizontal waves, and the fact that nearly all the walls fell outward, verifies this statement. The central line of the force undoubtedly passed through or very near Corinth and Kalamaki, in a direction about E. N. E. and W. S. W. On either side of this central line the force must have diminished in very rapid proportion, as Hexamilia, not two miles distant from it, appeared to have been visited by a shock considerably less violent, and a village five or six miles westward from Corinth, suffered but little damage. At Megara, on one side, and Argos on the other, the earthquake was sensibly felt, but without producing the slightest effect.

The shocks, which still continued, were confined to the neighborhood of Corinth. They did not pass the Geranean Mountains on the north, or that range on the south which divides the valley of Nemea from the plain of Argos. This limitation of the operations of the earthquake is its most singular feature, enabling us to determine very nearly the central point of the subterranean forces, which coincides with the centre of the Isthmus at its narrowest part. The Government decided to remove the town of Corinth to a new site on the plain two or three miles nearer the Gulf. No commencement had been made, however, and I doubt whether the people will second this measure. The Isthmus is undoubtedly the best site for a commercial city in all Greece, and the King and his advisers committed a great oversight in establishing the capital at Athens, instead of building up a new one here. Athens never can be an important city; its life depends only on that of the Court. It is a very small sort of a Washington—a village with public buildings. Here, however, is the saddle of Greece, whose warm flanks are bathed in the Mediterranean, and whose head, snorting for Constantinople, is thrust into Thessaly. A city mounted here, would have one foot in either sea, taking the commerce of the Adriatic from Patras, that of the Orient from Syra, and yet uniting the conflicting interests and jealousies of Greece as nothing else could have done. Ah, what a chance was lost through the classic taste and practical stupidity of old Ludwig of Bavaria!

We paused awhile before the seven ancient Doric columns of the temple of Neptune, or the Corinthian Jove, or Minerva Chalcidis, or whatever else they may be. Rough as these monoliths are, evidently erected long before the perfect period of Grecian architecture, one nevertheless finds the simple grace of the Doric order in their worn, unwieldy masses. One of them has been violently split by the earthquake, and a very slight impulse would throw it against its nearest fellow, probably to precipitate that in turn.

Passing around the giant Acropolis, whose summit was enveloped in clouds, we entered the valley of a stream which comes down from the Nemean Hills. It rained slowly and steadily, and the deserted landscape was doubly dismal under the lowering sky. We toiled on for four hours, and finally took refuge from the weather in the khan of Kourtessa, near the site of Cleonæ. This place, too, had suffered from the earthquake. Of the three houses, two were uninhabitable, the largest belonging to an officer of the gend'armerie, being terribly shattered, with both gable-ends thrown outwards. The young keeper of the khan, Agamemnon by name, received us kindly, and we whiled away the evening in listening to the songs of a blind, wandering Homer, who sang violently through his nose, accompanying himself with a cither, equally nasal and discordant. The character of the music was entirely Oriental—monotonous, irregular, and with a prolongatio of the final syllables of every line, which always interrupted the *tempo*. Some of the more lively airs suggested Irish melodies. There were admirable things in the themes—especially in a song of the *Klepts*—but they needed to be reduced to order and harmonized. After dinner came the same terrific, rumbling sound we had heard in the morning, with a sudden strong vertical motion, which made the house rock like a reed in the wind. The shock lasted from twenty to thirty-seconds, and the vibrations continued at least a minute longer. The timbers cracked, and the walls gave signs of splitting. A very little additional force would have brought the house down upon our heads.

During the night, I was awakened by the crash of a falling wall belonging to the large house; the shock was already over. But at daylight we were visited by the most powerful of all. The violence of the upward and downward motion caused the walls on either side of us to crack open and separate, with a horrid, grinding sound, while many of the smaller stones fell around us. We were in bed, and felt rather concerned for our safety, but were too intent on watching the phenomenon to take measures of escape. I felt relieved, however, on finding that the storm was breaking away, so that we could soon put ourselves on a more stable soil than that of Corinth.

By ten o'clock we had climbed to the crest of the hills, and the plain of Argos, crossed by long streaks of golden morning light, lay below us. On the right the mountains of Arcadia rose in a rampart of glittering snow, with the hills of Erymanthus and the pyramidal peak of Cyllene still further to the west. Beyond the emerald pavement of the plain rose the Acropolis of Argos against the purple line of the Argolic Gulf. The glorious landscape swam in a transparent vapor, which still further softened its exquisite harmony of color. The pink mountain headlands, painted with the tenderest streakings of silvery-gray shadow, had a play of light like that upon folded silk, and the whole scene was clear and luminous in tone, as if painted upon glass. It is difficult to picture in words the pure, aerial delicacy and loveliness of coloring which tinted the Argive world below us—and I have not the magic pencil of Turner, who alone could have caught its transitory splendor

CHAPTER XV.

ARGOLIS AND ARCADIA.

I HAVE nothing to add to the descriptions of the ruined fortresses of Argolis, given by previous travellers. Of course, we sat in the Gate of Lions, at Mycenæ, and, as in duty bound, thought of bully Agamemnon, Orestes, Electra, and all the other renowned old creatures who either were or were not (see Grote's History), admired the grand Pelasgic masonry of Tiryns, and climbed the seventy-two rows of rock-hewn seats in the theatre of Argos. To one who has seen Egypt, Baalbec, and Elephanta, these ruins, apart from their historical interest, are not very impressive. Athens, Sunium, Egina, and Phigalia, comprise all that is left of the architectural splendors of Greece; the rest is walls, foundations, cattered stones, and a few very dilapidated theatres. The traveller must bring the magic of immortal associations with him, or he will be disappointed.

I found the "thirsty Argos" a rich, well-watered plain—at least in March. The Inachos rolled a full, swift stream to the Gulf, and the lush grain was shooting up so vigor ously that two or three weeks more would see it in head Argos is a mean, filthy town, with a most indolent population, if the crowds of loafers at all the coffee-houses might be taken as a specimen. The country people were pitching quoits in the streets, and at a café where we stopped to rest, twenty-five men were playing cards. A Greek officer, who spoke some French, accosted us. I learned afterwards that he had been banished from Athens on account of his peculations being discovered. The richness of the soil, he said to me, makes the people idle: they raise two crops a year, have amply sufficient for all their wants, and work no more than they can help. "You want a Governor despotic enough," I said to him, "to take all these able-bodied idlers and make them clean the Augean stable in which they live." In fact, all the labors of Hercules need doing over again in Greece. The Hydra inhabits the Lernæan marsh; the lion crouches in the valley of Nemea; and there is more than one wild boar in the forests of Erymanthus. Fever, flood, drouth, and fire are at their old ravages, and they are doubly ferocious when they have reconquered a territory once wrested from them.

We spent a night in Nauplia, and climbed the embattled rock of the Palamidi. The town is small, being squeezed into a narrow space between the lower fortress and the water. The houses are lofty, well-built, and dirty, as in Italian seaports, and there are two diminutive squares, one of which has a monument in honor of Demetrius Ypsilanti. It has been decreed to erect another to Capo d'Istria—the only efficient ruler Greece has had—but some years have passed, and the first block of marble is not yet cut. In place of it, we found triumphal arches of calico commemorating the recent festival, and an Ionic pillar with an astonishing capital supporting a pasteboard figure of the King. Workmen were just taking to pieces the Doric columns of lath and muslin which had been erected in the principal streets. Outside the gate there was another triumphal arch, the supports of which had given way, so that it leaned at an angle of forty-five degrees, threatening to fall and block up the road. I could not look upon these monstrous decorations without intense disgust. One does not expect Greece to build new Parthenons all at once, but such pitiful gimcrackery is worthy only of Ashantee or Timbuctoo.

The morning was mild and cloudless. A light breeze blew from the west, scarcely rippling the beryl sheet of the Argolic Gulf, while the wide, amphitheatric plain basked in the fairest sunshine. We mounted the steps of the fortress—860 in all—and were well repaid, not so much by the fortifications as by the glorious Argive panorama around us. The position is one of immense strength, the rock being almost precipitous on the sea side. Eastward, it falls into a narrow ridge, connecting it with two hills of nearly equal height, but too distant to command it. The fortress, like all Venetian works of the kind, is much larger than necessary, consisting of several detached forts inclosed within one wall of circuit. The principal batteries bear the names of Phocion, Epaminondas, and Miltiades. The place is now used as a State Prison, and we had the satisfaction of seeing some ten or twelve manacled brigands in a dirty court-yard.

We were two days in riding from Nauplia to Tripolitza. There is a broad carriage-road the whole way, a distance of nearly forty miles, the construction of which is due to local enterprise, 300,000 drachmas having been subscribed in Tripolitza alone. The only fault in the work is that it is too well done for the needs of the country. It is carried over two branches of the Parthenian Mountains by zigzags of so easy a grade that the actual distance is trebled, and horsemen stick to the old road in preference. The workmanship is good, although a little ragged in places, and the bridges are admirable. The Government newspaper, the *Elpis*, recently stated, in its summing up of the benefits which Greece has derived from the reign of Otho, the amount of the roads which have been made. I find the total length of these roads to be less than 120 miles; while, if we subtract those which have been constructed simply for the convenience of the Court, and not for the good of the country, there will remain barely fifty miles. The Greeks say, and their friends say: "Don't ask too much of us; we are young and poor; we have not the means to accomplish more." Yes; but you build a palace for two millions of dollars; you support a useless army of military and naval leeches; you give to the Court whenever the Court asks, and you give nothing to the people. You adopt the policy of Venice, the Eastern Empire, Turkey even, instead of looking for example and guidance to the countries which now lead the van of civilization.

Riding southward along the beach, after leaving Nauplia, we passed the Government stud, established for the purpose of rearing cavalry horses. François knew the *Stallmeister* a Mecklenburger named Springfeldt, who had long been in Russian service at Warsaw. We spent an hour with the tall, strapping, good-humored fellow, who was delighted to talk German again. He had been there three months, and seemed very well satisfied with his situation. The stallions, he said, were mostly of Arabic blood, some of them very fine animals; but no judgment had been exercised in the breeding, and the colts were generally inferior. He entertained us with "pitch-wine" (as he called it), of excellent quality, at five cents a bottle.

At the end of the Argive plain is the little village of Miles, where Ypsilanti gained a splendid victory over the troops of Ibrahim Pasha, and Col. Miller greatly distinguished himself. On the left is the Lernæan marsh. The road now climbed across the Parthenian mountains, with a glorious backward view from the summit ridge. Nauplia, the gulf and plain, lay at our very feet, bathed in a flood of airy gold, while the summits at hand rose dark and cold under the descending folds of a heavy rain-cloud. Beyond the ridge opened a stony basin, six miles in diameter, and arid enough to be the home of the Danaïdæ. Passing the ruins of a pyramid, we descended to our resting-place for the night, the khan of Achladókambos (the pear-garden). At the village of the same name, on the hill above, the people stole the King's silver plate when he breakfasted there on one of his early journeys through the Morea.

The next day we crossed a second range of the mountains The road was thronged with asses laden with bar-iron or bales of dry-goods, bound inland, while an equal number, carrying skins of oil or great panniers of eggs—provision for the approaching Easter days—descended to the coast. We also met a convoy of mules, laden with money, protected by a guard of soldiers. From the top of the ridge we saw the great central plain of Arcadia, which is between two and three thousand feet above the level of the sea. Here the season was nearly a month later than on the plain of Argos, and the country had a gray, wintry look. There is no sufficient drainage for this plain, and hence parts of it are marshy and miasmatic. One to whom poetry has made the name of Arcadia a golden sound, the key to landscapes of ideal loveliness, skies of perpetual Spring, and a pure and happy race of men, will be bitterly disappointed as he descends from the gusty Parthenian Hills. In this bleak region, surrounded by cold, naked mountains, with its rough barbaric Slavonian population, and its filthy den of a capital, he will not recognise one feature of the Arcadia of his dreams. But so it is: the "*bella età dell' oro*" of Tasso and Hesiod never existed and never can exist, and Arcadia, which is for us the musical name of a beautiful impossibility, signifies no more to the modern Greek than Swampscot or Sheboygan.

Tripolitza soon appeared in sight, at the foot of the mountains which inclose the plain on the west. It is an immense straggling village—a mere mass of red tile-roofs—and we found the interior even less attractive than the distant view. Crooked streets, heaped with filth and interrupted by pools of black mud, lead between rows of roughly-built, dirty stone houses, inhabited by people as rough and dirty as they. On entering the place, we were assailed by a multitude of beggars: all the children seemed to have adopted this profession. The female costume is picturesque, and struck me as being truly antique in character. It consists of a white muslin petticoat, over which is a short tunic of blue cloth, with a bright red border, open in front ; a girdle around the waist, sleeves of yellow or some gay color, and a loose white handkerchief enveloping the head. Most of the men have Slavonic features, but I saw, in all, perhaps half a dozen true Hellenic faces.

In the afternoon we set off for Mantinæa, distant eight miles to the northward. Four miles from Tripolitza, the plain turns westward around an angle of the mountains, disclosing a higher and drier level, abounding in vineyards which were separated by hedges of thorn and blackberry. Our road was upon green meadow turf, straight across the plain. The low, white walls of Mantinæa now met the eye, at the foot of a round, gray hill, over which towered the snow-streaked summit of Orchomenos. On approaching the place, we could readily imagine the spot where Epaminondas fell, and the part of the hill from which he directed the battle in his dying moments, until a second daughter of victory was born to perpetuate his lineage. The foundations of the turreted walls can be traced throughout their whole extent, the first three courses being as perfect in many places as when first laid. It is conjectured that the remaining portion was of brick.

Black sun-clouds rested on all the mountains, as we rode away from Tripolitza. For three hours we followed a rocky bridle-path, crossing the ridge at an altitude of about 4,000 feet. By noon the chilly uplands were passed ; the hills suddenly fell away, and we saw far below us, warm in the sunshine, and stretching off to the blue Lycæan Mountains, which girdled it with a splendid belt, the valley of the Alpheus. Dense copses of shrubbery, studded with gnarled oak trees, covered the mountain sides; the blue crocus and pale star-flower spangled the sunny banks; fresh grain-fields and meadows of sprouting turf brightened the immense valley, and the red roofs of towns, with cypresses rising from their midst, dotted it here and there. Away to the right was Karytena, the rock-fortress of Colocotroni; in front Sinanu, on the site of ancient Megalopolis; and to the left, at the entrance of a defile commanding the road to Sparta, Leondari.

Descending to the floor of the valley, we rode over the oozy turf to Sinanu, a scattering town, with broad, grassy streets. We met many shepherds in shaggy sheepskin capotes and with long crooks in their hands. The people came in a body to the dirty little café where we halted, in order to stare at us. Three or four spruce young palikars offered to accompany us to the theatre of Megalopolis, which is about half a mile to the north of the town. As François had told them that I spoke both ancient and modern Greek, they plied me with questions the whole way, and I was sorely troubled to keep up my reputation for scholarship. These people were almost entirely of Slavonic blood, which is no doubt the predominating element in Greece. Groups of villagers sat in the sun — happy Arcadians!—and skilfully explored each other's heads. Both Sinanu and Leondari were very rich places under the Turks, but are now miserably poor, or seem to be so. The country Greeks hide their money, and are therefore often richer than they appear.

CHAPTER XVI.

FOUR DAYS AMONG THE SPARTANS.

LEONDARI, where we passed the night, is on the frontier of Sparta, but still in Arcadia. Here Alpheus, from his "glacier cold" on Taygetus, rushes down the hills in pursuit of his Dorian Arethusa. Here is still the rural paradise of ancient Greece, with its pure air, its sweet waters, its seclusion and peace—but alas! the people. We overlooked long tracts of oak forests—nothing but oak—some ancient trunks, gnarled and hoary with a thousand years, and younger woods covering the gently-rounded knolls. The morning was divinely clear and brilliant, but cold, with a thin sheet of ice on standing water. In an hour and a half, after threading scattering groves of oak and ilex, we passed a low bar connecting Taygetus with Menælus on the north, and this, as I rightly guessed, was the water-shed between the Alpheus and the Eurotas—the boundary of Sparta. In the splendor of the day, every feature of the landscape had its clearest form and its richest coloring, and from the beds of daisy and crocus at our feet to the snowy pyramids of Taygetus, high above us, everything spoke of life and of Spring. There is a village called Longaniko, in a very wild position, high up under the very crest of the mountain, which supplies the Morea with physicians. The boys are even sent to France and Germany to complete their studies. During the day we met with numbers of peasants, driving asses laden with bundles of young mulberry and olive trees, from the nurseries of Sparta. There was refreshing evidence of improvement, in the amount of new ground brought under cultivation.

As we approached Sparta, the road descended to the banks of the Eurotas. Traces of the ancient walls which restrained the river still remain in places, but, in his shifting course, he has swept the most of them away, and spread his gravelly deposits freely over the bottoms inclosed between the spurs of the hills. The clumps of poplar, willow, and sycamore which lined the stream, and the thickets of blackberry, mastic, ilex, and arbutus through which our road wound, gave the scenery a charmingly wild and rural aspect. The hills—deposits of alluvium left by the pre-Adamite floods—took the most remarkable forms, showing regular terraces, cones, pyramids, and bastions, as they fell off towards the river. Towards evening we saw, at a distance, the white houses of modern Sparta, and presently some indications of the ancient city. At first, the remains of terraces and ramparts, then the unmistakable Hellenic walls, and, as the superb plain of the Eurotas burst upon us, stretching, in garden-like beauty, to the foot of the abrupt hills, over which towered the sun-touched snows of Taygetus, we saw close on our right, almost the only relic of the lost ages—the theatre. Riding across a field of wheat, which extended all over the scene of the Spartan gymnastic exhibitions, we stood on the proscenium and contemplated these silent ruins, and the broad beautiful landscape. It is one of the finest views in Greece—not so crowded with striking points, not so splendid in associations as that of Athens, but larger, grander, richer in coloring. The plain, watered by the unfailing Eurotas, is covered with luxuriant vegetation, and opens its fruitful lap to the noonday sun. In warm countries water is the great fertilizer, and no part of Greece is so well supplied in this respect as Sparta.

Besides the theatre, the only remains are some masses of Roman brickwork, and the massive substructions of a small temple which the natives call the tomb of Leonidas. I walked over the shapeless rubbish which covers the five hills, without a single feeling of regret. There were great fighters before Agamemnon, and there are as brave men as Leonidas to-day. As for the race of military savages whom Lycurgus—the man of ice and iron—educated here, who would wish to restore them? The one virtue of the Spartans—bravery—is always exaggerated, because it is their only noble trait. They were coarse, cruel, treacherous, and dishonest, and while they acted in two or three instances as a shield to Greece, they dealt the perfidious stabs through which she perished at last. In art, literature, science, and philosophy, we owe nothing to Sparta. She has bequeathed to us only a few individual examples of splendid heroism, and a code which, God be thanked, can never be put in practice again.

We spent the night in a comfortable house, which actually boasted of a floor, glass windows, and muslin curtains. On returning to the theatre in the morning, we turned aside into a plowed field to inspect a sarcophagus which had just been discovered. It still lay in the pit where it was found, and was entire, with the exception of the lid. It was ten feet long by four broad, and was remarkable in having a division at one end, forming a smaller chamber, as if for the purpose of receiving the bones of a child. From the theatre I made a sketch of the valley, with the dazzling ridge of Taygetus in the rear, and Mistra, the mediæval Sparta, hanging on the steep sides of one of his gorges. The sun was intensely hot, and we were glad to descend again, making our way through tall wheat, past walls of Roman brickwork and scattering blocks of the older city, to the tomb of Leonidas. This is said to be a temple, though there are traces of vaults and passages beneath the pavement, which do not quite harmonize with such a conjecture. It is composed of huge blocks of breccia, some of them thirteen feet long.

I determined to make an excursion to the mountain district of Maina, which comprises the range of Taygetus, and the promontory of Tenarus, between the Laconian and Messenian Gulfs. This is a region rarely visited by travellers, who are generally frightened off by the reputation of its inhabitants, who are considered by the Greeks to be bandits and cut-throats to a man. The Mainotes are, for the most part, lineal descendants of the ancient Spartans, and from the decline of the Roman power up to the present century, have preserved a virtual independence in their mountain fastnesses. The worship of the pagan deities existed among them as late as the eighth century. They were never conquered by the Turks, and it required considerable management to bring them under the rule of Otho. A Greek poet, fifty years ago, writes of them: "Let all honest men fly from them as from a serpent. May the plague and the drought blast them all!" Dr. Kalopothakes, a born Mainote, who received his medical education in Philadelphia, assured me, however, that I should not meet with the least difficulty in travelling through the country. My principal object was to ascertain whether the ancient Greek face and form still exist among those whose blood may be presumed to be purest of all the fragments of the ancient stock. A thorough investigation of the character and habits of the people necessarily requires a familiar knowledge of the language.

Starting at noon, we passed through the modern Sparta, which is well laid out with broad streets. The site is superb, and in the course of time the new town will take the place of Mistra. We rode southward, down the valley of the Eurotas, through orchards of olive and mulberry. In one place some thirty men were at work, digging up the plain with large hoes, in order to plant a vineyard. The proprietor, a handsomely-dressed palikar, with pistols in his belt, was directing the labor. We now entered a tangled maze of rough alluvial hills, threaded by frequent streams which came down from Taygetus. Here we met a procession of ragged but very good-humored young fellows, the last of whom carried a cross decorated with gilt paper and laurel leaves. A Spartan, who was riding with us, said they had been celebrating the festival of St. Lazarus. There was the greatest diversity of character in the faces we saw. A very few were of the antique type, some Turkish, many Albanese or Slavonic, and some actually *Irish* in every respect. Our sailors are accustomed to call the Irish *Greeks*, and the term is more than a mere chance. There are very striking points of resemblance in character—the same vanity, talent for repartee, tenacity of religious faith, and happy lack of forethought. If the Greeks, on one hand, are more temperate, the Irish, on the other, are more hospitable; if the former blunder less, the latter cheat less.

We stopped for the night at the little khan of Levetzova. When François last visited this place, fourteen years before, he found the khanji lying dead upon the floor, having just been murdered. It was a case of blood revenge, and the assassin came all the way from Smyrna to effect his purpose. I asked the present khanji whether the country was quiet. "Here it is very quiet," said he, "but as for foreign parts, I don't know how it is." I saw some cows pasturing here, quite a rare sight in Greece, where genuine butter is unknown. That which is made from the milk of sheep and goats is no better than mild tallow. The people informed me, however, that they make cheese from cow's milk, but not during Lent. They are now occupied with rearing Paschal lambs, a quarter of a million of which are slaughtered in Greece on Easter Day.

The next morning we rode over hills covered with real turf, a little thin, perhaps, but still a rare sight in southern lands. The red anemone mantled the slopes as with a sheet of fire; the furze bushes shone with a shower of golden blossoms, which wholly concealed their prickly stems, and on moist banks the daisy, violet, buttercup, crocus, and star wort formed mosaics of spring bloom. The hills were dotted with groves of the oak which produces valonia or nutgalls. But for the mastic and oleander, and the carob-trees, with their dark, glossy foliage, I could have believed myself among the German hills at the end of May. In two hours we entered the territory of Maina, on the crest of a hill, where we saw Marathonisi (the ancient Gythium), lying warm upon the Laconian Gulf. The town is a steep, dirty, labyrinthine place, and so rarely visited by strangers hat our appearance created quite a sensation. François, as usual, was furious at being catechised, and snubbed the highest officials in the most despotic manner. When I remonstrated, he replied, "What can one do? If I ask, 'Where is the khan?' instead of answering, they cry out, 'Where do you come from? where are you going to? who are the strangers? what are their names? how old are they? what do they travel for?' *Diable!* If it was a Turkish country, I should not be bothered in this way. We should be entertained, we should eat, drink, and smoke, before we heard a question; but good manners among the Turks and Christians are two different things!"

We took refuge in a café, and ate our ham and eggs in public, to the horror of the orthodox spectators. I made acquaintance with the teacher of the Government school, who gave the people an excellent character, but lamented their slowness in learning. François also found an old acquaintance, a former fellow-soldier in Fabvier's expedition against Scio, who took us to his house and regaled us with coffee and preserved quinces. His daughter, a slender, handsome girl of sixteen, waited upon us. The father complained that he had not yet saved enough for her dowry, as he could not expect to get her married for less than two thousand drachmas ($333). For this reason sons are more profitable than daughters to Greek parents, and of course much more welcome.

As the road beyond Marathonisi is impracticable for laden horses, we engaged two mules, and set out for Tzimova, on the western side of the Mainote peninsula. This is the only road across Taygetus which is passable in winter, as there is a very sudden and singular break in the high snowy range between the two ports. After leaving Marathonisi and the barren little isle (50 by 200 yards in extent) where Paris and Helen passed the first night after their elopement, the scenery suddenly changed. A broad, rich valley opened before us, crossed by belts of poplar and willow trees, and inclosed by a semicircle of hills, most of which were crowned with the lofty towers of the Mainotes. In Maina almost every house is a fortress. The law of blood revenge, the right of which is transmitted from father to son, draws the whole population under its bloody sway in the course of a few generations. Life is a running fight, and every foe slain entails on the slayer a new penalty of retribution for himself and his descendants for ever. Previous to the Revolution most of the Mainote families lived in a state of alternate attack and siege. Their houses are square towers, forty or fifty feet high, with massive walls, and windows so narrow that they may be used as loopholes for musketry. The first story is at a considerable distance from the ground, and reached by a long ladder which can be drawn up so as to cut off all communication. Some of the towers are further strengthened by a semicircular bastion, projecting from the side most liable to attack. The families supplied themselves with telescopes, to look out for enemies in the distance, and always had a store of provisions on hand, in case of a siege. Although this private warfare has been suppressed, the law of revenge exists.

From the summit of the first range we overlooked a wild, glorious landscape. The hills, wooded with oak, and swimming in soft blue vapor, interlocked far before us, inclosing the loveliest green dells in their embraces, and melting away to the break in Taygetus, which yawned in the distance. On the right towered the square, embrasured castle of Passava, on the summit of an almost inaccessible hill—the site of the ancient Las. Far and near, the lower heights were crowned with tall white towers. The men were all in the fields plowing. They were healthy, tough, symmetrical fellows, and there was old Hellenic blood in their veins. They greeted us in a friendly way, and one whom I questioned concerning the road to Tzimova, answered: "It is four hours yet, but I pray you to forgive me, for the road is very bad." For two or three hours we threaded a terrific gorge, through scenery as rugged and grand as that of Norway. On every side were unusual evidences of industry—enormous heaps of stone removed to make room for little grain-plots, barren slopes reclaimed by artificial water courses, and terraces climbing the mountains until the loftiest strips of green seemed to be stuck against the sheer walls of rock. On expressing my delight at seeing such signs of patient labor, François, who shares the usual Greek prejudice against the Mainotes, answered: "But all this is the work of the women. The men are lazy vagabonds, who sit all day in the villages, and smoke paper cigars. The country is too poor to support its population, and you will find Syra and Smyrna full of Mainote porters." There may be some truth in this accusation, but it is exaggerated.

At sunset, after climbing a rocky staircase, we reached a little platform between the opposing capes of Taygetus, whence we saw both the Laconian and Messenian Gulfs. A still more dreary landscape lay before us, and there were no signs of Tzimova. The dusk fell, we dismounted and walked behind our spent horses, and so two hours passed away. François heaped anathemas upon the head of his friend in Marathonisi. "The stupid beast!" he exclaimed; "he told us it was only four hours to Tzimova, and we have already been six upon the road." I gave him a cigar, the moral effect of which was soon made manifest. "After all," he added, with a milder voice, between the whiffs, "Demetri meant well enough, and if he was mistaken bout the distance, it is perhaps not his fault." "So, François," I remarked, "you find that smoking improves your temper?" "Ah, yes," he answered, "my body is to blame for all the sins I ever committed. I can trace every one to the fact of my having had no tobacco, or not enough to eat, or too much to drink." At last we came upon olive groves, glimmering in the moonlight like the ghosts of trees, and then the scattered towers of Tzimova. I had

neglected to procure letters from Dr. Kalopothakes in
Athens to his relatives here, and François had but one
acquaintance, whom he had not heard of for fourteen years;
so we were doubtful whether we should obtain quarters
for the night. Reaching a little open place, however,
where some men were assembled, we asked whether any
one would receive us into his house. Thereupon stepped
forth a man with instant and cordial assent—and to our
wonder he proved to be, not only the old friend of
François, but one of the relatives of my friend, the
Doctor! In five minutes we were installed in the clean and
comfortable abode of his Holiness, the Bishop, who was
absent, and F., as he set about preparing one of his
marvellous soups, whispered to me: "This is what the
Turks call destiny, and, *ma foi!* they are right. An hour
ago I was on the brink of despair, and now the gates of
Paradise are opened."

In the morning we visited the other members of the
house of Kalopothakes, and were very courteously received.
The people collected to stare at us, and a pack of boys
tramped at our heels, but their manners were entirely kind
and friendly. Here the Slavonic element predominated, there
being few Greek faces except among the women. The
name of the place has recently been changed to Areopolis,
though I cannot find that any ancient city of that name
ever existed here. As we started in the morning on our
way up the western base of the Taygetus, a fierce-looking
palikar in fustanella and scarlet drawers came towards us,
jumping over the stone fences of the gardens. He shook
hands with us, scanned us from head to foot, and then,

turning to the Tzimovites who were escorting us, asked, 'Who are these?' "They are Englishmen—travellers," was the answer. "You will go to Vitylo: that is my town," said he to me—"*echete egeian!*" (may you have health) and forthwith strode away. He was the chief of Vitylo, which is only about three miles north of Tzimova, although we were two hours on the way, so terrific is the mountain road.

Vitylo is built on the brow of a precipice, more than a thousand feet above the sea. Our road, winding back and forth along the face of the rock, was like a path made by the infernal powers over the mountains which guarded Eden. Far up, apparently trembling in the air, as if giddy with their position, the tower-dwellings of the town overhung us, but the sheer yellow rocks, piled upon each other like huge steps, were draped with all manner of wild vines, flowers, and ivy, and every narrow shelf between was a garden of velvet soil, out of which grew olive and fig trees of enormous size. The people at work in these gardens were all armed. They wore a costume something like that of the Cretans, and the stamp of ancient Greece was upon their faces. A handsome, fierce boy, who was leaning over the edge of a rock above the road, looked me full in the face, and asked, with a sort of savage suspicion, "What do you want here?" The town was crowded with idlers, with knives in their belts and cigars in their mouths. Some twenty girls, who came down from the mountains, each with a donkey-load of furze upon her back, resembled antique goddesses in a menial disguise. No dirt or labor could conceal their symmetry, and the barbarism of a thousand years had not destroyed the type of their ancient race.

There is a curious story connected with Vitylo. About a hundred and fifty years ago, say the people, emigration from Mania into Corsica was frequent; among others, the family of Kalomiris, or Kalomeros (both names are mentioned), from Vitylo, who, soon after their settlement in Corsica, translated their name into Italian—*Bonaparte*. From this family came Napoleon, who was therefore of Mainote, or ancient Spartan blood. Pietro Mavromakhalis, it is said, when he visited Napoleon at Trieste, claimed him as a fellow-countryman on the faith of this story. The Mainotes implicitly believe it: the emigration at the time mentioned is a matter of history, and the fact that the name of Bonaparte previously existed in Italy, is no proof that the Corsican Bonapartes may not originally have been the Kalomeros of Maina. The thing is possible enough, and somebody who is sufficiently interested in the present race of Bonapartes to make researches, would probably be able to settle the question.

Our road for the remainder of the day was indescribably bad. For several hours we traversed a stony, sloping terrace on the side of Taygetus, 1,500 feet above the sea, and crossed by great yawning gorges, which must be doubled with much labor. The people said: "The road is very good, since our Bishop has had it mended. Formerly it was bad." What is a bad road in Maina? Mix together equal portions of limestone quarries, unmade pavements, huge boulder-stones, and loose beach shingle, and you will have a mild idea of the present good one. There were many villages scattered along the terrace, frequently so close to each other as almost to form a continuous town. The clear water-veins of Taygetus burst to light in spacious stone fountains, over which arose large arches of masonry festooned with ivy. There were also a great multitude of churches, many of unmixed Byzantine style, and several centuries old. The people—true Greeks, almost to a man —accosted us with the most cordial and friendly air. The universal salutation was "*Kalos orizete!*" (welcome), instead of the "*Kali emera sas!*" (good-day to you!) which is used in other parts of Greece. Although many of the natives were poor and ragged, we saw but four beggars in all Maina, while on entering Kalamata, the next afternoon, we encountered twelve in succession.

The descent to the sea-level was by a frightful ladder, which it required all the strength and skill of our poor beasts to descend. We had dismounted long before this, as riding had become a much greater labor than walking. Pericles, one of our *agoyats*, exclaimed: "I was never in this country of Maina before. If I should happen to be fettered and brought here by force, I might see it again · but of my own will, never!" We passed many traces of ancient quarries, and the sites of the Laconian towns of Thalamæ and Leuctra, but a few hewn blocks are all that remain. After twelve hours of the most laborious travel, and long after night had set in, we reached the little town of Skardamula. A shepherd on his way to the mountains turned back on learning that we were strangers, and assisted us to find lodgings. But this was not difficult. Almost the first man we met took us into his lofty tower of defence, the upper room of which was vacated for us. The people were curious, but kind, and I found my liking for the Mainotes increasing with every day. François, however, would know no good of them, and the Athenians opened their eyes in astonishment when they heard me praise those savage mountaineers.

We had a lenten supper of fish and vegetables, and slept securely in our lofty chamber. In the morning we received a visit from the Demarch, who courteously offered us refreshments. The people who assembled to see us off were very handsome—of the ancient blood, almost without exception. On crossing the river beyond the village I was so struck with the magnificent landscape that I halted an hour to sketch it. Before us lay Skardamula, its tall towers rising above the mulberry and sycamore trees which lined the bank. Hills covered with fig and olive, and crowned with the dark shafts of the cypress, rose beyond, a Mainote fortress on every commanding point. On our left issued the river from a gigantic gorge between precipices of pale-red rock: a line of bastion-like hills stood in front of the high purple peaks around which scarfs of morning vapor were continually twisting and unrolling themselves, while, through the gaps between them, glimmered like fields of frosted silver the snowy cones of the Taygetus.

Climbing a high headland of the coast by a rocky ladder, we descended on the other side into a lovely valley, in the lap of which, embowered in cypress groves, lay the village of Malta. Another castle was placed at our disposal, for breakfast, but we could get nothing except a few eggs

François was especially ill-humored on finding that no wine was to be had. "I suppose," said he to the people, "your priest here uses brandy when he celebrates mass." Presently, however, we had a visit from the captain of the gend'armes, who politely inquired whether he could assist us in any way. "Not unless you could give us some wine," answered François, rather scornfully. To my surprise, the captain instantly despatched a villager to the priest, who soon came, accompanied by a jar of the desired beverage. The captain now received the most courteous replies to his inquiries, a very genial conversation followed, and we parted from the company in the most friendly manner.

The journey to Kalamata occupied six hours, through scenery as rich and magnificent as that of Italian Switzerland. The eye ranged from orange orchards and groves of cypress on the rocky terraces near the sea, to forests of fir on the higher hills, bristling with robber towers, while, far above, the sharp white peaks flashed and glittered in the blue. While descending to the plain at the head of the Gulf, where we left the Mainote territory, I met Ariadne, carrying a load of wood on her back. Even in this position, bent under her burden, she exhibited a more perfect beauty, a more antique grace, than any woman you will see in Broadway in the course of a week. If such be the Greek race now, in its common forms, what must have been those refined Athenian women whom Phidias saw? Since I beheld Ariadne, ancient art has become a reality.

Early in the afternoon we reached Kalamata, a large, straggling, busy town, with a dismantled acropolis, and took up our quarters in the "Grand Hotel of Messenia." The filthy rooms of this establishment were not a pleasant change from the airy towers of Maina. All the afternoon, as I sat at the window, the boys tormented an idiot in the treet below, and all night there was such a succession of discordant noises through the house, that we got but little sleep.

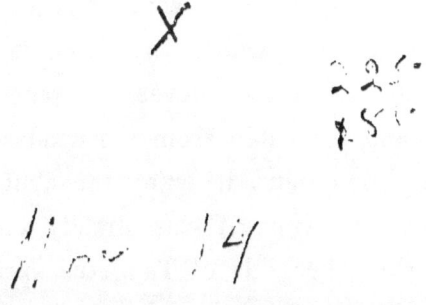

CHAPTER XVII.

MESSENIA, ELIS, AND ACHAIA.

The plain of Messenia, over which we rode, after leaving Kalamata, is the richest part of the Morea. Although its groves of orange and olive, fig and mulberry, were entirely destroyed during the Egyptian occupation, new and more vigorous shoots have sprung up from the old stumps, and the desolated country is a garden again, apparently as fair and fruitful as when it excited the covetousness of the Spartan thieves. Sloping to the Gulf on the south, and protected from the winds on all other sides by lofty mountains, it enjoys an almost Egyptian warmth of climate. Here it was already summer, while at Sparta, on the other side of Taygetus, spring had but just arrived, and the central plain of Arcadia was still bleak and gray as in winter. As it was market day, we met hundreds of the country people going to Kalamata with laden asses. Nine-tenths of them, at least, had Turkish faces. The Greek type suddenly ceases on leaving Maina, and I did not find it again, except in a few scatter ing instances, during the remainder of our travels in the Peloponnesus. And yet some travellers declare that the bulk of the population of Modern Greece belong to the ancient stock! On the contrary, I should consider 200,000, or one-fifth of the entire number, a very high estimate.

We crossed the rapid Pamisos with some difficulty, and ascended its right bank, to the foot of Mount Evan, which we climbed, by rough paths through thickets of mastic and furze, to the monastery of Vurkano. The building has a magnificent situation, on a terrace between Mounts Evan and Ithome, overlooking both the upper and lower plains of the Pamisos—a glorious spread of landscape, green with spring, and touched by the sun with the airiest prismatic tints through breaks of heavy rain-clouds. Inside the court is an old Byzantine chapel, with fleurs-de-lis on the decorations, showing that it dates from the time of the Latin princes. The monks received us very cordially, gave us a clean, spacious room, and sent us a bottle of excellent wine for dinner. We ascended Ithome and visited the massive ruins of Messene the same day. The great gate of the city, a portion of the wall, and four of the towers of defence, are in tolerable condition. The name of Epaminondas hallows these remains, which otherwise, grand as they are, do not impress one like the Cyclopean walls of Tiryns. The wonder is, that they could have been built in so short a time—85 days, says history, which would appear incredible, had not still more marvellous things of the kind been done in Russia.

The next day, we rode across the head of the Messenian plain, crossed the "Mount Lycæan" and the gorge of the

Neda, and lodged at the little village of Tragoge, on the frontiers of Arcadia. Our experience of Grecian highways was pleasantly increased by finding fields plowed directly across our road, fences of dried furze built over it, and ditches cutting it at all angles. Sometimes all trace of it would be lost for half a mile, and we were obliged to ride over the growing crops until we could find a bit of fresh trail. So far as I can discover, the Government neither makes nor guards any road in this part of the Morea. Two or three times a year a new track must be made.

The bridle-path over Mount Lycæus was steep and bad, but led us through the heart of a beautiful region. The broad back of the mountain is covered with a grove of superb oaks, centuries old, their long arms muffled in golden moss, and adorned with a plumage of ferns. The turf at their feet was studded with violets, filling the air with delicious odors. This sylvan retreat was the birthplace of Pan, and no more fitting home for the universal god can be imagined. On the northern side we descended for some time through a forest of immense ilex trees, which sprang from a floor of green moss and covered our pathway with summer shade. Near here, François was once stopped by robbers, to whom he gave some wine and tobacco in exchange for a sheep, and persuaded them to spare the baggage of two travellers whom he was conducting. We were now in the heart of the wild mountain region of Messenia, in whose fastnesses Aristoménes, the epic hero of the State, maintained himself so long against the Spartans. The tremendous gorge below us was the bed of the Neda, which we crossed in order to enter the lateral valley of Phigalia, where lay Tragoge. The path was not only difficult but dangerous—in some places a mere hand's breadth of gravel, on the edge of a plane so steep that a single slip of a horse's foot would have sent him headlong o the bottom.

We intended to stop with the priest, from whom François hoped to coax some of his sacramental wine. On hailing a peasant, however, on approaching the village we learned that the good man had been dead for some months. "What was the matter with him?" asked F. "Nothing was the matter with him," answered the man, "he died." We thereupon went to the father of the deceased, who received us kindly, and gave us a windy room, with a number of old silver-mounted yataghans and muskets hanging on the walls. During the evening a neighbor came in, whose brother was shot as a bandit a few years ago. In the kitchen there was a segment of a hollow sycamore trunk, used as a grain chest. Thirty or forty bee-hives, in a plot of ground near the house, were in like manner composed of hollow trees, and covered with broad flat stones.

In the morning, a terrible *scirocco levante* was blowing, with an almost freezing cold. The fury of the wind was so great that in crossing the exposed ridges it was difficult to keep one's seat upon the horse. We climbed towards the central peak of the Lycæan Hills, through a wild dell between two ridges, which were covered to the summit with magnificent groves of oak. Starry blue flowers, violets and pink crocuses spangled the banks as we wound onward, between the great trunks. The temple of Apollo

Epidarius stands on a little platform between the two highest peaks, about 3,500 feet above the sea. On the morning of our visit, its pillars of pale bluish-gray limestone rose against a wintry sky, its guardian oaks were leafless, and the wind whistled over its heaps of ruin; yet its symmetry was like that of a perfect statue, wherein you do not notice the absence of color, and I felt that no sky and no season could make it more beautiful. For its builder was Ictinus, who created the Parthenon. It was erected by the Phigalians, out of gratitude to Apollo the Helper, who kept from their city a plague which ravaged the rest of the Peloponnesus. Owing to its secluded position, it has escaped the fate of other temples, and might be restored from its own undestroyed materials. The cella has been thrown down, but thirty-five out of thirty-eight columns are still standing. Through the Doric shafts you look upon a wide panorama of gray mountains, melting into purple in the distance, and crowned by arcs of the far-off sea. On one hand is Ithome and the Messenian Gulf, on the other the Ionian Sea and the Strophades.

We rode for nearly two hours along the crest of the mountain, looking down into the deep-blue valley of the Alpheus, and then descended to Andritzena, which lies in a wild ravine, sloping towards the river. This is a poor place, with less than a thousand inhabitants. We passed the night at a small village, two hours beyond, and the next day pushed on down the valley to Olympia. As the streams were swollen with melted snows, we had some difficulty in finding a place where the Alpheus was fordable. It was about thirty yards wide, with a very swift current, and the *agoyats* were in mortal fear during the transit, although the water did not reach above our saddle-girths. Having safely reached the northern bank, we now had the Ladon and the Erymanthus to cross, both of which were much swollen. Pericles and Aristides crossed themselves, after these streams had been crossed, and really had the water been six inches deeper, we should have been swept away. There is no bridge over the Alpheus, and communication is frequently cut off during the winter.

We now trotted down the valley, over beautiful meadows, which were uncultivated except in a few places where the peasants were plowing for maize, and had destroyed every trace of the road. The hills on both sides began to be fringed with pine, while the higher ridges on our right were clothed with woods of oak. I was surprised at the luxuriant vegetation of this region. The laurel and mastic became trees, the pine shot to a height of one hundred feet, and the beech and sycamore began to appear. Some of the pines had been cut for ship-timber, but in the rudest and most wasteful way, only the limbs which had the proper curve being chosen for ribs. I did not see a single sawmill in the Peloponnesus; but I am told that there are a few in Euboea and Acarnania. As we approached Olympia, I could almost have believed myself among the pine-hills of Germany or America. In the old times this must have been a lovely, secluded region, well befitting the honored repose of Xenophon, who wrote his works here. The sky became heavier as the day wore on, and the rain, which had spared us so long, finally inclosed us in its misty circle. Towards evening we reached a lonely little house, on the banks of the Alpheus. Nobody was at home, but we succeeded in forcing a door and getting shelter for our baggage. François had supper nearly ready before the proprietor arrived. The latter had neither wife nor child, though a few chicks, and took our burglarious occupation very good-humoredly. We shared the same leaky roof with our horses, and the abundant fleas with the owner' dogs.

In the morning the clouds broke away, and broad sunshine streamed down on the Olympian vale. A ride of twenty minutes brought us to the remains of the temple of Jupiter—substructions only, which have been discovered by excavation, as they are entirely beneath the level of the soil. The vast fragments enable one to guess at the size and majesty of the perfect edifice. The drums of the Doric columns, only two or three of which remain *in situ*, are nearly eight feet in diameter. The stone employed is the same hard, coarse, gray limestone as that of the temple of Apollo Epicurius. The soil of Olympia—a deep alluvial deposit—undoubtedly contains a rich fund of remains of ancient art; but when shall they be brought to light? Prince Pückler-Muskau proposed to the Greek Government to make excavations at his own expense, and to place whatever he found in a museum which he would build on the spot, but his generous offer was refused, out of a mean jealousy of permitting a foreigner to do that which the Greeks themselves will not do for a hundred years to come. The latter boast of their descent from the old heroes, but (old Pittakys excepted) they are greater Vandals than the Turks towards the ancient monuments of their country. *Foreign* influence has preserved the Acropolis from being still further despoiled; foreign scholars have discovered the lost landmarks of Greece; and foreign money is now paying for the few excavations and restorations which are being carried on. Athenian boys hurl stones from their slings at the choragic monument of Lysicrates and mutilate its exquisite frieze, and the sportsmen who pass Colonos pepper with shot and ball the marble tombstone over Ottfried Müller's grave. During my residence in Athens, Sir Thomas Wyse prevented the builders of the new Cathedral from plundering the Theatre of Bacchus, and it is fear of the opinion of the world, rather than reverence for the Past, which saves many a venerable relic from the like fate.

The hills surrounding Olympia are low, and picturesquely wooded with pine. The scenery has a pleasing air of seclusion and peace. Broken stones and bricks mark the position of the city, which stood on a shelf of the valley next the hills, out of the reach of inundations from the river. The temple stood very nearly in the centre, opposite an arm of the valley which enters the hills to the north, at right angles to the course of the Alpheus. Here was the stadium, no trace of which now remains. At one end is a small Roman ruin of brickwork, resembling a bath. We here found a wild olive-tree, from which we robbed enough of leaves to make a victor's crown. The vale is nearly deserted, and most of its mellow loam is lying fallow. And this is Olympia, whence, for nearly 1,200 years, the chronology of the ancient world was computed—which has witnessed the presence of a greater number of great men than any other spot in the world!

A journey of two days across the wild mountain country of Erymanthus took us to Kalavryta, in Achaia. We left the valley of the Alpheus at Olympia, and struck into a hilly district, covered with forests of splendid pine. A number of lumbermen were at work, wasting more than half the wood for the want of saws. After a gradual ascent of about a thousand feet, we reached a summit ridge, but instead of finding a corresponding descent on the other side, we saw a broad table-land stretching away to the foot of a second ridge of hills. On this fine plain was the little village of Lala, built on the site of one destroyed during the war. The place was very rich, but now, although about one-tenth of the number of the former inhabitants own the same region, they are miserably poor. The fields for miles around, once bounteous with corn and wine, are lying waste and covered only with a thick carpet of ferns and asphodel. Ascending the second range of hills, we came upon another table-land, covered with an immense forest of oaks. We rode for more than two hours through this forest, which extends to the foot of the high range of Erymanthus, a distance of eight or ten miles, and even spreads up the mountain sides as far as the region of snow. Most of the trees are less than fifty years old, but interspersed among them are noble old trunks of many centuries. The open spaces were carpeted with soft, green turf, and every sunny bank gave a breath of violets to the air. The ground was covered with limbs and trunks, slowly rotting away. I saw enough of waste wood during the ride to supply all Athens for five years, but there it will lie and rot, so long as there are no roads in Greece

It is saddening to see a country so rich in natural resources neglected so shamefully.

Leaving the forest at last, we entered the deep, abrupt gorge of the Erymanthus, and spent the night in a lonely khan in the woods, high on the mountain side. It was a long day's journey thence to Kalavryta, over the back-bone of Erymanthus. This is the main line of communication between the Gulf of Corinth and the south-western portion of the Peloponnesus. The King and all his ministers have travelled it, the people have sent, literally, hundreds of petitions in regard to it, yet not a solitary drachma, so far as I could learn, has ever been expended on it. Near the khan there is a wild mountain stream, which frequently cuts off communication for days. A good bridge over it could be built for 10,000 drachmas; the poor people of the neighborhood have raised among themselves nearly half the amount, yet all their clamor and entreaty cannot pro- cure the remainder.

Our *khanji* was evidently of Turkish blood; the Greek face is very rare in these parts. We had an exceedingly rough ride of three hours, up the gorge of the Eryman- thus to Tripotamo. The mountains rose on either side to a height of 300 feet above the stream, which thundered down a precipitous defile. Tripotamo is a khan, lying, as its name denotes, at the junction of the three branches of Erymanthus. A few foundation walls still remain from the ancient city of Peophis, which stood on a rocky height, commanding the valley.

We now followed the middle branch of the Erymanthus up a warm, narrow valley, planted with tobacco and vines.

The banks were purple with the dark-hued violet, and the air balmy as the breath of Paradise. At the end of the valley we mounted the central ridge of the Erymanthean chain—a sharp comb, which appears to connect the group of Panachaïacum with that of Cyllene. From the summit we had a glorious view backwards, down the gorge of the Erymanthus, between the blue foldings of whose mountains we saw the level line of the wooded table-land overlooking the Olympian plain. Before us stretched a similar valley, closed on the north by another mountain range, while the hoary summit of Cyllene sparkled near us on the right, through the crystal ether. Of the four monasteries which we passed, between Tripotamo and Kalavryta, but one was inhabited. The others, so François said, had been sequestrated by the Government.

Kalavryta is situated at the eastern end of a high mountain basin, which discharges its waters into the *katabethra* (cañon) where lies the monastery of Megaspelion. Over it towers the snowy head of Cyllene, in which are the fountains of the Styx. It is a busy, picturesque little place, with better houses than one usually finds in the country towns. There was no khan, but the Chief of Police directed us to a house where we obtained quarters. As it had a second story, chimney, and small glass windows, we considered ourselves luxuriously lodged. The next day we went no further than Megaspelion, two hours distant. Our youngest *agoyat*, Pericles, was quite ill, from the effect of Lent. He had eaten nothing but bread, olives, and raw onions during the whole trip. A single good meal would have cured him, but I believe he would sooner have died than have eaten meat before Easter. Our host refused to drink wine, because he had once brought a load of fish from Lala to Kalavryta in one day, and is certain he would never have accomplished it, if he had not strictly observed his fasts at the proper time. What has Christianity become? Is it, as practised by one-half of Christendom, much better than the ancient Paganism?

Entering the gorge of Megaspelion, we had a succession of grand mountain pictures, the naked rocks rising high overhead, almost to the very clouds, while there was barely space between their bases for the Kalavryta River. We saw the monastery, far up on the mountain side, stuck against the face of tremendous cliffs of dark-red rock. A long and steep ascent leads into the amphitheatric hollow which it overlooks, the buildings being hidden from view by a projecting spur until you are close upon them. It is certainly one of the wildest and most singular places in the world. The precipice, which is nearly five hundred feet perpendicular, is hollowed out at the bottom into three crescent-shaped caverns, penetrating ninety feet into the rock. In front of these, a massive wall, sixty feet high, has been built up, and on the summit of the wall, and the rocky floor of the topmost cavern, are perched the chapel and dormitories of the monks—for all the world like a lot of swallows' nests, of all forms, colors, and dimensions. The mountain slope below the monastery is terraced and devoted to gardens, of which every monk has a separate one, and there are nearly three hundred when they are all at home. The staircases and passages in the interior of this hive are mostly hewn in the solid rock, and so dark and labyrinthine that you must have candles and a guide.

The monks—to whose piety I will testify, since I saw how dirty they were—received us rather coldly, but did not refuse us a room, nor prevent François from cooking a bit of mutton. They hurried us off to the church, supposing that we must be impatient to behold the portrait of the Holy Virgin, sculptured in very black wood, by St. Luke himself. If the portrait be correct, she was a very ordinary person. I prefer, however, to throw the blame on St. Luke, whose pictures are quite as hideous as this bas-relief. The rooms of the monks were in harmony with their persons. All the offal of the monastery is thrown out of the windows, and lies in heaps at the foot of the wall, whence its effluvia rise to mingle with the incense in the chapels above. The most spacious part of the building was the wine-cellar, which was well stored. There was no temptation to stay and witness the Easter festivities—indeed, we were too anxious to reach Athens. Two Englishmen, however, who had arrived before us, were spending every night in the church and sleeping in the day-time. The monotony of the nasal chanting is something terrible, and how they endured it six hours a night was beyond my comprehension.

So we left Megaspelion on *megalo sabaton* (Great Saturday), in the beginning of a rain. Our path climbed the mountain behind the monastery, and followed the crest of a long ridge running towards the Gulf of Corinth. Clouds were above and below us, and a wild, black abyss of storm hid both Cyllene and the gulf. These mountains were thickly clothed with firs, the first we had seen in Greece

The most of them were young, but here and there rose a few fine, tall trunks, which both War and Peace had spared. The appearance of this region showed conclusively how easy it would be to restore the lost forests of Greece—and through them the lost streams. After four or five hours up and down paths so difficult that they would have been very dangerous with horses unaccustomed to such travel, we reached the hamlet of Akrata on the coast, wet, sore, and hungry.

A crowd of village idlers collected about the little shop where we stopped to breakfast, and thronged in to see us eat and to ask questions. They had sharp, eager, intelligent faces, but all with a greater or less mixture of the Slavonic element. Among them was a handsome boy of sixteen, who, having studied at the gymnasium of Patras, was put forward as spokesman. We were the first Americans they had seen, and they were curious to learn something about America. I pointed out one of the boys present as having a genuine American face, whereupon the smart youngster remarked, "That is almost like an insult —it is as much as to say that he don't look like a Greek." "You should, on the contrary, take it as a compliment to your country," I answered; "the people of a free country have a different expression from those who live under a despotism, and if he resembles an American, he resembles a free man." He was a little abashed; and one of the men asked: "But if it is a free country, what despot (*tyrannos*) rules you?" I thereupon, with the help of François, gave them a brief description of our Government and country, to which they listened with the greatest attention, asking questions which showed a clear comprehension of my explanations. I am sure that a group of German or French peasants would not have understood the subject half as readily.

By this time the rain had not only ceased, but the clouds parted, allowing splendid gaps of sunshine to stream down on the dark-green gulf, and light up the snowy top of Parnassus, nearly opposite. Before sunset we reached the village of Stomi, where we spent the night very comfortably in a two-story house. The next day was Easter Sunday, which we had promised to spend with our friend, the Demarch of Hexamilia. The storm had delayed us considerably, but we still hoped, by starting early, to arrive in season for the Paschal lamb. The way, however, was longer than we had counted upon. Following the shore of the gulf, we witnessed the Easter festivities in twenty villages, saluted by everybody with the glad tidings. "*Christos aneste*" (Christ is arisen,)—to which we gave the customary reply: "*Alethos aneste*" (Truly he is arisen.) All were dressed in their gayest garments, and the satisfaction which a hearty meal of meat—the first in fifty days—spread over their countenances, was most refreshing to behold. There was a continual discharge of musketry from the young palikars; and, in the afternoon, the women danced slowly on the shore, in long semicircular companies to the sound of their own screechy voices. The short mantles which they wore, over their white petticoats, were of the gayest colors, bordered with an ornamental pattern of truly antique and classical form. One of them was an exact copy of that worn by Ristori, as Medea.

Sending our baggage direct to Hexamilia, and intrusting Pericles with a message to the Demarch, that a Paschal lamb should be bought and roasted for us, we left the shore, and mounted to the rocky platform whereon stood Sikyon, the forerunner and rival of Corinth. We spent a quiet hour in the grass-grown theatre, looking on the sapphire gulf, and the immortal peaks of song beyond it. It was nearly sunset when we reached Corinth, but I determined to improve the occasion by climbing to the acropolis, which we had been unable to do on our former visit, on account of the rain. From the huge rock, nearly two thousand feet in height, you have a panorama extending from Sunium, the eastern headland of Attica, on one side, to the mountains of Etolia, on the other.

It was after dark when our weary horses halted at the Demarch's door, in Hexamilia. The lamb was on a spit, truly enough, and Pericles and Aristides were turning him with expectant eyes. The Demarch opened an amphora of red, resinous wine (which, having once learned to drink, we preferred to all other), and late at night, by the light of lanterns, we sat down to our Easter feast. The house was still shaken by the throes of the lingering earthquake, but none of us heeded them. The Demarch, whose red face and starting eyes already told of repletion, tore a rib from the lamb with the remark: "I have already eaten three times to-day, but on Easter one can hold a double portion." It is a fact that there are more cases of illness after this festival, than at any time in the year. We were all ravenously hungry, and the Demarch was finally left behind in the race. Pericles and Aristides devoured an entire quarter, besides an immense omelette, with silent rapture.

Returning by way of Megara and Eleusis, in two days more, we hailed again the beloved Acropolis from the brow of Daphne.

CHAPTER XVIII.

BYRON IN GREECE.

No poet of modern times—not even Scott among the lochs of the Highlands—has left so lasting an impress of his own mind on the scenes he saw and sang of, as Byron. Whether on the Rhine, in Switzerland, Venice, Rome, Albania, Greece, Stamboul, or Gibraltar, the first lines that bubble up from the bottom of Memory's pool, as some feature or expression of the landscape agitates it, are sure to be his. Epithets struck off like the lucky dash of an artist's pencil, cling so tenaciously to the scenes themselves, that mountain, cape, cataract, and temple hurl them back to you. "The Acroceraunean mountains of old name," "Leucadia's far-projecting rock of woe," Soracte heaving from the plain "like a long-swept wave about to break," Lake Nemi "navelled in the woody hills," the "exulting and abounding" Rhine—are all illustrations of this. It is not, as somebody observes, that Byron expresses the average sentiment of cultivated travellers, but rather from the intrinsic excellence and aptness of his descriptive epithets, that he is so constantly quoted. Nothing can be finer than the images —rarely more than a line in length—with which Childe Harold is crowded. The disciples of Wordsworth have attempted to depreciate Byron as a poet, as Pollok and other Pharisees have blackened his character as a man—but no one can visit Greece without recognising how wonderfully the forms and colors of her scenery, the solemn sadness of her ruin, are reproduced in his pages.

It is a severe test of a description to read it on the actual spot. The twilight medium of words pales in the broad blaze of Nature; and as mountain, city, and river flush into living color before your eye, the life-blood seems to be drained from the page in your hand. Only when you become familiarized with a landscape, can you venture to open a book in its presence. Classical travellers, it is true, carry their Homers with them to read on the mound of Troy—or their Sophocles, for the Gate of Mycenæ; but this is a bit of agreeable sentiment which we must pardon. In Chamounix, before sunrise, you would scarcely think of reading Coleridge's "Hymn;" Schiller's "Diver" would sound but tamely in the Calabrian Strait; and I should like to see the man who could repeat any of the many feeble addresses to Niagara, on Table Rock!

Why is it, then, that so many of Byron's descriptions, when you have once read them, are given back to you again by Nature herself? Because he wrote in the presence of Nature: impression and expression were simultaneous; and his pictures, like the open-air studies of a painter, however deficient in breadth, depth, or atmosphere, have the unmistakable stamp of truth. Scarcely any other poet painted so directly from the model. His thunder storm on Lake Leman, written, as one might say, by the flashes of lightning, reminds us of Turner lashed to the foremast of a steamer, in order to study a snow-squall at sea. The first and second books of Childe Harold were written almost entirely in the open air. In wandering about Athens, on a sunny March day, when the asphodels are blossoming on Colonos, when the immortal mountains are folded in a transparent purple haze, and the waveless Ægean slumbers afar, among his islands, I never failed to hear a voice steal upon the charmed silence—a young, manly voice, ringing with inspiration, yet subdued by the landscape to a harmony with its own exquisite rhythmus, chanting:

> "Yet are thy skies as blue, thy crags as wild,
>   Sweet are thy groves, and verdant are thy fields,
>   Thine olive ripe as when Minerva smiled,
>   And still his honeyed wealth Hymettus yields;
>   There the blithe bee his fragrant fortress builds,
>   The free-born wanderer of thy mountain air;
>   Apollo still thy long, long summer gilds,
>   Still in his beam Mendeli's* marbles glare:
>   Art, Glory, Freedom fail, but Nature still is fair."

Here the simple thought is neither new nor profound but when the blue sky of Greece is over your head; when the thick olive groves shimmer silverly before you down the valley of the Cephissus; when the bee rises from his bed in the bells of the asphodel, and the flavor of the thymy

---

* Pentelicus.

honey of Hymettus is still on your palate; when the marble quarries of Pentelicus gleam like scars on the blue pediment of the mountain—then these lines sing themselves into your brain as the natural voice of the landscape.

Although fifty years have elapsed since Byron first visited Greece, his connexion with the later struggle for independence has kept alive some memories even of that earlier period. No foreign name is so well known to the Greeks as that of *Veeròn* (as they pronounce it); his portrait always has a prominent place in the Pantheon of the Liberators. Mrs. Black, to whom he sang "*Zoe mou, sas agapo*," still lives at the Piræus, and has transmitted her charms to a lovely Greco-Scottish daughter; and Mavrocordato, his friend and ally, though blind and octogenary, was living at the time of my visit. I knew the physician who attended him at Missolonghi—the same in whose arms Ottfried Müller breathed his last. Mr. Finlay, the historian of Mediæval Greece, knew him both at Cephalonia and at Missolonghi, and related to me the circumstances under which he contracted his fatal illness. Some of the particulars were new to me; and as Mr. Finlay informed me that portions of his statement had already been published, I feel no hesitation in repeating them here.

It is well known that after Byron reached Missolonghi, he was greatly annoyed and perplexed by the turbulent horde of half-robbers among whom he was thrown—a set of jealous, clamorous, undisciplined rogues, who were less zealous in the cause of Grecian freedom than in their endeavors to get a share of the poet's money. Ambitious to achieve some military distinction, and at the same time accomplish something for Greece, he enrolled a company of Suliotes under his own immediate command, and commenced a strict course of discipline. [Byron's helmet, with his crest, and the motto "*Crede Biron,*" is now in the possession of Dr. S. G. Howe, of Boston, who received it from Count Gamba. It is so small that few men could be found whose heads could be put into it.] He was very punctual in his attendance at the drill, and disregarded a proper protection from the weather, fearing that an appearance of effeminacy would weaken his influence over his men.

Mr. Finlay, then a young and ardent Philhellene, was sent with dispatches from Athens to Missolonghi, about the close of March, 1824. After remaining a few days he prepared to return; but heavy rains had swollen the river Achelous, and he was obliged to delay his departure. His plan was, to cross the Gulf of Corinth in a small boat, so as to avoid the risk of being captured by the Turks at Lepanto, and then push on eastward, through the defiles of the Achaian Mountains. One morning, at last, the weather seemed better, and he set out. Riding eastward over the plain, towards the Achelous, he met Byron on horseback. The latter turned and rode along with him for two or three miles, conversing on the prospects of the cause. Finally, Byron said: "You'd better turn back; the river is still too high." "I think not," said Mr Finlay; "but, at least, I'll try it." "You'll be wet to the skin, at any rate," urged Byron, pointing to a heavy black cloud, which was rapidly approaching. "*You* will be wet, not I," Mr. Finlay answered, whereupon Byron saying: "I'll see to that,' turned his horse and galloped back towards the town.

In a few minutes, however, the cloud broke, and the rain fell in torrents. Byron's house was at the western end of Missolonghi, so that, in order to avoid the breakneck streets, he was in the habit of crossing the harbor in a boat, and mounting his horse outside the eastern wall. On this occasion, he reached the boat in a dripping state, and, being obliged to sit still during the passage, received a violent chill, which was followed by an attack of fever Mr. Finlay, finding the river still too high, returned to Missolonghi, where he was obliged to wait two days longer. Byron then lay upon the bed from which he never arose. "One evening," related Mr. F., "he said to Col. Stanhope and the rest of us: 'Well, I expected something to happen this year. It's all owing to the old witch.' We asked for an explanation. 'When I was a boy,' said he, 'an old woman, who told my fortune, predicted that four particular years would be dangerous to me. Three times her prediction has come true; and now this is the fourth year she named. So you see, it won't do to laugh at the witches. He said this in a gay, jesting voice, and seemed to have no idea that his illness would prove fatal. Indeed, none of us considered him in a dangerous condition at that time."

During his first visit to Greece, Byron resided for several months at Athens, and every fair or inspiring feature of the illustrious region was familiar to him. Two points seem to have especially attracted him—the ancient fortress of Phyle, in the defile of Parnes, through which passed one of the roads into Bœotia, and the sunset view from the Propylæa, or pillared entrance at the western end of the Acropolis. The latter is frequently called "Byron's View," by the English, and no poet's name was ever associated with a lovelier landscape. Seated on a block of marble opposite the main entrance, which steeply climbs the slope, you look down between the rows of fluted Doric columns, to the Hill of the Nymphs, rising opposite, across the valley of the Cephissus, twinkling with olives and vines, over the barren ridge of Corydallus, the mountains of Salamis and Megara, and away to the phantom hills of the Peloponnesus, whose bases are cut by the azure arc of the Saronic Gulf. Here was written the often quoted description of a Grecian sunset, commencing:

> "Slow sinks, more lovely ere his race be run,
> Along Morea's hills the setting sun—"

and every feature of the picture is correct. In the south, you see Egina, crowned by the Panhellenic temple of Jupiter, Hydra, and Poros; while the "Delphian cliff" on the west, behind which the still triumphant god sinks to rest, though hidden from sight by a spur of Parnes, is nevertheless visible from the sides of Hymettus.

To me, this view had an indescribable charm. Apart from the magic of its immortal associations, it is drawn and colored with that exquisite artistic feeling, which seems to be a characteristic of Nature in Greece, and therefore takes away from the almost despairing wonder with which we should otherwise contemplate her perfect temples. We the more easily comprehend why Proportion should have been an inborn faculty of the Grecian mind—why the laws of Form, with all their elusive secrets, should have been so thoroughly mastered. The studied irregularity of the

Parthenon, the result of which is absolute symmetry, was never attained by mathematical calculation. It sprang from the inspired sagacity of a brain so exquisitely educated to Order, that it could give birth to no imperfect conception. Ictinus caught the magic secret (which all Apostles of the Good Time Coming would do well to learn), that Nature abhors exact mathematical arrangement—that true Order and Harmony lie in a departure from it. By violating the apparent law, the genuine law was found.

A few days before leaving Athens, I rode out to Phyle, which is about eighteen miles distant. The weather was intensely hot, thermometer ninety-one degrees in the shade, and a strong sirocco wind, blowing directly from Africa, wrapped the mountains in a fiery blue film. A rapid trot of two hours brought us to an Albanian village at the foot of Parnes, where we halted for breakfast, and to rest our exhausted horses. The inhabitants have the reputation of being robbers, and probably deserve it. They seemed to have no regular occupation, and the number of well-armed, lusty, yellow-moustached, and long-nosed fellows lounging about, was, in itself, a suspicious circumstance. They were, however, very courteous to us, and I have no doubt we might have lived for weeks among them with entire security.

At the little inn, where we ate our cold chicken and *caviar*, moistened with resinous wine, several of the villagers were collected, in lively conversation with a keen, quick-eyed fellow from a distant village, whose witty remarks and retorts diverted them exceedingly. One wild, young scamp jumped up at intervals, and executed steps of the palikar dance, or *romaïka*, and another, lolling lazily in a corner, sang fragments of a song he had learned in Crete:

> "All on a Sunday morning,
> On Easter and New-Year's day,
> The bells of Holy Constantine
> They ring so loud and gay."

The tide of fun ran high; and I regretted that my imperfect knowledge of the language did not allow me to enjoy it with them. Finally, however, one of the villagers called out to the jolly stranger: "Nicolà, tell us that story of your second marriage. Giorgios here, and Costandi, and Kyrie François have never heard it." "Oh, yes!" shouted the others; "that was a capital trick of Nicolà's. You must all hear it." Nicolà thereupon began the story —his quick blue eyes dancing in wicked delight under his shaggy brows at the very thought of the trick.

"You must know," said he, "that my first wife died about a year and a half ago. Well, she had not been dead long, before I found out that I must fill her place with somebody else. It's poor business living without a wife, especially when you've been used to having one. But I was as poor as the Holy Lazarus, and how to get a handsome girl, with a good dower, was more than I knew. At last I remembered Athanasi, the fat innkeeper in Kuluri, where I had spent a night a year or two before. He had a daughter, handsome and nimble enough; and five hundred drachmas, they said, would go with her. I must be Athanasi's son-in-law, I said to myself. Now, I am no fool and presently I hit upon the right plan. I washed my fustanellas, put on my best clothes, and started on my horse (it's not a bad animal, you know) for Kuluri. But first, I took my big saddle-bags, and filled them with broken horse-shoes and other such bits of iron. Then I threw in all the money I had—about ten or twelve silver dollars—locked the bags, and hung them over my saddle. As I jogged along the road, with the metal jingling under me I said to myself 'Ho! Papa Athanasi, get the bride ready; your son is a-coming!'

"When I drew near Kuluri, I put my horse into a trot, so that everybody heard the jingle as I rode. I went straight to Athanasi's, hung my saddle-bags up in a place where I could always keep my eye on them, and ordered dinner. 'The best that can be had,' said I, 'it will be paid for!' The dinner was fit for a bishop, I must say, and no lack of wine. When I was satisfied, I asked Athanasi, 'Who cooked for me?' 'Oh,' says he, 'it was my daughter, Heraclea.' 'Let her come, then,' says I: 'I must tell her how good it was.' Then I unlocked my saddle-bags before their eyes, gave a dollar to Athanasi, and another to his daughter. I jingled the bags well as I carried them out—and heavy enough they were—and then rode away.

"The next week, I came back and did the same thing, but when Heraclea had gone to the kitchen, I said to Athanasi: 'Your daughter pleases me; I should like to marry her, and even if her dowry is not so high as I have a right to ask, I will take her.' He looked at me, then at my saddle-bags, brought another bottle of wine; and so the thing was settled. It wasn't a month before Papa Anagnosto blessed us as man and wife; and I felt easy and comfortable again. Her dower was—well, I won't say how much; but I might have done worse.

"When my wife went home with me, I hung the saddle-bags over my bed, and cautioned her against allowing any one to come near them. She did everything as I wanted it, and was quiet and steady enough for a week or two But a woman, you know, is never satisfied. I knew it would come and come it did. 'What is the use of all that money hanging there,' she thought, 'when I might have the heaviest gold ear-rings in the village?' 'Nicolà, my life,' said she [here the speaker imitated a woman's voice, in the most irresistibly droll way], 'I should like to get a new pair of ear-rings for the Easter dances.' 'Very well,' says I, 'here's my key. Go to the saddle-bags and take as much money as you want.' She hopped into the bed-room like a cat, while I went on cleaning my gun, as cool as could be. In a minute, she was out again, looking scared and pale. 'Money!' she screamed; 'that's not money—it's bits of iron!' 'Why, you're a fool:' said I, trying to look as wild as I could. When I went in with her, and looked into the saddle-bags, I threw my gun on the floor, stamped, howled, and cursed like a thousand dragons; while Hera clea, sitting on the bed, could only say: 'Holy Spiridion. what has happened?' 'Why,' I yelled, 'that cursed Alexandros, that wizard, that devil—whom I offended last week —he has gone and turned all my bright silver dollars into iron!' Then, when she found I was so furious, she tried to quiet and console me. So I got out of the difficulty then; but I guess she begins to suspect how it really was. However, she likes me well enough, and I am now the father of a little Athanasi; so it don't much matter."

Nicola's story—to the truth of which some of the villagers testified—gave great amusement to his auditors. We shook hands with the jolly band of miscreants, and rode up the hot, narrow gorge for an hour or more, until the road approached the summit ridge of Parnes, where, upon a narrow, precipitous cape, stood the ancient fortress of Phyle. The blocks of tawny marble of which it is composed are entire to the height of ten to twenty feet, and picturesquely overgrown with glossy draperies of ivy. Sitting on the parapet, the savage defile, dark with pine trees, yawns below you; while, between its scarped walls of orange-colored rock, you look out over the warm plain of Attica, as far as Hymettus and the sea. In the central distance rises the Acropolis, distinct with all its temples. Here, as in the Propylæa, you have a foreground and a frame for the picture; and the wonderful coloring of the landscape, thus confined to an extent which the eye can take in at a single glance, assumes a purity and depth which is always wanting in a wide panoramic view.

On the Propylæa, perfect Art inframes the harmonious landscape; at Phyle, it is savage Nature. Different in features, the views nevertheless make a similar impression. Nothing could better illustrate the integrity of Byron's appreciation of Nature than his selection of these two points. And, while sitting among the lizard-haunted ruins, gazing through the hot film of the sirocco upon Athens, and reflecting upon her flimsy Court and degenerate people, I could not but admit that he might still say:

"Spirit of Freedom! when on Phyle's brow
　Thou sat'st with Thrasybulus and his train,
Couldst thou forebode the dismal hour which now
　Dims the green beauties of thine Attic plain?"

CHAPTER XIX.

THE HAUNTS OF THE MUSES.

WE left Athens on the 13th of April, for a journey to Parnassus and the northern frontier of Greece. The company consisted of François, Braisted, myself, and Ajax and Themistocles, our *agoyats*, or grooms. It was a teeming, dazzling day, with light scarfs of cloud-crape in the sky, and a delicious breeze from the west blowing through the pass of Daphne. The Gulf of Salamis was pure ultramarine, covered with a velvety bloom, while the island and Mount Kerata swam in transparent pink and violet tints. Greece, on such a day, is living Greece again. The soul of ancient Art and Poetry throbs in the splendid air, and pours its divinest light upon the landscape.

Crossing the sacred plain of Eleusis for the fourth time in my Grecian journeys, our road entered the mountains—lower offshoots of Cithæron, which divide the plain from that of Bœotia. They are now covered with young pines, to the very summits, and François directed my attention to the rapidity with which the mountains were becoming wooded, since the destruction of young trees has been prohibited by law. The agricultural prosperity of the country, in many districts, depends entirely on the restoration of the lost forests. The sun was intensely hot in the close glens, and we found the shade of the old Cithæronian pines very grateful. We met a straggling company of lancers returning from the Thessalian frontier, and many travellers in the course of the afternoon. Among the baggage animals following the lancers we were surprised to find Pegasus and Bellerophon, the lean horses which had carried us through the Peloponnesus; and soon after, Aristides himself resplendent in clean Easter garments. He was greatly disappointed at seeing us under way, as he had intended to carry us to the Mounts of Song on his own winged steeds.

Towards evening, we descended into the valley of the Eleusinian Cephissus, at the foot of Cithæron, passing the remains of an ancient tower, twenty feet high. At sunset, when the sky had become overcast and stormy, we reached the solitary khan of Casa, at the foot of a rocky, precipitous hill, crowned by the acropolis of Œnoë, and were heartliy glad to find shelter in the windy building, from the more violent wind outside. The keepers of the khan were two women—old friends of François—who received us with great cordiality. There was a military barrack a few paces off, containing a corporal's guard, who were supposed to keep down brigandage. The setting sun built a magnificent rainbow upon the bases of heavy clouds, which moved away upon Athens with thunder and lightning. Our lodging was in a loft, among heaps of grain and piles of dried herbs; but F.'s convenient camp-beds, as we knew from experience, were as comfortable in a stable as any where else; and his famous *potage aux voyageurs* would have made a hungry Lucullus shriek with satisfaction. Benevolence prompts me to communicate the receipt for this soup, which anybody can make, with a little practice. Boil two fowls for the broth: add a sufficient quantity of vermicelli, and, when nearly done, the yolks of four eggs, beaten up with a gill of water. Then squeeze into the mixture the juice of half a lemon: and, lo! it is done. If any lady can make a better soup, with fewer materials, I should be glad to possess her autograph.

We awoke to a cloudless sky; and, after coffee, climbed the hill of Œnoë, or Eleutheria, whichever it may be. I suppose Leake is most likely to be right; and so I shall call it Œnoë. A hard pull of fifteen minutes brought us to the lower part of the wall, which is composed of immense blocks of gray conglomerate limestone—the native rock of the hill. The walls are eight feet thick, and strengthened by projecting square towers. On both the northern and southern sides, the natural precipices assist the plan of defence. Following the northern wall up the hill to the northwestern angle, we were surprised to see before us a range of tall square towers, which, with the connecting curtains, appear to be in nearly a perfect state. Of the nine towers which defended this side of the city, six are still from twenty to twenty-five feet in height. We walked along the top of the wall, and passed through them all in succession. There are loop-holes in the sides, for arrows or javelins; and I noticed mortices in the stones, for the joists which supported the upper floors. On the southern side the wall overhangs the deep gorge, through which flows the main branch of the Cephissus. There were two massive postern gateways to the town. The walls are better preserved, without exception, than any which I saw in Greece. They date from the time of Alexander the Great. The position of the place, among the wild peaks of Cithæron, makes it one of the most picturesque ruins in the country.

We now climbed the main ridge of the mountains; and, in less than an hour, reached the highest point—whence the great Bœotian plain suddenly opened upon our view. In the distance gleamed Lake Copaïs, and the hills beyond; in the west, the snowy top of Parnassus, lifted clear and bright above the morning vapors; and, at last, as we turned a shoulder of the mountain in descending, the streaky top of Helicon appeared on the left, completing the classic features of the landscape. We descended to the *kalyvia*, or summer village of Vilia, whose inhabitants cultivate part of the plain during the winter. The want of water obliges them to retire to another village in the mountains during the summer; so that their lives are passed in a regular alternation between the two places— each village being deserted half the year. This is a very common mode of life among the Greek peasants. As we entered the plain, taking a rough path towards Platæa, the fields were dotted, far and near, with the white Easter shirts of the people working among the vines.

Another hour, and our horses' hoofs were upon the sacred soil of Platæa. The walls of the city are still to be traced for nearly their entire extent. They are precisely similar in construction to those of Œnoë—like which, also they were strengthened by square towers. There are the substructions of various edifices—some of which may have been temples—and on the side next the modern village lie four large sarcophagi, now used as vats for treading out the grapes in vintage-time. A more harmless blood than once curdled on the stones of Platæa now stains the empty sepulchres of the heroes.

> "It was a bright immortal head
> They crowned with clustering vine;
> And o'er their best and bravest dead,
> They poured the dark-red wine."

We rode up to the miserable little village, took our seats in the church-door, and ate our breakfast there, gazing on the hollow plain below the ruins, which witnessed, probably, the brunt of the battle. In the intense glare of the sunshine no illusion was possible. The beggarly huts about us; the uncouth piles of stones, lying here and there among the springing grass; the bare, deserted hills beyond—what was there to remind one of ancient valor and glory in all these? The landscape was like a worn-out garment, which the golden mist of sunset, or the magic of moonshine, may touch with deceptive color; but, seen at noon-day, with every rent and patch obtruded to your gaze, it is simply—rags.

Nevertheless, we rode over the plain, fixed the features of the scene in our memories, and then kept on towards the field of Leuktra, where the brutal power of Sparta received its first check. The two fields are so near, that a part of the fighting may have been done upon the same ground

The landmarks of Leuktra are so uncertain, however, that I trusted entirely to François, who had conducted travellers thither for thirty years, and plucked some field-flowers on the spot he pointed out. I then turned my horse's head towards Thebes, which we reached in two hours.

It was a pleasant scene, though so different from that of two thousand years ago. The town is built partly on the hill of the Cadmeion, and partly on the plain below. An aqueduct, on mossy arches, supplies it with water, and keeps its gardens green. The plain to the north is itself one broad garden to the foot of the hill of the Sphinx, beyond which is the blue gleam of a lake, then a chain of barren hills, and over all the snowy cone of Mount Delphi, in Eubœa. The only remains of the ancient city are stones; for the massive square tower, now used as a prison, cannot be ascribed to an earlier date than the reign of the Latin princes. A recent excavation has disclosed the foundations of a mediæval building, constructed of ancient stones. Can it be the palace of that Theban merchant who bought the Duchy of Naxos and made himself the equal of kings—the architectural wonder of Greece during the Middle Ages? The site of the town is superb. Both Helicon and Parnassus tower in the south and west, and even a corner of Pentelicus is visible. While I sat beside the old tower, sketching the Mountain of the Sphinx, a Theban eagle—the spirit of Pindar—soared slowly through the blue depths above. The memories of Pindar and Epaminondas consecrate the soil of Thebes, though she helped to ruin Greece by her selfish jealousy of Athens. It is not an accidental circumstance that she has so utterly disappeared, while the Pro pylæa of the Athenian Acropolis, which Epaminondas threatened to carry off, still stand—and may they stand for ever!

A scholar from the French Academy at Athens joined us in the evening. He was out hunting inscriptions. The French scholars are always hunting inscriptions, and it is wonderful what a lot of archæological eggs (addled) they discover. This time he had certainly heard of a nest, and was on his way at full gallop, to secure the prize. The next night he rejoined us at Livadia, wet to the skin, without an *alpha* or a *beta* about him, and rather disposed to find the secret of the Pindaric measure in the red Bœotian wine, than to grope any longer in empty cellars.

The next morning we rode down from the Cadmeion, and took the highway to Livadia, leading straight across the Bœotian plain. It is one of the finest alluvial bottoms in the world, a deep, dark, vegetable mould—which would produce almost without limit, were it properly cultivated. Before us, blue and dark under a weight of clouds, lay Parnassus; and far across the immense plain the blue peaks of Mount Œta. In three hours we reached the foot of Helicon, and looked up at the streaks of snow which melt into the Fountain of the Muses. Presently a stream, as limpid as air, issued from the cleft heart of the mountain "*O fons Bandusiæ, splendidior vitro!*" I exclaimed; but it was a diviner than the Bandusian wave which gurgled its liquid dactyls over the marble pebbles. Ajax and Themistocles had halted in the shade of a garden on the bank; François was unpacking his saddle-bags; so I leapt from Erato, my mare, knelt among the asphodels, and drank

The water had that sweetness and purity which makes you seem to inhale, rather than drink it. The palate swam in the delicious flood with a delight which acknowledged no satiety. "What is this?" I said, as I lifted up my head "Can it be the Muses' Fountain coming down from yonder mountain? Whence this longing unsuppressed in my breast—this desire that is springing to be singing? My veins are on fire—give me a lyre! I'll beat Apollo all hollow!"

"Pshaw!" said François (who had just taken a draught). "He now can drink who chooses, at the Fountain of the Muses. Why, you know, the gods and goddesses, and the nymphs in scanty bodices, are now no more detected in the shrines to them erected. That was only a superstition unworthy a man of your position. To such illusions you're no dupe: this water's very good for soup!"

"Sound the hew-gag, beat the tonjon!" exclaimed Braisted, who had not been thirsty: "I believe you are both crazy." But the mare, Erato, who had taken long draughts from the stream, whinnied, whisked her tail, and galloped off one line of hexameter after another, as we continued our journey. So I devoutly testify that Helicon is not yet dry, and the Fountain of the Muses retains its ancient virtue.

In the afternoon we turned the spur of a mountain—a sort of outpost between Helicon and Parnassus—and saw before us Livadia, on the northern slope of a high hill. A ruined Turkish fortress, with two round towers, gave the place a wild, picturesque air, while the green gardens and mulberry orchards below, relieved the sterility of the gray cliffs which towered above it. Clear, bright, mountain water gushed in full streams down the glen, and wandered away into the rich plain, fructifying the pregnant soil wherever it went. We reached a large, dreary khan, as the rain began to fall; and, having established ourselves there for the night, set out to visit the cave of the oracle of Trophonius. It lies at the upper end of the town, in a ravine which is buried almost below the sunshine by precipitous rocks that tower more than a thousand feet above. The grand, savage aspect of the spot might well have given rise to the ancient superstition that he who once entered the cave never smiled again. Notwithstanding its reputation, I took refuge in one of the hollow chambers from the torrents of rain which drove down the awful gorge.

A ride of three hours the next day brought us to Cheronœa, the battle-field where the Bœotians made their last desperate stand against Philip of Macedon. The ruins of the city have disappeared, with the exception of the theatre, the seats of which are hewn in the solid rock, and some fragments of marble and breccia; but the monument to the Bœotians who fell in the battle is one of the most interesting in Greece. The colossal lion, placed in the sepulchral mound, had gradually become imbedded in the earth, and thus preserved, when it was discovered and blown to pieces with gunpowder by the guerilla chieftain, Odysseus, during the war of independence. The head remains entire, with the eyes upturned in the agony of death, and the teeth set in the last howl of mingled rage and despair. I have never seen a more grand and touching memorial. The mutilated face embodies the death-cry of Greece. It expresses a despair so awful, yet so heroic, that a man need not blush if he should find sudden tears starting into his eyes as he gazes upon it

CHAPTER XX.

PARNASSUS AND THE DORIAN MOUNTAINS.

THE khan at Cheronæa was a mere hovel, where the only place for our beds was in the stable among the horses. Our hoofed friends were tolerably quiet, however, and nothing disturbed our slumber except the crowing of the cocks. But the landlord of this hotel demanded no less than three dollars for our lodgings; and thereupon ensued one of those terribly wordy battles in which François was a veteran combatant. Epithets struck and clashed against one another like swords; the host was pierced through and through with furious lunges, and even our valiant dragoman did not escape some severe wounds. Then some peasants, whose horses had been stalled for the night in our bed-room, demanded to be paid for the feed of the animals, because, they said, we had fed ours in the stable, which obliged them to feed theirs, unnecessarily. The Greeks believe, that if one horse sees another eat, without eating himself, he will fall sick, and perhaps die. Until I discovered this fact, I was surprised to find that when we reached a khan all the horses were removed from the stable until after ours had been fed, when they were brought back again.

In the morning, tremendous black clouds were hanging over Parnassus; and deep-blue gloom, alternating with streaks of fierce sunshine, checkered the broad, level valley of the Cephissus—the highway through which the Persians and the Macedonians marched upon Greece. As we skirted the plain, riding towards the south-eastern corner of Parnassus, François pointed out a village, hanging on the dark, rocky slope. "That is Daulia!" said he. The ancient Daulis, the birth-place of the nightingale! The thickets by every stream resounded with the exquisite songs of the bird of passion and of sorrow.

> "Dost thou once more essay
> Thy flight; and feel come over thee,
> Poor fugitive, the feathery change
> Once more; and once more make resound.
> With love and hate, triumph and agony,
> Lone Daulis and the high Cephissian vale?"

We now entered a deep defile, leading along the southern base of Parnassus to Delphi. The country was stony and barren, overgrown only with broom and furze, and reminded me of some of the wilder parts of Scotland. This is the home of brigands, and they still abound in these rocky fastnesses. A shepherd-boy, tending his flock of black goats, called out to us: "The robbers have come down—have you met any of them?" He informed us that, five days before, they had carried off a rich Greek, whom they were keeping in a cavern somewhere in the rocks overhanging the defile. They demanded thirty thousand dollars for his ransom, and would not give him up until the money was paid.

Passing the spot where Œdipus killed his father, and the wild gorge of Schiste, we reached, about eleven o'clock, the khan of Ismenos, tolerably high up on the side of Parnassus, whose snowy peak cleft the sky, wrapt in a misty veil of drifting snow. The wind was frightful. It blew with tremendous force and icy coldness, stiffening our limbs and freezing the very blood in our veins. A snow-storm raged around the topmost summit of Parnassus, which shone now and then with a blinding white gleam, as the clouds parted. While we were breakfasting, a company of shepherds arrived. Instead of Arcadian crooks they carried muskets and daggers, and I have no doubt looked after something else besides their sheep. They were fierce, splendid fellows, with a strong dash of the ancient Hellenic blood in their veins. Two of them had come to appeal to the keeper of the khan as an arbitrator, one accusing the other of having stolen two sheep, while the latter claimed compensation for the damage done to his grain by eight sheep belonging to the former. It was a double case, not easily to be decided, and the mild little umpire quite lost his wits in the storm that raged around him. Fists were clenched, furious words flung back and forth, daggers drawn, and every moment I expected to see blood flow. It was a wild, exciting scene, in singular keeping with the hurricane outside, which made the house rock to its foundations.

As we continued our journey along the southern side of

Parnassus, high over the gorge between it and a cluster of barren peaks, forming a cape between the bays of Salona and Aspropitia, I was several times almost unhorsed by the violence of the wind. One of the first poems I read, as a child, was Mrs. Hemans' "Storm at Delphi," commencing:

> Far through the Delphian shades
> A Persian trumpet rang;"

—and, though forgotten for years, it returned to my memory as we faced the gusts which seemed still to protect the shrine of the god. In two hours, however, we reached the village of Arachova, which is situated most picturesquely on the steep mountain side, in the midst of a vast amphitheatric sweep of terraced vineyards. The place was almost entirely deserted, the inhabitants being in the fields or upon the mountain with their flocks. The few whom we saw, however, verified the correctness of the statement that on Parnassus, as on the sides of Taygetus, may still be found traces of the ancient blood of Greece. Here still live the forms of Phidias—the rude plebeian type of that ennobled and perfected beauty which furnished him with the models of heroes, demi-gods, and deities. Yon barefooted girl, filling her pitcher at the fountain, would have been a Venus of Milo, in a higher social sphere; the shepherd, asleep on a sheltered bank under the rocks, is already a Faun of Praxiteles, and might be a Theseus or a Perseus; and these children need but the loveliness of nudity to become Cupids, Ganymedes, and Psyches. The clear-cut symmetry of the features, the low brow, short upper lip and rounded chin, the beautiful balance of the limbs, and that perfect modelling of the trunk, which neither conceals nor exhibits too much the development of the muscles, are all here—so far as the body can be seen through its disguise. The true Greeks differ from the Albanians and the mongrel Turco-Slavic-Venetian race, which constitute the bulk of the population, in everything—in character, form, features, and movement—and I cannot understand why it is that enthusiastic travellers persist in seeing in every one who bears the name of Greek a descendant of Pericles, or Leonidas, or Homer.

As we left Arachova, proceeding towards Delphi, the deep gorge opened, disclosing a blue glimpse of the Gulf of Corinth and the Achaïan mountains. Tremendous cliffs of blue-gray limestone towered upon our right, high over the slope of Delphi, which ere long appeared before us. Our approach to the sacred spot was marked by tombs cut in the rock. A sharp angle of the mountain was passed; and then, all at once, the enormous walls, buttressing the upper region of Parnassus, stood sublimely against the sky, cleft right through the middle by a terrible split, dividing the twin peaks which give a name to the place. At the bottom of this chasm issue forth the waters of Castaly, and fill a stone trough by the road-side. On a long, sloping mountain-terrace beyond, facing the east, stood once the town and temples of Delphi, and now the modern village of Kastri.

François conducted us up the hill to the house of Mr. Triandaphylli (Rose), a good-humored old fellow, who, with his wife, received us in the most cordial manner

They occupied a second story, with two rooms, one of which had a broad chimney-place, where they were cooking dinner. The shelter and the fire were most welcome to us, and so were the bowls of red, resinous wine, which Dame Rose, with the air of a Pythoness, presented to us. An old soldier, who has nominal charge of the antiquities—an easy way of pensioning him upon travellers—had scented us from afar, and now offered his services as guide. We were at first disinclined to move; but the warmth and the Delphian wine soon restored all the enthusiasm which the Parnassian winds had blown out of us, and we sallied forth.

As you may imagine, our first walk was to the shrine of the Delphic oracle, at the bottom of the cleft between the two peaks. The hewn face of the rock, with a niche, supposed to be that where the Pythia sat upon her tripod, and a secret passage under the floor of the sanctuary, are all that remain. The Castalian fountain still gushes out at the bottom, into a large square inclosure, called the Pythia's Bath, and now choked up with mud, weeds, and stones. Among those weeds, I discerned one of familiar aspect, plucked and tasted it. Water-cress, of remarkable size and flavor! We thought no more of Apollo and his shrine, but delving wrist-deep into Castalian mud, gathered huge handfuls of the profane herb, which we washed in the sacred fount, and sent to François for a salad.

We then descended to a little monastery, on the opposite slope of the glen. In the court-yard, at the door of a small, fantastic church, leaned three or four ancient bas-reliefs. One was the torso of a man, life size, and very well modelled: a smaller one, full of spirit, represented four horses attached to a chariot. The monastery stands on an ancient terrace, of fine square blocks, which the soldier said had once supported a school, or gymnasium—who knows? All through and around Kastri are portions of similar terraces, some of very early masonry. Of the temple of Apollo there only remain blocks, marble drums, and the inscription which cost poor Ottfried Müller his life.

As the sun sank, I sat on the marble blocks and sketched the immortal landscape. High above me, on the left, soared the enormous twin peaks of pale-blue rock, lying half in the shadow of the mountain slope upheaved beneath, half bathed in the deep yellow lustre of sunset. Before me rolled wave after wave of the Parnassian chain, divided by deep lateral valleys, while Helicon, in the distance, gloomed like a thunder-storm under the weight of gathered clouds. Across this wild, vast view, the breaking clouds threw broad belts of cold blue shadow, alternating with zones of angry orange light, in which the mountains seemed to be heated to a transparent glow. The furious wind hissed and howled over the piles of ruin, and a few returning shepherds were the only persons to be seen. And this spot, for a thousand years, was the shrine where spake the awful oracle of Greece! And yet—what was it? A hideous nest of priestcraft—of jugglery, delusion, and fraud. Only the ideal halo thrown over it by the Mount and the Fountain of Song, has given to the name of Delphi such wonderfu music. The soil where Plato's olives grew is more truly hallowed. When you stand before the naked shrine, you think less of the cloudy sentences uttered there, the words of fate for Greece, than of the secret passage laid bare below the Pythia's niche—the trickery under the inspiration. But as it then was, so it is now; so will it always be Does not the blood of St. Januarius become liquid once a year? Do not pictures weep and bleed, and skeleton bones fall upon doctors' tables?*

When we returned to the Triandaphylli mansion, we found the Roses, old and young, at their supper. Their meal consisted of a stew of veal and onions, with bread and good wine. The old lady handed me her glass, and her husband picked out and extended to me on his fork, a choice fragment of meat, as a token of hospitality. While we had been absent, François had improved the opportunity, and gratified his own and their love of gossip, by giving all manner of information concerning us. When, therefore, I took the glass of wine, Mrs. Rose arose, like a Pythia, with extended arms, and moved by the Delphic spirit, uttered a prophetic sentence. What she said, you, reader, have no right to know: it suffices that the oracle is not yet dumb. It spake to me: and, under the spell of the place, I believed it. Was it fulfilled? you ask. Well—no.

François slept among the Roses, and we in an outer room, lulled by a wind which threatened to shake down the house. In the morning, it still blew so violently, that I gave up my intention of visiting the Corcyrean Cave, especially as we learned that the upper plateau of Parnassus was still covered with snow. We went, however, to the stadium of the Delphic games, which lies along the hillside, above the village. Parting with our friendly hosts,

---

* See the Annals of Spiritualism in New York.

we passed out by the ancient gate of Delphi, which was hewn out of the solid rock. On rounding the corner of the mountain, there opened upon us a glorious view of the rich, olive-covered Chrissean plain below, the Gulf of Corinth with Erymanthus and Pan-achaïcum beyond, and the dazzling Dorian mountains to the westward. The descent to the valley, which was rough and difficult, occupied two hours.

On the slope of the opposite mountain, lay the flourishing town of Salona. We did not visit it, but bore to the right, up the course of the stream, into the Dorian hills. The valley gave cheering evidence of improvement, being covered with young olive orchards and thriving vineyards, to the extent of which the people are adding every year At the bottom of each field was a square basin of masonry with a hole leading to a sunken vat—a primitive but very serviceable wine-press. The gorge now became narrow and wild, overhung by precipices of blue limestone, stained with the loveliest orange tints. Turning a sudden angle, we saw before us the village of Topolia, built up a steep cape of the mountain, at the intersection of two valleys, rich with fine old olive groves. Sparkling streams gushed down the rocks in silver foam, and hedges of fig and pomegranate embowered the paths. Here the blast of war which has elsewhere in Greece left such desolating traces seems never to have reached. It was an idyl of the ancient Doris.

The houses were large, two-storied, and comfortable, and the people, who thronged the narrow, tortuous streets in Sunday idleness, had mostly faces of the old Hellenic stamp. Some children, gathered about a fountain, were as beautiful as anything in ancient art. After a search, we found a large country store, better stocked than any we saw in Greece. Here we breakfasted, gazed upon by a curious, but good-humored and friendly crowd. The people asked many questions, and seemed delighted that I was able to converse a little with them in their own language. I was considerably puzzled for awhile by their speaking of Delphi as *Adelphous*. Among others, a dumb man came in, and made piteous attempts to talk to us, accompanying his gestures with uncouth, inarticulate noises. We took special notice of him, which seemed to gratify the others very much. I gave him a tumbler of wine, which he flourished around his head, and then drank, placing one hand upon his heart, with signs of extravagant joy. I was delighted to find that here, as in Sparta, the character of the people improved in proportion as they approached the purity of the ancient blood.

After leaving Topolia, our road took to the hills, crossing the summit of the lower ridges, connecting Parnassus with the Dorian Mountains. We passed a most picturesque old mill, with a lofty race, raised on a wall, from which the water was carried to the wheel in curious wicker tubes, plastered with clay. It was a ride of nearly four hours to the khan of Gravia, over the wild, uninhabited hills, sparsely dotted with fir-trees on their northern side. As we descended towards the upper valley of the Cephissus, Œta, the boundary of Thessaly Phthiotis, came in sight. Following the course of a rapid stream, we descended into the valley, which opened green and lovely before us, shining softly in the mellow gleam of the sun, already dropping behind the Dorian snows. The place contained only half a dozen houses, each one of which was anxious to offer us lodgings. Our room was large and dirty, but the evening soup was better than ever, and besides, our Topolian wine was of that kind which cheers the heart, but not inebriates the brain.

CHAPTER XXI.

THE FRONTIER OF THESSALY.

WHEN we left the khan of Gravia at sunrise, hundreds of nightingales were singing in the green thickets, and the light already lay warm on the glorious plain. After crossing Cephissus, we rode for two hours across the low hills along the western base of Œta, which were completely covered with forests of oak, in full foliage. Although our bridle track was rough and muddy, I enjoyed greatly those sweet Arcadian woods, brightened by the purple sprays of the Judas-tree, and fragrant with the odors of the flower-spangled turf. The ground was covered with fallen trunks and dead limbs—an immense supply of fire-wood, rotting idly in a country where it is exceedingly scarce and dear. François affirmed that the Dorians were mostly bandits, and that their laziness accounted for the ruined and neglected appearance of the country. As we climbed the sides of Œta, plunging up and down great ravines, there were fine views of Parnassus across the plain. Another hour of ascent brought us to the summit, and we saw, through the mountain gateway opening before us, Mount Othrys, an off-shoot of Pindus, and the modern as it was the ancient frontier of Greece on the north.

On the topmost peak of Œta, which rose on our right, near at hand, is the spot where Hercules died, wrapped in the poisoned shirt of the Centaur. But how dim seemed those grand old traditions in the clear, unillusive light of a spring morning! Hercules was as far away as if that were the Alleghanies, and not Œta, and the only association which came readily to my mind was an absurd one. A few months before, I had been reading Immermann's novel of "Münchausen," wherein, under the disguise of goats upon Mount Œta, he holds up the transcendentalists and reformers of Germany to the most exquisite and unmerciful ridicule. These goats and their socialistic pranks obstinately thrust themselves on my memory, and instead of sighing sentimentally, I laughed profanely. O heroes and demi gods! pardon me; and yet not only Aristophanes, but Plato, would have done the same thing. Let us be honest, if we cannot be ideal. When a man always feels the proper emotion at the right place, suspect him!

Descending for a mile or two through groves of fir, oak, and beach, we came upon the open side of Œta, whence a superb panorama is suddenly unfolded to the view. The great plain of the Spercheios, tinted with all the softest colors of spring—a shifting web of pink, green, and gold—lay unrolled beneath from its far source at the feet of Pindus to the broad arc in which it embraces the Malian gulf. Beyond the valley ran the long gray ridge of Othrys, terminating, far to the east, in the snowy summit of Pelion

The town of Lamia, sprinkled in a hollow at the base of the hills, glimmered faintly in the distance. The blue mountains of Eubœa bounded the view on the east, and deep down on our right, at the base of Œta, lay the pass of Thermopylæ. A long and rough descent followed, but the path was shaded with oak, ilex, laurel, mastic, and pine, among which were the first beeches we had seen in Greece. We breakfasted at a fountain, half-way down: then, leaving the baggage to take the direct road to Lamia, descended to the corner where Œta of old jutted into the gulf, forming the pass of immortal name.

Thermopylæ is not so formidable now. The deposits of the Spercheïos have, in the course of twenty-three hundred years, formed a marsh, from one to three miles in width, between the base of the mountains and the sea. The Persian army was encamped upon the broad valley of the Spercheios, while the Greeks had posted themselves a mile or more *within* the pass, near the hot-springs whence it devives its name. Here the Spartans were seen by Persian scouts, on the morning of the battle, washing their faces and combing their long hair. They seem to have advanced to the mouth of the pass, and there met the first onset; but gradually fell back to a low hill near their first position, where the last of them were slain. The similarity between Thermopylæ and the field of Issus, where Alexander defeated Darius, is quite remarkable.

We gathered a few wild flowers from the spot, and then turned about for Lamia. Some peasants came out of their cane huts, built on the edge of the marsh; and one of them handed me a common copper coin of the Eastern Empire, begging me to tell him what it was. He said that his father, who had found it when plowing, had been offered two dollars for it, but had refused. "If anybody offers you *ten* dollars," said François, "don't sell it; but hang it by a string around the neck of your oldest boy, and it will bring him good luck." "What do you mean by deceiving the poor man in that manner?" I asked. "Oh!" answered my inveterate guide, "he is a beast; if you told him the coin was worth ten lepta (two cents), he would be offended. He wished to sell it to you for five dollars: better make him happy, and save yourself from being bored, by confirming him in his own stupidity." With which practical, but not very commendable doctrine, François lighted a fresh cigar.

We crossed the Spercheios on a high Venetian bridge; and, after passing the marsh, which was a wilderness of the pink and white *spiræa*, in full bloom, rode on over level grain-fields to Lamia. This town has been compared to Athens, and there is, in fact, considerable resemblance between the two places. The Acropolis is very similar in form and position; and there are even suggestions of the Nympheion, the Museion, and Lycabettus, between which the town occupies the same relative position. The fortress on the Acropolis is Venetian, but made picturesque by the addition of a Turkish mosque and minaret. Two other minarets in the town still remain; and these, with the camels which travel back and forth from the port of Stylida, called to mind the Moslem cities of the Levant.

On entering Lamia, we inquired for a khan, which, it seems, the place does not afford. While engaged in seek ing lodgings, we were accosted by a soldier, who bore a pressing invitation from the Commander of the gen-d'armerie, that we should come and take up our quarters at his house. I declined — saying that we had already found rooms; and, while we thanked the Commander for his courtesy, would not be obliged to trouble him. "Oh! but he expects you," said the soldier: "he has been looking for your arrival all day." "Then it is a mistake," I answered; "and he takes us for somebody else." By the time our pack-horses were unloaded, however, a second messenger arrived. "The Commander begs that you will come immediately to his house, he expects you, and has letters for you from Athens." Again I asserted that there was some mistake. "No, no." said the messenger; "you are the very ones. He received letters two days ago about you. He will not accept any refusal."

I thought it barely possible that General Church, Mr. Hill, or some other good friend in Athens might have written to Lamia in my behalf, after my departure, and finally decided to accompany the messenger. He conducted us at once to the commander's residence, a neat, comfortable house on the slope of the hill, and ushered us into the presence of Major Plessos, who received us with great cordiality. "My friend, Gen. Church," said he, "has written to me announcing your arrival, and I am very glad to welcome you to my house." I then remembered distinctly that Gen. Church had spoken to me of his friend Plessos, in Lamia, and had offered me letters of introduction, which I had neglected to bring with me. Presuming, therefore, that all was right, I accepted the proffered hospitality, and sent François after the baggage. But I was presently undeceived. The major handed me a letter saying: "This is for you — it arrived several days ago!" Behold! it was for Mr. Gardner, M. P., who was travelling somewhere in Eubœa. I at once explained the mistake, and proposed to retreat; but the friendly commander would not hear of such a thing. "I have you now," said he, "and here you shall stay until you leave Lamia. A friend of Gen. Church, and an American, is always a welcome guest."

Lieutenant Mano, a nephew of Mavrocordato, joined us at dinner, and in the evening came in a Mainote captain — a strikingly handsome, agreeable fellow. As they all spoke French and Italian, we had a very animated conversation on the political condition of Greece. My new acquaintances were enthusiastic patriots, as was proper; but the admissions they made tended to confirm my previous impressions. Major Plessos has the task of suppressing brigandage on the Thessalian frontier, which he appears to have done very effectually. The room in which we slept was hung with trophies taken from the robbers — long Albanian muskets, ornamented with silver, pistols, yataghans, splendid silver belts, and even richly-ornamented cases of the pure metal, designed to contain a copy of the New Testament! The robbers, you must know, are gentlemen and Christians; and although they cut off the noses of shepherds, and pour boiling oil on the breasts of women, I have often heard them spoken of by the Greeks with a certain degree of admiration and respect.

After we had got into bed, François, whose tongue had been loosened by the Phthiotan wine, redder than the blood spilt at Thermopylæ, sat down upon a chest of arms, and became confidential. The sight of the glittering weapons suspended on the wall carried him back to the struggles for Grecian independence, in which he had borne his part. He had fought in Doris and Etolia; had taken part in Fabvier's unfortunate expedition to Scio; and had been for years a captive in Stamboul. "Ah!" said he, with his eyes fixed on the crossed yataghans, "we came over ground to-day that I know but too well! I fought the Turks, many a day, on those hills, as you go from Gravia towards the ruins of Orchomenos. We had a little battery—three guns only—but it annoyed the Turks very much; and they made a desperate struggle to get hold of it. Out of two hundred men, I don't believe we had sixty left. They wouldn't have taken it, after all, if we had not lost our captain He was a mountaineer from Acarnania, one of the handsomest men you ever saw; tall, with a head and shoulders like a lion, blue eyes, and a magnificent beard, as blonde as a Muscovite's. We were working the guns with all our might, for the Turks were coming down upon us. He sprang upon a parapet to give orders, and I was leaning back, looking at him, and waiting for the word. His sword-arm was stretched out, his eyes flashing, and his mouth opened to shout—when, all at once, I saw his forehead break in. He did not waver, his arm was still stretched; but instead of words, a sound like '*Zt—zzt—zzt!*' came from his mouth. Then his knees suddenly bent, and he fell down, stone-dead. We fought like devils; but each man for himself, after that—no command anywhere—and the Turks got the battery."

"Were you wounded?" I asked.

"Not then, but a few days afterwards. I escaped, picked up a horse, and joined a body of lancers. We kept up a sort of guerilla warfare about the plains of Orchomenos, avoiding large bodies of the enemy. But one day the Turkish cavalry surprised us. When a man is desperate, he loses his wits; and I have not much recollection of what followed. There was dust, there were sabres, pistol-shots, yells, and mad riding. I tumbled a Turk off his horse with my last pistol, and threw it at the head of another who rode full tilt upon me. Then my own horse jumped, and I lost my senses. When I opened my eyes, it was dark night. I was in a hut, on my back, and a woman sat beside me. It was a peasant's wife, whom I knew; but I could not imagine what I was doing there. I tried to rise, but felt as if every bone in my body was broken. 'Where am I? What's the matter?' I asked. 'Oh,' she cried, 'we are beaten!' Then I remembered all. I had a bad lance wound in my leg, and was dreadfully bruised, but knew that I was not going to die. 'Where are the others?' I asked. 'Where is Giorgios? Where is Constantinos? Where is Spiridion?' She only clasped her hands and cried aloud, and I knew that they were dead. I got well after awhile, but saw no more service until I joined Fabvier. Ah, Dieu! to think of the blood we shed — and what has come of it?" Thereupon François relapsed into a fit of melancholy musing — pending which I fell asleep.

In the morning, the Major proposed riding to the summit of Othrys, in order to look upon the plains of Thessaly

but the weather was so calm that I feared we would be
delayed in crossing to Euboea, and reluctantly gave orders
to proceed to the port of Stylida. After breakfast we set
out, accompanied by the Major and Lieut. Mano for the
first few miles. A carriage-road to Stylida has been commenced, and is about half finished: 200,000 drachmas
($33,000) have also been raised for a road across the marsh
to Thermopylæ; but it is impossible to get laborers.

Stylida, the port of Lamia, ten miles distant, is a picturesque, pleasant little place. Our first business, on arriving,
was to secure a boat, and we were not long in finding one.
It was a solidly built sloop, about thirty feet long, which
had just arrived from one of the outer islands, with a load
of maize, brought to Stylida, to be ground; after which,
it would be taken back as flour. Ajax and Themistocles,
who, at first, positively refused to cross with their horses,
preferring to give up the remainder of the contract, and
return home, now declared that they would go with us.
We were obliged to wait until evening for the land-breeze,
and in the meantime furnished some entertainment to the
good people of the town, who inspected us during the
afternoon with a friendly curiosity.

The sloop was decked fore-and-aft, but there was an
opening in the hold, midships, about six by eight feet in
dimensions, and into this place all our five horses were
stowed. They were gotten aboard without a great deal
of trouble, a little frightened but submissive. As there
was a dead calm, the captain's two boys towed us out of
the harbor in a little boat. Braisted and I crept into the
after-hold, a hot, cramped place, where we lay until nearly

suffocated; then went on deck, smoked, and watched the sails for an hour, and finally, turned in at midnight to sleep.

The night was quiet, with an occasional puff from the land. Towards morning, the captain anchored under an island off the extreme north-western point of Eubœa, whence at dawn he rowed to the beach, where we anchored broadside on. At sunrise, we commenced discharging the cargo, which was a work of some difficulty; but by dint of patience, main force, and the whip, the horses were, one after another, made to rear, plunge over the sloop's side, and take to the shore. The first one cleared the gunwale in good style, but all the others caught with their hind legs, and were thrown headlong into the water. The poor beasts were rejoiced to get upon firm earth again; nor were we less so, for we were all tired and hungry. But we were now upon Eubœa—the Negropont of the Middle Ages—the largest of the Grecian isles.

CHAPTER XXII.

ADVENTURES IN EUBŒA.

On landing in Eubœa, our first care was to find food and rest. Taking the first donkey-path, over fields and through mastic thickets, we reached, in about an hour, a scattering village, high up on the side of the mountain. The approach to it was through lanes of pomegranate-trees. Streams of water gushed down the hill-side, fertilizing wherever they touched; and the vegetation was not only more luxuriant, but further advanced than that of the mainland. Just above the village there was a magnificent fountain of water, in a grove of enormous plane-trees. Two of the trunks which Braisted measured, were twenty-eight and a half and thirty-five feet in circumference. It was a fresh, lovely spot, full of broken light and shade, and musical with the sound of falling water and the singing of nightingales in the pomegranate thickets. After resting two hours (during which I made a sketch of the place), we breakfasted, and then started for Edipsos, five hours distant.

The day was fair, hot, and with a sultry haze in the air

After ascending the steep ridge of the mountain which forms this corner of Eubœa, we had a long and rugged descent on the northern side, overlooking a splendid panorama of the Artemisian strait, the mountains of Thessaly, and the snowy peak of Pelion in the background. The path was lined with clumps of myrtle, mastic, laurel, and other glossy and fragrant trees; while flowers of all hues spangled the banks.

Edipsos is a most picturesque village, at the base of a lofty mountain, from the cleft gorges of which issues a fine stream. Channels of swift, clear water traverse the place; and the houses are embowered in mulberry and fruit trees. In the centre of the village is an immense plane-tree, the trunk of which is encircled by a bench for summer loungers. We found good lodgings in the house of the schoolmaster. A *gend'arme*, who persisted in talking Greek to me, informed me that there are a number of fine mineral springs up the glen. Bottles of the water, sent to Germany to be analysed, were found to contain highly medicinal properties.

The next morning, we rode across the hills to the splendid plain of Xirochori, the rich northern extremity of Eubœa. The whole Artemisian strait, and the island of Skiathos, in the Ægean, were visible. The valley and village of Agios Joannes, into which we descended, are the property of M. Mimot, a French gentleman, whose mansion, surrounded with orchards, occupies a commanding situation on one of the lower hills. Here we had a slight evidence of what may be done in Greece by the exercise of a little knowledge and industry. Stone walls or neat wooden fences bordered the road; orchards of thrifty olive-trees, grafted on the wild stock, covered the hills, and the village, in its neatness, comfort, and the tidy, prosperous air of its inhabitants, seemed to be Swiss rather than Greek. A number of the European Philhellenes settled in Euboea after the independence of Greece had been acknowledged. The rich Turkish proprietors were allowed a few years to dispose of their estates; and, when the time drew to an end, were forced to sell out for a mere song, on account of the scarcity of purchasers. Thus, tracts comprising from five to ten square miles of the richest land were sold at prices ranging from $5,000 to $10,000. Under the present miserable administration of government, these purchases are not such great bargains as might be supposed.

Crossing the plain of Xirochori, we endeavored to strike the main road leading thence down the centre of the island to Chalsis; yet in this, the richest district of Greece, a road has never been located! Every spring, the peasants plow up the ground, and the horse-path with it. We wandered about two or three hours before finding a trail, but were abundantly repaid by the beauty of the valley into which it conducted us. The hills were covered with noble pine-trees. A handsome mansion, belonging to a rich Greek, stood on a knoll above the stream, and an avenue of young trees led to a cheerful summer-house on the height, commanding a lovely view to the northward. Where were we? This was not the bare, barren, savage Greece we knew: it was a warm dell in southern Germany — the home of ease, taste, rest, and security. So completely is it in the power of man to transform the impression of a landscape. The mansion, the avenue, and the summer-house banished from mind the ancient Eubœa, the granary of Athens; or, if I remembered the fact, it was but to notice how easily classic associations are outweighed by the amenities of modern life. But when we reached the summit of the mountain, and looked backward, there stood, as if to rebuke us, not only Pelion, silvered with snow, guarding the gulf whence Jason sailed with his young Argonauts, but Ossa behind him, overlooking the Vale of Tempe, and far, far away — the dream of a peak, in the vapory slumber of the air, the home of the gods, the immortal mountain — Olympus of Thessaly!

We now entered a deep, wide gorge, leading southward to the Euripean strait. Tall, dark pines feathered the mountain sides to the very summit, and abundant streams of water gushed down every rocky hollow. The road was a faint trail, difficult to find, and perilous in the extreme. In some places it was a mere thread, notched along the face of a precipice, where one slip would have sent horse and rider down the awful gulf. With each one of these dangerous passes, the chances of our safety seemed to diminish; and when, at last, we reached a spot where the path was not more than four inches wide, resting on points of rotten-looking rock, Ajax and Themistocles turned back with the pack animals, the intrepid François dismounted, and the mare Erato stopped short. My nerves were in a tingle, but the sensation was more agreeable than otherwise. Come, Erato, said I, this is not much worse than those poetical chasms over which your divine namesake has often carried me. François went first, leading Boreas of the shaggy mane. I did not dismount, but dropped the reins on Erato's neck. As softly as a cat stealing upon a bird, she put out one paw, tried her foothold, then bracing herself upon it, brought forward the next foot and planted it in the same way, and thus, inch by inch, crept along. I sat perfectly still, keeping a just equilibrium, and looking at the path ahead—not for worlds into the yawning gulf. Millions of the finest needles were sticking into the pores of my skin; but when we reached the opposite side they fell out suddenly, and I felt as refreshed as if I had bathed in a tub of liquid electricity. Braisted followed in the same way; and after incredible labor, Ajax and Themistocles brought their horses around over the rocks.

For an hour and a half more we descended the left side of the grand gorge, which gradually contracted so as to form an impassable *cañon*. The path was delightfully shaded with pines, ilexes, oaks, and laurels: and the air, filled with warm odors of scented leaves and the flowering gorse and cistus, was delicious to inhale. Finally, we reached the last knee of the mountain, which commands a wide prospect of the Eubœan Gulf and the Locrian mountains beyond. A long upland terrace lay before us, and we rode for an hour and a half over its wooded undulations without seeing any signs of the port of Limni, our destination. The sun was setting in a bed of threatening vapors, and we were very tired and hungry, when at last the path led down a ravine to some fields of olive-trees near the seashore. But there were no signs of habitations: only some piles of sawed timber on the beach. We followed the windings of the indented coast for nearly two hours longer, before we came upon the wished-for haven, which is snugly

hidden away in a little triangular nook between two capes
In my map (that of Berghaus, published by Perthes) the
place was given about four miles too far to the northward
—which was the only example of inaccuracy I found during
all my journeys in Greece. On my return to Germany, I
pointed it out to Mr. Berghaus, who made the correction
at once. In all other instances, I found his map a miracle
of accuracy.

We were famishing, and sore from eleven hours in the
saddle, and the appearance of the well-built, compact village, with its large houses fronting the beach, promised
us welcome quarters. The people gathered about us curiously, for a traveller was a rare sight there. There was
no khan; but we procured lodgings in the house of the
richest inhabitant. The mayor and other dignitaries kept
my Greek in use, while I enjoyed a refreshing narghileh
before dinner.

In the morning, while we were taking some black coffee,
I was accosted in very bad English by a young sailor of
the place, who had made a voyage to Liverpool and thence
to Calcutta. Presently appeared a rough old fellow with
an unmistakable odor of salt about him, who hailed us
with: "Good morning! How do you come on? Are
you Scotchmen or Irishmen?" On hearing our reply, he
seemed greatly surprised and delighted. "You Americans! Why, *I* am a Yankee, too!" In fact he had
served six years in the American Navy, two years of
which he had spent at the Norfolk and Washington Navy
Yards. "Ah!" said he, "that is a great country: you
don't see any such piles of rock as here—all plain, without

stones, and good for wheat." He was a native of Limni, where he had a family, otherwise he would have gone home with us, and never returned to Greece again. "An American sailor," said he, "is a gentleman, but the Greeks are all liars and scamps. They are my people, but I hate 'em."

The health-officer informed me that some remains of the ancient town of Argæ still existed in the village, and conducted us thither, followed by quite a concourse of villagers. We found the foundations of a small but very handsome bath of the Roman time. The Mosaic floors of four chambers still remain in a tolerable state, with some fragments of stone and brick work, and broken marble columns. By this time our horses were ready, and the crowds of villagers assembled to see us off, our would-be countryman shaking hands and swearing in sailor fashion, as he lamented his inability to accompany us.

Our path led up the sides of rough, broken hills for about an hour, when we reached the summit ridge of the island, and saw before us the rich eastern valleys, the Ægean, and the scattered islets of the *eparchia* of Skopelos. The view was northern, in its abundance of piny hills and green intervening vales; but southern, almost tropical, in the hot, dim, silvery atmosphere in which they were clothed. It was really inspiring to find such lovely Arcadian scenery in Greece, and my summer memories of the forests of the Mysian Olympus came back vividly to mind. The richness and beauty of Eubœa would never be suspected by the rapid traveller, who satisfies himself with a view of dusty Attica, or the thirsty Argolis.

After breakfasting beside a picturesque mill, in a lovely little dell, we started for the estate of Mr. Noel, an English gentleman, who for twenty years has made his home in this solitude. Riding on through low valleys, hedged in with forested hills, we soon saw, by the evident care with which the young trees had been protected, that we were within the boundaries of his domain. Presently we came upon the track of a cart—a most unusual sight, in Greece. Following this, we emerged from the woods, and saw before us Mr. Noel's mansion, which stands on a gentle knoll, commanding a superb view of meadow and forest-land, sweeping into hills in the distance, and crowned by the snowy summit of Pyxario! We rode into the court and dismounted, while a servant went to seek Mr. Noel, who was below in the village. His son, a boy of twelve, who spoke English with a little hesitation, showed us, in the meanwhile, a large tame deer, of a species which is still quite abundant on the mountains. He was a noble beast, much larger than the ordinary European deer, and so completely tamed, that it was difficult to keep him out of the house. While sitting in Mr. Noel's library, in the afternoon, I was startled by the thumping of his antlers on the door. Having effected an entrance, he marched deliberately around the table, snuffing at the books, and finally seizing upon a number of *Galignani*, which he would have devoured in a very literal sense, had he not been ejected by main force.

Mr. Noel soon appeared, leading with him our baggage-horses, which he had met on their way to the khan. The cordiality of his reception left us no choice but **to stop**

there for the night. While he went off to the forest to
superintend the lumbermen, I improved the time by making
a sketch of the magnificent landscape. The Judas-trees
gushed up like pink fountains among the tender green of
the thickets; violets and wild thyme scented the air, and
the bees hummed their sleepy songs. The stream flowing
through the valley was bordered by a double row of enormous plane-trees, and the distant mountains, instead of
lifting their limestone crags naked in the sunshine, were
clothed with the cool robes of the evergreen pine. All the
landscape, from the unseen Ægean, behind the eastern hill,
to the summit of Pyxario, belonged to Mr. Noel. He was
lord of a princely domain, in a land of immortal name—yet
I commiserated him. It was a lonely life, among a horde
of ignorant, superstitious, ungrateful peasants, under a
miserable government, where his example availed nothing,
and all his attempts at improvement were frustrated. I
confess, the sight of so much cultivation and refinement as
Mr. Noel possessed, buried in such a wilderness, impressed
me with a feeling of melancholy. Everything spoke of
exile and isolation. His daughter, a sweet English rose
bud, soon to blossom into womanhood, seemed far out of
place among the frowzy Ariadnes and Iphigenias of the
village, whose companionship, even, could not take away
from her that quiet grace and self-possession which she
inherited from the mother who now sleeps in Grecian soil.

In almost any other country in the world, Mr. Noel's
labors would have produced more hopeful results. Not
only has he built more comfortable houses for his tenantry,
established a school for their children free of cost, and fur-

nished them with ample employment, but he has also introduced better agricultural implements, and endeavored to teach them a more rational system of farming. He has made a wagon-road ten miles in length, from the forests to the sea-shore, and occupies himself principally with the felling of timber, which is shipped from his own beach to Syra and the other island ports. The natives, however, only laugh at his good advice; and all that he has done for them emboldens them to make new demands on his generosity. He almost despairs of improving their condition so long as they are under the sway of a creed which turns half the days of the year into festivals, and deprives them of sufficient nourishment during the other half. Of all the absurdities of Paganism, there is none quite so irrational and injurious as these ordinances of the Eastern Church. A Greek Empire in the Orient is simply impossible while they continue in practice.

It was a great comfort to sleep in clean beds, and enjoy the abundant appliances of an English toilet. The morning was cool and gusty, and as we had determined to reach Chalcis, we took leave of our kind host immediately after breakfast. As the avenue of sycamores in the valley hid from view his mansion, and the noble landscape it commands, I repeated Tasso's "*bella età dell' oro*," and sighed to think how dreary life would be in such an Arcadia, without the company of congenial minds — but with such a company, what a paradise on earth! How, far away from the storms and commotions in which we live, within the sheltering circle of those purple hills, all pure tastes and simple virtues might flourish — how the years might pass, fair and soft as Grecian days, until death would be unwelcome, were it not for the resignation which such peace would breed!

O Zimmerman! thou sentimental imposter! O solitude! thou immortal humbug! It is very fine to talk of communion with Nature when you have a home and family, books horses, and amusements to fall back upon: but Nature, without Man, is a sorry teacher. Four years more of solitude would have made Selkirk a brute or an idiot, and even your Plato would go a long way on the same downward road. What are the lonely shepherds on Alpine heights? What were the anchorites of the early Christian ages? No! better a garret in the Five Points than a cave in the Theban Desert.

Our road was a beautiful shaded path, following the stream to its source in the mountains, whence we climbed the spinal ridge of the island—a cold, windy region, overgrown with pines. From the summit we saw, shimmering in the distance, the wheat-plains of Chalcis, and far to the south-east the snowy wedge of Mount Delphi, which is between five and six thousand feet in height. The descent occupied two hours, and the afternoon was far advanced before we caught sight of the yellow walls and white minarets of the city. Our wanderings in Euboea were now at an end, and a distance of only fifty miles separated us from our home in Athens.

The afternoon and evening were intensely hot. We clattered through the stony streets, in the full glare of the sun, and finally found a sort of hotel, kept mainly for the accommodation of the officers in the fortress. Here we obtained a room, and in the course of time a dinner, con sisting of beefsteaks and English ale—smoked a narghileh on the quay among a lot of dirty sailors, watched the funeral of a soldier from the windows—tried to write, and gave it up on account of the heat, and finally came to the conclusion that Chalcis was the dullest and stupidest town in all Greece. The three Mohammedan mosques, however, were some relief to the eye. This, we believe, is the only place in the kingdom where a residence is permitted to the Turks. The only incident which occurred during our stay was the visit of a Greek, having in charge the horses of an English traveller, who had sailed from Sunium for the southern end of Euboea ten days before, and had not been heard from. The man was in great distress—because, if the Englishman had been lost, he would be obliged to pay for the keep of his horses. We could give him no consolation, but we were glad to learn, a week afterwards, that the traveller finally turned up.

Starting the next morning bright and early, we crossed the Euripean Strait by a new drawbridge, over which all Greece rejoices, as it is almost the only public work which the government has accomplished. It had been solemnly inaugurated by the king and queen two months previous—on which occasion their majesties fared no better than persons of common clay. A storm came on, the house in which they were lodged took fire, they were obliged to sleep in rooms half full of drifted snow, and even the queen's wet robes of ceremony were ironed dry without being taken off her royal person! This memorable bridge once passed, we were on the mainland again, and in half an hour rode along the strand of—Aulis! Yes, this little bay this stony hill, these few blocks of hewn limestone, gnawed by the teeth of three thousand years, witnessed the assemblage of the armament destined for Troy—that is, provided such a thing ever took place. At any rate, this is Aulis, the golden, the Homeric name—a trumpet-word in Grecian song.

Trotting rapidly onwards three hours over rich plains of wheat, three more over hills and hollows, spotted with plane-trees and huge Bœotian oaks, and two more over stony, broken heights, we at last reached the northern side of Parnes, beyond whose pines lay Attica, now almost as much a home to us as it was to Pisistratus and Solon. The baggage, guarded by Ajax and Themistocles, was far behind; our three horses, Erato, Boreas, and Chiron, were pretty well spent, but five or six hours more would bring us to Athens, and we still cheered them on. We received news on the way that the robber-chief, Kalabaliki, the terror of northern Greece, had just been captured near Thebes and his band broken up. On the top of Parnes we were joined by three soldiers, who were lounging in the rear, when three armed men suddenly emerged from a thicket. I did not for a moment doubt that they were members of Kalabaliki's band: we confronted them boldly, and passed, and as the soldiers came into view, they retreated again into the woods. A little before sunset we emerged from the forest, and saw the plain of Attica stretching away before us until it was blended with the Ægean Sea in the distance. The turf, on the upper slopes of the mountain around us, was as green as in Switzerland; clumps of pine were sprinkled over the knolls, and this fresh northern foreground gave an exquisite charm to the glorious landscape, painted with the purple and violet tints of the Grecian air. Far away—a golden speck against the sky—rose the Acropolis, beckoning us on.

And on we went. Down to the plain, spurring the exhausted horses, while the sunset waned away. Past dusty villages, past dark wheat-fields, dim olive groves and vineyards, fragrant with the newly-stirred earth, until we reached the well-known houses of Patissia. Then the horses knew where we were, and resigned themselves to the task. In half an hour more, just as the moon rose behind Hymettus, and struck in gleaming sparkles on the scarred pillars of the Parthenon, we jumped from our saddles at the door of the House of Vitalis, thus terminating the ride through Northern Greece.

Ajax and Themistocles made their appearance towards noon the next day—the former having been seized by the valiant guard on Mount Parnes, and detained all night on suspicion of being a robber.

CHAPTER XXIII.

PEOPLE AND GOVERNMENT.

Except Acarnania, Etolia, and some of the Cyclades, I had now visited all parts of Modern Greece, and, so far as personal observation and inquiry might accomplish in the space of four months, considered myself tolerably familiar with the condition of the country and its inhabitants. In summing up my impressions and throwing them together in the form of a general statement, I shall endeavor to be just, believing myself to be unprejudiced. I have lately looked over several recent works on Greece, and have been surprised to find so much of a partisan spirit in them—as if the position and character of Greece and the Greeks were a question to be debated rather than a picture to be drawn. One author is too favorable, another too severe, and I foresee that, inasmuch as my path lies between the two extremes, I shall be, to some extent, discredited by both sides.

The fact is, a few deeds of splendid heroism have thrown a deceitful halo over the darker features of the Greek War of Independence, and most of those who bend in reverence to the name of Marco Bozzaris do not know that his uncle Nothi stole supplies from his own troops to sell to the Turks—that, while Canaris and Miaulis were brave and incorruptible, Colocotroni filled his purse and made cowards of his men—that, while Karaïskakis was honorable, others broke the most solemn oaths of their religion, and murdered the captives they had sworn to spare. One can say that the Greeks are what the Turks made them—that we should not expect to find in slaves the virtues of freemen; but treachery and perjury were never characteristics of the Moslem. It is the corrupt leaven of the Lower Empire which still ferments in the veins of this mixed race. I have already said, and I repeat it, that not one-fifth of the present population can with justice be called *Greeks*. The remainder are Slavonians, Albanians, and Turks, with a slight infusion of Venetian blood. Only in Maina, on the slopes of Parnassus and in parts of Doris, did I find the ancient type in any considerable amount. In the war, the Albanian blood—the Suliotes, Hydriotes, and Spetziotes—achieved the greatest distinction.

Owing to this admixture—when not always of race, yet still of character and association—there is a great diversity in the nature of the modern Greeks, and their number is still so small that one must be cautious in stating general characteristics. Some features of the ancient race are still preserved: they are vain, talkative, fond of argument, and fond of display. Their appreciation of Art, however, has utterly perished. Most of them profess a leaning towards democratic principles, yet they are pleased as children at the tawdry pomp which surrounds a throne. They are passionately fond of gain, yet, with the most elastic temperament in the world, dislike manual labor. One of their best general traits is their eagerness to learn, but, unfortunately, it ceases as soon as they are capable of obtaining an office under government. Official corruption is as prevalent in Greece as—as—as in the United States, but there is not the same means of preventing it in the former country. There is not an *honest society* sufficiently large to brand the genteel pickpockets, and so the great bulk of the population are in no better condition than the Christian subjects of the Sultan, while a horde of leeches, military, naval, and civil, thrive and fatten upon them. More than one prominent man in Athens, with whom I conversed on the state of the country, said to me: "We want more people. What can we do with a million of inhabitants?" Yet at this moment numbers of Greeks are emigrating from Acarnania into Turkey! There might have been, long ago, a considerable influx of German emigrants, yet the Government refused to permit it.

The Greeks have three leading virtues, which, alone, form a basis of good almost sufficient to redeem them. They are remarkably chaste, for a southern race; they are probably the most temperate people in the world; and they are most unselfish and devoted in their family relations. Their vanity, also, while it retards their progress in many respects, is a chord which may nevertheless be touched to their advantage. Being very sensitive to the judgment pronounced upon them by others, they sometimes become better for the sake of being thought better. Hence, nothing injures them so much as injudicious praise. I know a family who have acted on this principle in their treatment of servants, and their confidence has never been abused. In this case, however, an unfavorable sentence would have been a lasting misfortune, and the incitement to honesty was proportionately greater. Some Greek servants, I have reason to know, are great scamps, and the reputation of the whole class is none of the best. The honesty of the country Greeks, I think, is quite up to the average of people in their condition—in fact, I am not sure that they do not deserve credit for not being worse, seeing that the most outrageous arts of cheating are taught them by those above them.

For instance, the agriculturist is not taxed by assessment upon the value of his property, but by a tithe of what his land produces. The abominable Turkish system prevails, of farming out the entire tithes of the country to a pack of contractors, who pay a certain sum to the Government, and then make the most of their bargain. In measuring the grain, the law requires that it shall be poured lightly into the measure, and the top scraped off level, but the contractors are in the habit of shaking and settling it repeatedly, and then heaping the measure. This is only one example of their practices, and the tithes are only one form in which the people are taxed. Frequently there are special taxes levied for special objects. The money is always collected, and that is the last of it. Even the sum contributed by Government for the relief of the sufferers at Corinth melted away in passing through different hands, until less than the half of it reached its destination.

The Greeks are patriotic enough *in principle*, but in practice no enemy could injure Greece more than they do. There is not one who does not see the abuses under which the land is groaning, but I have yet to find the first man actively opposed to these abuses. One hears only such laments as these: "What can we do with such narrow means? We are not responsible for our condition. The Great Powers took away from us Crete, Chios, Epirus, and Thessaly, to which we were justly entitled, and which would have given the basis for a strong and successful kingdom. We are hopelessly weak, and more could not be expected of us." But when I have said in reply: "If you do not achieve the most possible with the resources you have, you will never be in a situation to command greater resources. You talk of poverty, yet spend more upon your Court, proportionately, than any country in Europe. Your revenues are large enough, if properly applied, not only to meet all really necessary expenditures, but to open means of communication for the want of which the industry of your country languishes."—I have more than once heard the feeble plea: "Our Court must be suitably kept up There cannot be a throne without a large expenditure We Greeks are democratic, but the Great Powers gave us a throne, and since we have accepted it, the country would be disgraced if the usual accessories of a throne were wanting."

The Royal Palace at Athens cost two millions of dollars. For this sum the Greeks have an immense, ugly pile of Pentelican marble, as large as Buckingham, or the *Residenz* at Berlin. One fourth of the money would have built a beautiful structure, proportioned to the size and means of the country. The King has a salary of one million of drachmas ($166,666) per annum, which, to his credit, he spends in and about Athens. The Court alone swallows up about one-twelfth of the entire revenues. Then there is a list of salaried and pensioned officials—civil, military, and naval—such as no country in Europe, relatively, exhibits. In the Navy there is just about one officer to every two-and-a-half men; in the Army, which numbers 9,000, all told, there are no less than *seventy* generals! The revenues of the country amount to something more than $3,000,000 annually, which, for a population of 1,000,000, is a sum sufficient not only for the machinery of Government, but the rapid development of the present neglected resources; yet it is easy to see how, between useless expenditure and official venality, the whole of it is swallowed up. Norway, with a smaller revenue and a larger population, supports her roads, schools, colleges, steamship lines, army, navy, and police, and keeps out of debt.

The absurd jealousy of the Greeks tends still further to retard anything like Progress. There might have been a large immigration of German farmers to the uncultivated lands of the Isthmus and Morea, but no! the pure Hellenic stock must not be corrupted by foreign grafts. The first thing the Legislative Assembly did, after Greece received a Constitution, was to pass a law, depriving all *heterochthones* (Greeks born in Crete, Chios, Constantinople, or anywhere outside the limits of the present kingdom) of equal civil rights. Yet the greatest private benefactors of Greece—Arsakis, Rhizari, Sina, and others, who have founded or supported her institutions of learning, science, and charity — are *heterochthones!* This shameful law has since been repealed, but the same selfish policy prevails, and instead of making Greece a rallying point for the pride and national feeling of the entire Hellenic race, the result has been to alienate its scattered fragments. The Greeks dream of a restoration of the Byzantine Empire, rather than of the ancient republics or confederacies. They are itching to grasp Thessaly and Macedonia. Constantinople, more or less distant, lies in the plans and hopes of every Greek — and they will never get it.

Some travellers point to the Constitution of Greece, and by enumerating a few sounding features, such as suffrage, free speech, a free press, religious liberty, education, &c., give the impression that the Government is strongly Democratic in its character. But the fact is, the King does not understand a representative government — he does not even comprehend its first principles; and ever since he was compelled to sign away a portion of his power, at the cannon's mouth, his whole study has been to recover it again. Thanks to the facilities afforded him by the Constitution itself, he has succeeded. The Senate is not only named by the King, but the Nomarchs also, and he has the right of choosing the Demarchs out of the three candidates who have the largest vote. One of these three is sure to be in the interest of the Court, and thus the whole government of the country is thrown back into his own hands. A distinguished citizen of Athens once said to me: "It is hopeless to expect anything like a just and decent administration of Government under the present system. We once, here in Athens, after great labor, and not a little intrigue, succeeded in presenting three candidates for the Demarchy, two of whom were just, enlightened men, of our own party. The third was a stupid ass, whom we prevailed upon the Court party to select, believing it to be morally impossible that he would obtain the office. But it was all in vain; the King appointed the ass." During my stay in Athens, a Court favorite was appointed to the chief rank in the Navy, over the head of the venerable Canaris, whose name will be remembered as long as the world honors a deed of splendid heroism. The true old man immediately resigned, and sent back to the King every order or token of honor he had received at the hands of the Government.

It is a wearisome task to wade through the long list of abuses, which are kept alive by the indolence and apathy, no less than the corruption of the Greeks, nor can I refer to them without the humiliating consciousness that my Hellenic friends have the right to ask, referring to our own legislators: "Are *you* without sin, that you should cast stones at us?" The rapid decline of political morality at home (I speak without reference to party) makes every honest American abroad blush with shame and mortification.

The avidity of the Greeks for learning has often been referred to, and justly, as one of their most hopeful traits. It is general, pervading all classes, and the only qualification to be made with regard to it is that in a great many instances it arises from the desire of escaping manual labor and obtaining the consideration which place under government affords. Hence Greece abounds with half-educated men, who cease their studies, satisfied, at a certain point. There have been no scholars produced since the Liberation equal to Coray, or Æsopios, who still lives. The Kleptic songs are still the best poetry of Modern Greece. In History and Law something has been done; in Art, nothing at all. Nevertheless, this thirst for education promises well, and to the honor of the Greeks be it said that the first thing they did on becoming free was to make provision for schools. At present the total number of scholars in the kingdom amounts to nearly forty-five thousand, or about one in twenty-four. The University of Athens is in a very flourishing condition, the Arsakeion (under the charge of Madame Mano, a sister of Alexander Mavrocordato) numbers three hundred female pupils, and the well-known school of Mr. and Mrs. Hill, nearly four hundred. There are also excellent seminaries at Syra, Patras, Nauplia, and other places.

No persons have done more for Free Greece than our two countrymen, just named, and few things pleased me more during my journeys through the country than to notice the deep and abiding gratitude which the Greeks feel for them. They are now teaching the second generation — the children of those they taught from twenty to thirty years ago. I had every opportunity of witnessing the plan and operations of their school, and I know of no institution of the kind which is doing a better work. I have frequently had occasion to speak of the inadequate and unsatisfactory results of American Missions in foreign lands — results attributable, in many instances, to an excess rather than a lack of zeal. Mr. and Mrs. Hill have confined their efforts to educating for Greece a body of virtuous, refined, intelligent, and pious women, and they have fully succeeded. Proselytism is prohibited by the laws of Greece, and they have not attempted it. They, therefore, enjoy the love and confidence of the whole Greek people, and continue to plant the seeds of a better, purer, more enlightened life, leaving them to ripen in their own good time, and as God shall direct. Dr. King, who has been American Consul for the last seven years, occupies himself principally with the conversion of the Armenians. He has, besides, printed a great number of Greek tracts and school-books, some of which are extensively used in the schools of the country.

The principal progress which Greece has made since her liberation, has been in her commerce. The blue cross now floats, not only in every port in the Mediterranean and Black Seas, but in most of the ports of Europe. The trade carried on at Constantinople by Greek vessels is larger than that of all other nations combined. Greek houses are now common, not only in Trieste, Vienna, Marseilles, London, Paris, and Manchester, but are also springing up in the United States. In spite of what has been said concerning the commercial dishonesty of the Greek merchants in the Orient, those who settle in the Occident bear, generally, as good a character as their Frank brethren. The race has a natural aptitude for trade, and upon this feature one might also build a hope for the future of Greece. But what that future will be, we cannot even conjecture. I do not yet believe that the Hellenic race will regenerate the Orient. A Grecian Empire, with Constantinople for its capital, is as far off as the moon. Whether the present kingdom will continue to drag along a weary existence as a petty independent power, or whether it will ultimately become the limb of a more powerful body, is a matter upon which I shall not speculate. It is significant, however, that until quite recently, the political factions in Greece bore the names of the English, Russian, and French parties. Of these three, the Russian naturally was the strongest.

As the King and Queen are childless, the people are in great uncertainty as to their future ruler. According to the Constitution, the next monarch must belong to the National Church. Prince Luitpold of Bavaria, Otho's brother, has renounced his right of succession rather than change his religion. Adalbert, the youngest brother, is willing to comply, after he has possession of the throne—not before. But the son of Luitpold has a prior claim, and, in addition, the Queen is intriguing with might and main to make capital for her brother, the Protestant Prince of Oldenburg. In all these nice little plans and counterplans, Greece is the last thing thought of. The Queen is thoroughly selfish, but it is not to be denied that she is popular, and possesses considerable influence. The King is a truly amiable man, and I believe desires to do what he can for the good of Greece; but so long as he lives, he will never realize her actual condition and necessities. The best men of Greece at present—Mavrocordato, Psyllas, Argyropoulos, and Kalerges—are not in a position to make their influence felt as it deserves, and so the country goes on in a blind way, heedless of the Future so long as it can bear the weight of the Present without breaking down.

I write these things in sorrow, and wish that my impressions were of a more cheering character. I should hail the success of Greece with as sincere a joy as any of her citizens; I should be glad to know that more of the ancient blood and the ancient genius was still extant — but I must not give the reader what I cannot find. Is there really no resurrection of a dead nation? No enduring vitality in those qualities of the old race, which triumphed for a thousand years? Cannot those "arts of war and peace," which sprang from Greece and the Grecian Isles, flourish again in the arms of a purer religion and a more enlightened law? The answer may be given a century hence, but not now.

CHAPTER XXIV.

AGRICULTURE AND RESOURCES.

BEFORE returning to the North, a few words must be said in regard to Greece as a *productive* country, a subject concerning which the reader has doubtless heard very contrary opinions. The Greeks themselves are so much in the habit of saying, "We have a poor country," that the flying tourist, who stops four days at Athens on his way to Egypt and Palestine, and who sees only the bald sides of Hymettus and Pentelicus, and the dry plain of Attica, imagines the whole country to be barren, desolate, cursed — as it is customary to represent Judea. With the exception of Acarnania, Etolia, and parts of Euboea, it does indeed greatly lack water, but its soil is probably as productive, in other respects, as that of any country of Europe. The valleys are a fine mellow loam, which produces excellent crops of wheat, rye, and barley, although the system of agriculture is Homeric in its simplicity and rudeness. The lower slopes of the mountains, where they have been reclaimed, or have escaped the devastation of war, produce vines, as in Missolonghi, forests, as in Eubœa, or grain, as in Maina, while the sides of Parnassus, Taygetus, and Erymanthus are covered, up to the elevation of 6,000 feet, with woods of oak, fir, and pine.

But one thing fails, without which the Garden of Eden itself would be poor — the means of transporting produce to a market. All the roads in the Peloponnesus, with the exception of that from Nauplia to Tripolitza, are the roughest possible bridle-paths, crossed in many places by mountain torrents, which frequently interrupt the communication for days. In fact, one can hardly say that there are any roads at all in spring, when the plow obliterates all trace of the previous trail. In Northern Greece there is but one, from Athens to Thebes, which is now impassable, owing to fifty yards of it having been washed away in the pass of Œnoe, about six months before my visit. From Thebes to Livadia there is a bridle-track over the Bœotian plain, which is a quagmire when it rains. Formerly much barley was raised about Livadia, but the cost of transporting it to Athens upon asses was found to be just three-fourths of the value of what the ass carried, so that, unless the trader succeeded in doing a little highway robbery on his way back, he lost money by the trip. The peasantry around Athens now use carts, and with the present high prices, succeed in driving a very good business. The Government is at last making an effort to do something in the way of remedying this evil. We hear of roads to Chalcis, to Corinth, and other places. An engineer has been imported from France at a salary of 22,000 francs a year, notwithstanding there is an abundance of Greek

engineers idle. A large sum has been raised by special
taxation, but all that has yet been accomplished is the
grading of a few streets in Athens. But — "Do not expect
too much of us," say the Greeks.

A German botanist (Fraas, I think) has given a very
decided opinion that the lost forests of Greece can never be
restored, and that the land must consequently remain dry
and barren. From this decision I must wholly dissent. All
Greece, it is true, rests on a bed of blue limestone, which
refines into marble here and there, and the hills which have
been disforested are as bare and dry as the mountains of
Moab. Hymettus appears to be hopelessly naked, and
even Parnes hides his few remaining pines in the depth of
his savage gorges. Yet the least encouragement would
reclothe even this sterility. An example of what simply
letting the mountains alone will do, is seen at the pass of
Œnoe, between Cithæron and Parnes. Here the peasants
have been prevented, for a few years past, from touching
the young pines, and the heights are covered green and
thick, up to the very summit. As for forest culture, such
as is carried on with so much success in Germany, it is
unheard of. It is true, Inspectors, Foresters, &c., have
been appointed, and some 200,000 drachmas of the revenue
go in this way, but the only thing they do is to make the
peasants pay for tapping pine-trees for resin, instead of
taking it for nothing. If a Greek mountaineer wants a little wood for his fire, he cuts down twenty thriving saplings
rather than fatigue himself by felling a full-grown tree.
Eubœa, which was once a land of splendid forests, abounding with deer, is rapidly becoming denuded, and the moun

tain valleys, once plentifully and regularly watered, are now subject to alternate freshets and drouths.

Wood was sold in Athens during the winter of 1857-8 at the rate of a cent a pound, while the grand oak woods of Doris and Elis are lying full of rotting trunks. All over the country one sees noble trees wantonly girdled, even in the midst of forests, where they are never felled. It would seem that the people took a peculiar pleasure in the act of destruction. A large land-owner in Eubœa informed me that while superintending the cutting of pines in his woods, he directed the workmen to be very careful and fell the trees in such a direction as to injure the saplings under them as little as possible. The people laughed outright, and almost told him to his face that he was a fool. The saplings, they said, were little things, worth nothing except to burn, and it would be no harm to destroy them all. Where the forests have only been partially spared, there are fountains and running streams the whole year through. The Alpheus and the Eurotas, fed by the oak-covered hills of Arcadia, flow through summer heats, but in naked Attica the Cephissus and the Ilissus perish even before they reach the sea.

Agriculture, as I have said, is in the most imperfect state. I find, on repeated inquiry, that fifteen fold — that is, fifteen bushels reaped for one sown — is considered a large crop, and that the general average cannot be considered higher than eight fold. The soil is not manured, but relieved a little by a rotation of crops. It is scratched up to the depth of three or four inches with an antediluvian plow and then crosswise again, so that the soil is cut in smal cubes or dice. Then the farmer sits down and folds his hands, waiting for a rain that shall dissolve and break up these cubes, so that he can sow his grain. Sometimes a freshet comes in the meanwhile and carries them all off before they have had time to dissolve, leaving only the hieroglyphics made by the point of the plowshare in the hard surface below.

The other staple productions of Greece—oil, silk, currants, and wine—are more easily managed, and hence the yield from them is greater. The vines are pruned in the spring, the earth is dug up, raised into heaps between the stalks, and finely pulverized, and they are then left to their fate. Olive and mulberry trees are planted, and that is all. The produce both of silk and currants is slowly but steadily increasing, and the number of olive trees, which in 1833 was 700,000, now amounts to 2,400,000. Yet in spite of this apparent growth, the country is poorer now than it was under the Turkish domination. The little Province of Achaia alone yielded to the Latin princes, during the Middle Ages, a greater revenue than the whole kingdom of Greece at present. The fact is, the country is poor, only because the development of its resources has been most shamefully neglected.

A circumstance which more than anything else, perhaps, retards this development, is the *religious indolence* of the Greek farmers. A creed which turns *one half the days of the year* into saintly anniversaries, on which it is sinful to do any manner of work, would ruin any country in the world. In addition to these saints' days, there are four grand fasts, and a number of smaller ones, amounting, in all, to over one hundred and fifty days, or *five months* These are most rigidly kept, and though the temperate Greek satisfies his hunger with bread, olives, and onions, his capacity for labor is seriously affected. To crown his shortcomings as an agriculturist, add his egregious vanity, which prevents him from suspecting that there is any knowledge in the world superior to his own. An English gentleman, long settled in Greece, assured me that he found it almost impossible to teach his workmen, owing to this trait of character. Whenever he directed anything to be done, instead of being obeyed, he always received instructions from them as to how it might be better done. After twenty-four years' experience, he was almost ready to despair of their improvement.

I found the country Greeks generally honest. We met with two or three instances of downright imposition, but this might occur in any country — except in the northern and western provinces of Sweden. Those who have the worst reputation are the most friendly and agreeable. The Mainote robbers, as they are called, the Delphians, and the Dorians, are hearty, cheerful, hospitable people, and I shall long remember them with pleasure. The timid traveller need no longer hesitate to visit Greece, from a vision of fierce palikars levelling their long guns at him in the mountain passes. Northern Greece has long been overrun by a band of robbers under the command of the chief, Kalabaliki, but just before we left Athens, himself and the greater part of his men were shot by the Government troops, near Thebes. With the death of Kalabaliki brigandage is almost suppressed in Greece. From 1854 to

1858 the number of robbers shot or executed was 493! I must state, however, on the authority of the Minister of War, that only twenty of the whole number were born within the limits of the kingdom.

Besides her neglected fields and forests, Greece has also neglected mines. There is the material for a hundred Parthenons yet in Pentelicus; the white, waxy marble of Naxos and Paros; precious verde antique and rouge antique in Taygetus: coal in Euboea, sulphur on the Isthmus, and emery in Naxos. It is said that the treasures of Paros are to be exploited, but of the other mineral productions, sulphur and emery, only, are quarried to a limited extent. Agriculture, however, should be the first care of a nation, and until Greece has roads for the transportation of her corn, wine, and oil, she will scarcely be able to make her quarries available. I have not yet heard of any geological survey of the country, but I know an intelligent young officer who spent eighteen months, by the order and at the expense of the Government, in making a secret military reconnoissance of Turkey! Offer a plan for the irrigation of the Cephissian plain, and you will be politely snubbed. Offer another of the fortifications of Constantinople, and you will be well paid.

Enough of dry statement. Let me not lose the pensive sweetness and sadness of this last evening in Athens. The sun is sinking in clear saffron light beyond the pass of Daphne, and a purple flush plays all along the high, barren sides of Hymettus. Before me rises the Acropolis, with its crown of beauty, the Parthenon, on whose snowy front the sunsets of two thousand years have left their golden stain. In the distance is the musical Ægean, dancing with light-whispering waves to fill the rock-hewn sarcophagus of Themistocles. Plato's olives send a silver glimmer through the dusk that is creeping over the Attic plain. Many an evening have I contemplated this illustrious landscape, but it was never so lovely as now, when I look upon it for the last time. Every melodious wave in the long outline of the immortal mountains — every scarred marble in the august piles of ruin — every blood-red anemone on the banks of the Ilissus, and every asphodel that blossoms on the hill of Colonos — I know them and they know me. Not as a curious stranger do I leave Athens ; not as a traveller eager for new scenes ; but with the regret of one who knows and loves the sacred soil, to whom it has been at once a sanctuary and a home.

CHAPTER XXV.

RETURN TO THE NORTH.

We went direct from Athens to Constantinople in the French steamer Meandre. The voyage was a repetition of the two which I have described years ago, and I shall make no further note of it than to advise all my friends and readers who may visit the Orient to choose the steamers of the French *Messageries* in every possible case, rather than those of the Austrian Lloyd. Over the unrippled Ægean our trip was a luxurious one, and though we missed Sunium and saw the Trojan Ida by twilight, we steamed around Seraglio Point and into the Golden Horn in the full blaze of noon — a piece of real good fortune to those who see Constantinople for the first time. In this category were even Americans on board the steamer.

I noticed but three changes in Constantinople since I first saw it, in 1852 — to wit: Pera is lighted with gas, the hotels have raised their prices five francs a day, and the dogs of Stamboul no longer bark at Giaours. In all other respects, it is the same medley of unparalleled external splendor and internal filth, imperfect Europe and shabby Asia. The last change of the three is undoubtedly due to the wholesome training given to the dogs aforesaid by the soldiers of the allied armies. It is an astonishing fact that dogs of the most orthodox Moslem breed now tolerate the presence of the Frank, without a snarl. Moreover, St. Sophia, then accessible only through the all-potent seal of the Grand Vizier, now sees its doors turn on their holy hinges for an every-day bribe. Even at the mosque of Eyoub, standard-bearer of Mahmoud II., I was refused admission only because it was Ramazan. There is a Turkish theatre in Pera, Turkish plays (adapted from the Italian) are acted by Turkish actors, and — oh, shade of the Prophet! —Turkish women appear unveiled upon the stage. This, however, does not signify much. Polygamy and the seclusion of women are a part of the Moslem religion, and with that religion dies the prestige of the race. The fraternization of Turkey with the Western Powers has forced her to relinquish a few antiquated prejudices—and that is all.

The grand fête of the Night of Predestination took place two days after our arrival, and, with the recollection of its magical illuminations six years before, fresh in my mind, I promised my companions a spectacle such as they had never yet witnessed; but it turned out to be a comparative failure. The Turkish Government has wisely grown economical. The far-echoing thunders of a thousand cannon, booming up and down the length of the Bosphorus, were wanting; and though we floated in the midst of a crowd of caïques in the Golden Horn, the waters were dark underneath us, and the sky dark above—not lighted to red transparency, as I once saw them, with the minarets blazing like fiery lances around the fiery helmets of the domes.

We had rather an adventurous trip to the Sweet Waters of Europe. The wind was blowing strongly from the west, but I took a four-oared caïque, and after passing Cassim Pasha, where we were most exposed to its force, supposed that we should get on without further trouble. But on turning northward into the valley of the Sweet Waters, it came on a perfect hurricane. We could scarcely breathe, and the boatmen tried in vain to manage our egg-shell of a craft. We drove first upon a marshy island; then upon the shore; then down stream; then against a pier; and finally striking upon a rock, the caïque began to fill. We were in the edge of a swamp; Braisted and I lifted the lady out into the reeds, and we made the best of our way to firm land. All landmarks were lost in a cloud of dust; the tempest blew with such force that it was barely possible to stand; and when we at last wore round so as to scud before the wind, we were almost taken off our feet. After much search and the payment of a pound sterling, I procured a jolting Turkish araba to take us back to Pera, but on crossing the brow of the hill above the Sweet Waters, we were several times on the point of being overturned by the blast.

The steamer in which we took passage to Galatz proved to be our old friend the Miramar, with her gallant captain, Mazarevitch. We had soft spring sunshine for the glorious panorama of the Bosphorus, but the day became partially obscured as we entered the Black Sea, and about five in the afternoon, the sky being clear only to the

northward, a most singular mirage arose in that direction
Vessels were seen suspended in the air, about two degrees
above the horizon, with inverted images below them.
Beyond them ran a long line of low coast, which in the
north-east rose into hills, covered with patches of dark fir
trees. There was no land nearer than the Crimea in that
direction, and it was about 180 miles distant. What, then,
were these shores? They were no mere optical delusion,
for through a strong glass the outlines appeared very dis
tinct even to the projecting buttresses and receding gulf ot
the hills. I came to the conclusion, therefore, that it was
actually the mountain-shore of the Crimea which I beheld,
almost from the mouth of the Bosphorus. The wind was
blowing cold from the north-west at the time, with dull
clouds overhead, but the phantom picture was lighted with
strong sunshine, and the sails of the vessels appeared to
hang almost motionless.

After two disagreeable nights and one disagreeable day,
we reached the Sulina mouth of the Danube. The river
makes his muddy presence known far off shore, like the
Mississippi, the Ganges, and the Yang-tze-Kiang. The
land is as flat as a pancake, and Sulina, which consists of a
light-house and a long row of wooden buildings on piles,
resembles the skeleton of a town deposited there by some
freshet. You exchange the green plain of the sea for the
green plain of the Dobrudja marshes, through which the
Danube winds like a brown vein. Much was said about
the improvements for navigation at Sulina, in the Paris
Conferences, but the most I could discover was a long line
of posts to which vessels were moored, and which may be

the forerunner of a wharf. We passed through a **street of vessels** nearly three miles long, touching each other stem and stern, on both sides of the river, and then pursued our winding way towards Galatz, comparatively alone. By and by, however, the hills of the Dobrudja arose in the southwest, and the monotonous level of the swamps was broken by belts of trees. Vegetation appeared to be fully as far advanced as at Constantinople, although we were nearly five degrees further north.

In the afternoon, we passed the southern or St. George's arm of the Danube, which is now so closed up by a bar at its mouth as to be useless. The northern or **Kilia arm** enters a short distance higher up, and looking towards it at sunset, over the great levels, we saw the fortress-town of Ismaïl, built upon its northern bank. This was the famous citadel of the Turks, which fell before Suwarrow, after one of the bloodiest assaults recorded in history. We anchored for some hours during the night, but early the next morning were at Galatz, in Moldavia.

I cannot say much about this place, for we only remained long enough to exchange our Black Sea steamer for the river-boat of the Danube Company. It is a dull, common place town, built over the slope of a long, barren hill. Some travellers, who had been there several days, had nothing whatever to tell me about it. We were much more interested in our new steamer, which was built on the American plan, and very handsomely furnished. But—down with all monopolies! say I. Although the fare from Constantinople to Pesth—a voyage of seven days—is $70 this does not include a state-room on the river-boats, for which $52 additional is demanded! Nevertheless, I had taken the precaution to telegraph from Constantinople to Galatz to secure a room. A single message costs *twenty francs*, yet when we reached Galatz, six days afterwards, the message had not arrived. The nearest approach to this which I ever experienced was in Ohio, where a message which I sent was three days and a half in going two hundred miles. The engineer of the boat kindly offered to give me his cabin, containing one berth, for $50, but we preferred using the common cabins, which were as badly ventilated as on the American boats. These Danube steamers, however, were very swift, kept in admirable order, and the fare (what little there was of it) was unexceptionable.

From Galatz to the Iron Gates, in ascending the Danube, you have two days of monotonous scenery. On one side the low hills of Turkey,—heavy, ungraceful ridges, generally barren of wood,—and on the other the interminable plains of Wallachia. Except Giurgevo, the port of Bucharest, there are no towns on the northern shore, but on the southern you pass, in succession, Rustchuk, Silistria, Nicopolis, and Widin, besides a great number of shabby, red-roofed villages, nestled in the elbows of the hills. Immense herds of horses graze on the meadows; rough Wallachian boors in wide trowsers and low black hats lounge about their huts, which are raised on high piles out of the reach of freshets; guard-houses at regular intervals stud the bank, and three slovenly gray soldiers present arms as we pass; coal-barges and flat-boats descend the river in long black lines; and all these pictures, repeated over and over again, at last weary the eye. We passed Silistria at dusk, and I saw only an indistinct silhouette of its famous fort. But the scars of battle vanish soon from the earth, and Silistria is as quiet and orderly now as if it had not heard a cannon for a thousand years.

At Gladowa, we entered the celebrated Iron Gates, where a spur of the Transylvanian Alps, running southwestward through Servia to join the central mountain chain of Turkey, attempts to barricade the Danube. But, like the Rhine at Bingen, and the Potomac at Harper's Ferry, he has cut with his crystal sword the Gordian labyrinth he could not thread, and roars in a series of triumphant rapids through the heart of the terrible hills. Covered with forests of oak, beech, larch, and pine, the mountains tower grandly on either hand, while through the interlocking bases the river descends in watery planes, whose slant can be readily measured by the eye. The rocks have been blasted so as to afford a channel for the steamer, which trembles in every timber as she stems the foamy tangle of chutes and whirlpools. Let one of her iron muscles give way, and the river would have his will. A mile and a half of slow, trembling, exciting progress, and we have mounted the heaviest grade, but six hours of the same tremendous scenery await us. We pierce yet sublimer solitudes, and look on pictures of precipice and piled rock, of cavern and yawning gorge, and mountain walls, almost shutting out the day, such as no other river in Europe can show.

At Orsova, the northern bank becomes Austrian, and we were ushered into the Empire with the usual suavity. I must confess that much as I detest the Austrian Govern ment, there are few countries in Europe where a traveller meets with so little annoyance and so much courtesy. All day long, we sat on the hurricane deck, enjoying the superb scenery, but towards evening the mountains dropped into hills, and the hills on the northern bank flattened out into the great plain of Hungary. We passed Belgrade during the night, and early next morning were at Peterwardein, a fortress in southern Hungary. The contrast between Turk and German (or the races under German rule) was as surprising as it was welcome. I had not expected to see, here in the Banat, on the borders of Servia, so sudden a line drawn between the indolence, filth, and discomfort of the Orient, and the order, neatness industry, and progress of the Occident.

II.

POLAND AND RUSSIA.

CHAPTER XXVI.

CRACOW, AND THE SALT MINES OF WIELICZKA

The great Brandenburg Plain, or "Baltic Sand-sea," as Humboldt calls it, which accompanied us all the way to Breslau, did not cease until after we had crossed the border of Austrian Poland. The day was intensely hot, and the dust on the road stifling. These vast levels, where great grain tracts alternate with pine forests, are even more monotonous than our own prairies, because they are far less fertile. In many places, the desert sand of the lost ocean whose waves once rolled here pierces the thin coating of soil and defies all attempts at cultivation. The forests first reclaimed it, and much of it should be given back for a time to the keeping of the forests again. In this region rye is grown almost exclusively. As we penetrated further into Upper Silesia, the smoke of smelting furnaces blotted the air and sooty trails marked the way to the coal mines. An intelligent young Pole, in the cars, informed me that the country has also a good name for its agricultural condition—the province being full of large landed proprietors, who, it seems, have paid much attention to the improvement of the soil.

After passing Oppeln the Polish language begins to be heard, and Polish Jews, in rusty black caftans and shabby cylinder hats, are seen at the stations. The pine forests are more frequent, and some low undulating swells—the first faint ripples of the distant Carpathians—break the dead uniformity. "When you get beyond Myslowitz," said the young Pole, "you will see a bit of the Sahara, only instead of camels there are Austrians." Myslowitz is the last Prussian station, and really, for ten miles beyond, the country is a hopeless waste of sand, as yellow and bare as the Nubian Desert. After passing Szczakowa, where the Warsaw road branches off, the country gradually improved. The low swells rose into hills covered with dark forests, between which lay meadows, or rather immense flower-beds, sheets of glittering pink and yellow, threaded by tributaries of the Vistula. Polish peasants, in their high black hats, long jackets and wide Chinese trowsers, were at work in the fields, or tending the herds of horses. Strength, coarseness, and stupidity, occasionally relieved by a twinkle of cunning, were their prominent characteristics Some of the boys were Irish over and over.

The sepulchral mound of Kosciusko, on the summit of a long hill, denoted our approach to Cracow. It is visible far and wide, a noble landmark. The Austrians have commenced fortifying the city, and this monument, being on a commanding point, is now inclosed by a strong fort

Eastward, over a green belt of foliage—tall ash trees, avenues of Lombardy poplars, and locusts showered all over with blossoms—lies Cracow, in the lap of the valley of the Vistula, which stretches away to the south-west until its folding hills of green grow blue in the distance, and crouch at the feet of the high Carpathian mountains. Tall, fantastic, Tartaresque spires shoot up in pairs from the stretch of tiled roofs, and in the midst, on the mound of the Wawel, stands in massive and venerable ugliness, the ancient Palace of the Polish Kings. The novelty of the picture, no less than its exquisite beauty, took me by surprise. I seemed to be already far away from Europe, and in that strange central region which, in character, forms a continent by itself.

This impression was not weakened after arriving. A queer, bearded hackney-coachman took our baggage, repeating with great emphasis "*piet-nasty*" (or something like it), which I was afraid referred to my dusty appearance, but the German conductor explained that it was "fifteen," the number of the fiacre. Driving through an old tower-gate we entered the city, and were deposited at a hotel, where a room spacious enough for a king's audience-hall was given to us. Our first visitor was a black Jew, who wanted to do something in the exchange way. Then came a rosy Polish chambermaid, who asked whether we had brought our own bedding! The valet-de-place was also a Jew, rusty, black, and unwashed, whose company we were obliged to endure, during an inspection of the city.

The place has a modern air, with the exception of the churches, upon which rests the mellow weight of from two to five centuries. We were more interested in the people who happened to be celebrating a national and a religious festival at the same time, and thronged every street in their holiday clothes. Not only was all Cracow out of doors, but thousands of peasants from the neighboring villages had come into the city to share in the festivities. There was the most fantastic and picturesque mixture of characters and costumes. It was the last day of *Frohnleichnamsfest* (the Body of Christ), and religious processions, with tapers, shrines, and banners of white and crimson silk, were parading the streets. A company of boy choristers, in scarlet robes, and bearing a crucifix, generally led the way. Then came a group of young peasants, bare-headed, with wild, matted hair, and candles in their hands; next girls carrying a shrine and canopy, decorated with flowers, and lastly, priests and peasants mingled together, with a crowd of devout followers.

The civic festival was the anniversary of a victory over the Tartars, which has been annually celebrated for the last seven hundred years. It is characterized by a curious ceremony called the *Konik*, which came off in the evening. A man dressed to represent a Tartar chief, with a turban of preposterous size, terminating in a high, conical cap, with his face masked, and his body inclosed in an imitation horse, over which his false legs dangled, was conducted through the principal streets, preceded by the sound of trumpet and the banners of the city. He carried in his hand a sort of mace, with which he attacked every one who came near him, accompanying his blows with what must have been very humorous and telling remarks, to judge from the shouts and laughter of the crowd. The press of people was so great, in spite of the efforts of a double line of soldiers who accompanied this curious procession, that we had great difficulty in catching a glimpse of what was going on. We mounted the Wawel to the castle of the Polish Kings, which is now a military barrack. Two new towers and a wall of circumvallation have been recently added.

The frst court, high, and with arched galleries around every story, was formerly the residence of the nobles attached to the Polish court. Beyond this we entered a large open space, on the right of which stood the Cathedral, a lofty ancient pile, of no particular style of architecture. The Jew called our attention to the dome over one of the side-chapels. "See!" said he, "that is real ducat gold; you will not see the like anywhere else in the world." But the heavy gilding has been for the most part torn away, and the dome has rather a shabby look in consequence. An ox-faced Polish priest took us in charge, and showed us the monuments of many kings and more bishops—ringing historical names, some of which stir the blood. The catafalques of Casimir the Great, of Wratislaw, of Stephen Batory, of John Sobieski, and others, rich with marble and silver, fill the side chapels of this storied pile. There still exists the stall of precious marble, where the Kings of Poland attended mass, with wooden seats on either side for the ministers; while in the chancel, before the magnificent gilded altar, stands the velvet canopy under which they were crowned. The sepulchral monuments are poor, except two statues by Thorwaldsen—a repetition of his

Christ, and the Roman, half-nude figure of Prince Potocki.

We afterwards descended into the crypt of the church by a trap-door in the pavement. Here, groping along after the waxen torch in the priest's hands, we came to the massive silver sarcophagi of Wladislaus IV. and his queen. Beyond these glittering shells, at the end of the dusky vault, gloomed a sarcophagus of black marble, inscribed with the name of John Sobieski. The Saviour of Austria (who *repaid* his services a hundred years later!) lies in fitting company: on his right hand is Poniatowski, on his left Kosciusko, both in marble coffins. I went up reverently and placed my hand upon the stone which covers each—proud, noble, glorious hearts, now dust for ever!

Every boy who reads "The Wonders of the World" in the chimney-corner, in the long winter evenings, as I have done, has heard of the salt mines of Wieliczka. The account of this subterranean saline world made a profound impression upon me when a youngster, and I diverged a little from my direct route on purpose to visit it. All wonders which we first hear of in the dear, secluded nest of home, most attract us after our wings have grown and we have become restless birds of passage; but not all retain the old magic after we behold them. The Maelström turned out to be an immense exaggeration; Teneriffe and the Natural Bridges of Icononzo lie far out of my track, but here were the salt mines, within eight miles of Cracow, and I should have been false to every promise of youth if I had not visited them. If "The Wonders of the World" is still extant, and some of my youthful readers are acquainted with the book, I know they will not overlook this chapter. Talking is pleasantest when one is sure of an interested audience beforehand.

In company with a Professor from St. Petersburg, we left Cracow in the morning, crossed the Vistula, and drove eastward through a low, undulating country, covered with fields of rye, oats, and potatoes. The village of Wieliczka occupies a charming situation on the northern slope of a long, wood-crowned hill. The large store-houses for the salt, the Government offices, and the residences of the superintendents, on a slight eminence near the foot, first strike the eye. After procuring a permit from the proper official, we presented ourselves at the office, over the mouth of the mine, in company with five Prussian travellers, two of them ladies, and a wandering German mechanic, who had tramped out from Cracow in the hope of seeing the place. We were all enveloped in long, coarse blouses of white linen, and having bespoken a supply of Bengal lights, a door was opened, and we commenced descending into the bowels of the earth by an easy staircase, in a square shaft. Six boys, carrying flaring lamps, were distributed among our party, and one of the superintendents assumed the office of conductor.

After descending 210 feet, we saw the first veins of rock salt, in a bed of clay and crumbled sandstone. Thirty feet more, and we were in a world of salt. Level galleries branched off from the foot of the staircase; overhead, a ceiling of solid salt, under foot a floor of salt, and on either side dark gray walls of salt, sparkling here and there with minute crystals. Lights glimmered ahead, and on turning a corner we came upon a gang of workmen, some hacking away at the solid floor, others trundling wheelbarrows full of the precious cubes. Here was the chapel of St. Anthony, the oldest in the mines—a Byzantine excavation, supported by columns with altar, crucifix, and life-size statues of saints, apparently in black marble, but all as salt as Lot's wife, as I discovered by putting my tongue to the nose of John the Baptist. The humid air of this upper story of the mines has damaged some of the saints: Francis, especially, is running away like a dip candle, and all of his head is gone except his chin. The limbs of Joseph are dropping off as if he had the Norwegian leprosy, and Lawrence has deeper scars than his gridiron could have made, running up and down his back. A Bengal light burnt at the altar, brought into sudden life this strange temple, which presently vanished into utter darkness, as if it had never been.

I cannot follow, step by step, our journey of two hours through the labyrinths of this wonderful mine. It is a bewildering maze of galleries, grand halls, staircases, and vaulted chambers, where one soon loses all sense of distance or direction, and drifts along blindly in the wake of his conductor. Everything was solid salt, except where great piers of hewn logs had been built up to support some threatening roof, or vast chasms, left in quarrying, had been bridged across. As we descended to lower regions, the air became more dry and agreeable, and the saline walls more pure and brilliant. One hall, 108 feet in height, resembled a Grecian theatre, the traces of blocks taken out in regular layers representing the seats for the spectators. Out of this single hall 1,000,000 cwt. of salt had been taken, or enough to supply the 40,000,000 inhabitants of Austria for one year.

Two obelisks of salt commemorated the visit of Francis I. and his Empress in another spacious, irregular vault, through which we passed by means of a wooden bridge resting on piers of the crystalline rock. After we had descended to the bottom of this chamber, a boy ran along the bridge above with a burning Bengal light, throwing flashes of blue lustre on the obelisks, on the scarred walls, vast arches, the entrances to deeper halls, and the far roof fretted with the picks of the workmen. The effect was magical—wonderful. Even the old Prussian, who had the face of an exchange broker, exclaimed, as he pointed upward: "It is like a sky full of cloud-lambkins." Presently we entered another and loftier chamber, yawning downwards like the mouth of Hell, with cavernous tunnels opening out of the further end. In these tunnels the workmen, half-naked, with torches in their hands, wild cries, fireworks, and the firing of guns (which here so reverberates in the imprisoned air that one can feel every wave of sound), give a rough representation of the infernal regions, for the benefit of the crowned heads who visit the mines. The effect must be indeed diabolical. Even we, unexceptionable characters as we were, looked truly uncanny in our ghostly garments, amid the livid glare of the fireworks.

A little further, we struck upon a lake four fathoms deep, upon which we embarked in a heavy square boat and entered a gloomy tunnel, over the entrance of which was inscribed (in salt letters) "Good luck to you!" In such a place the motto seemed ironical. "Abandon hope, all ye

who enter here," would have been more appropriate
Midway in the tunnel, the halls at either end were suddenly
illuminated, and a crash, as of a hundred cannon, bellowing
through the hollow vaults, shook the air and water in such
wise that our boat had not ceased trembling when we
landed in the further hall. Read Tasso:

"'Treman le spazioso atro caverno,
E'l asr cieco in quel rumor rimbomba,"

if you want to hear the sound of it. A tablet inscribed
"heartily welcome!" saluted us in landing. Finally, at
the depth of 450 feet, our journey ceased, although we
were but half way to the bottom. The remainder is a
wilderness of shafts, galleries, and smaller chambers, the
extent of which we could only conjecture. We then
returned through scores of tortuous passages to some
vaults where a lot of gnomes, naked to the hips, were busy
with pick, mallet, and wedge, blocking out and separating
the solid pavement. The process is quite primitive, scarcely
differing from that of the ancient Egyptians in quarrying
granite. The blocks are first marked out on the surface by
series of grooves. One side is then deepened to the
equired thickness, and wedges being inserted under the
block, it is soon split off. It is then split transversely int
pieces of one cwt. each, in which form it is ready for sale.
Those intended for Russia are rounded on the edges and
corners until they acquire the shape of large cocoons, for
the convenience of transportation into the interior of the
country.

The number of workmen employed in the mines is 1,500, all of whom belong to the "upper crust"—that is, they live on the outside of the world. They are divided into gangs, and relieve each other every six hours. Each gang quarries out, on an average, a little more than 1,000 cwt. of salt in that space of time, making the annual yield 1,500,000 cwt.! The men we saw were fine, muscular, healthy-looking fellows, and the officer, in answer to my questions, stated that their sanitary condition was quite equal to that of field laborers. Scurvy does not occur among them, and the equality of the temperature of the mines—which stands at 54° of Fahrenheit all the year round—has a favorable effect upon such as are predisposed to diseases of the lungs. He was not aware of any peculiar form of disease induced by the substance in which they work, notwithstanding where the air is humid salt-crystals form upon the wood-work. The wood, I may here remark, never rots, and where untouched, retains its quality for centuries. The officer explicitly denied the story of men having been born in these mines, and having gone through life without ever mounting to the upper world. So there goes another interesting fiction of our youth.

It requires a stretch of imagination to conceive the extent of this salt bed. As far as explored, its length is two and a half English miles, its breadth a little over half a mile and its solid depth 690 feet! It commences about 200 feet below the surface, and is then uninterrupted to the bottom, where it rests on a bed of compact sandstone, such as forms the peaks of the Carpathian Mountains. Below this, there is no probability that it again reappears. The general direction is east and west, dipping rapidly at its western extremity, so that it may no doubt be pushed much further in that direction. Notwithstanding the immense amount already quarried—and it will be better understood when I tate that the aggregate length of the shafts and galleries amounts to *four hundred and twenty miles*—it is estimated that, at the present rate of exploitation, the known supply cannot be exhausted under 300 years. The tripartite treaty, on the partition of Poland, limits Austria to the production of the present amount—1,500,000 cwt. annually —of which she is bound to furnish 300,000 cwt. to Prussia, and 800,000 to Russia, leaving 400,000 cwt. for herself. This sum yields her a net revenue from the mines, of two millions of florins ($1,000,000) annually.

It is not known how this wonderful deposit—more precious than gold itself—was originally discovered. We know that it was worked in the twelfth century, and perhaps much earlier. The popular faith has invented several miracles to account for it, giving the merit to favorite saints. One, which is gravely published in "The History of Cracow," states that a Polish King, who wooed a Princess Elizabeth of Hungary (not the saint of the Wartburg) in the tenth century, asked what she would choose as a bridal gift from him. To which she replied: Something that would most benefit his people. The marriage ceremony was performed in a chapel in one of the salt-mines of Transylvania. Soon after being transferred to Cracow Elizabeth went out to Wieliczka, surveyed the ground, and, after choosing a spot, commanded the people to dig. In the course of a few days they found a salt-crystal, which the

Queen caused to be set in her wedding-ring, and wore until the day of her death. She must have been a wonderful geologist, for those days. The bed actually follows the Carpathians, appearing at intervals in small deposits, into Transylvania, where there are extensive mines. It is believed, also, that it stretches northward into Russian Poland. Some years ago the Bank of Warsaw expended large sums in boring for salt near the Austrian frontier. There was much excitement and speculation for a time; but, although the mineral was found, the cost of quarrying it was too great, and the enterprise was dropped.

On our return we visited Francis-Joseph's hall, a large salt ball-room, with well executed statues of Vulcan and Neptune. Six large chandeliers, apparently of cut glass, but really of salt, illuminate it on festive occasions, and hundreds of dancers perspire themselves into a pretty pickle. When we had reached the upper galleries, we decided to ascend to daylight by means of the windlass. The Prussian party went first, and the ladies were not a little alarmed at finding themselves seated in rope slings, only supported by a band under the arms. All five swung together in a heap; the ladies screamed and would have loosened themselves, but that moment the windlass began to move, and up they went, dangling, towards the little star of daylight, two hundred feet above. Under them hung one of the boys, to steady the whirling mass, and the little scamp amused himself by swinging his lamp, cracking his heels together and rattling his stick along the sides of the shaft. When our turn came, I found, in spite of myself, that such pastime was not calculated to steady my nerves

The sound of the stick was very much like that of snapping ropes, and my brain swam a little at finding my feet dangling over what seemed a bottomless abyss of darkness.

The arrival at the top was like a douche of lightning. It was just noon, and the hot, white, blinding day poured full upon us, stinging our eyes like needles, and almost taking away our breath. We were at once beset with a crowd of beggars and salt-venders. The latter proffered a multitude of small articles—crosses, stars, images, books, cups, dishes, &c.—cut from the native crystal, and not distinguishable from glass in appearance. I purchased a salt-cellar, which has the property of furnishing salt when it is empty. But it seemed to me that I should not need to use it for some days. I felt myself so thoroughly impregnated with salt, that I conceived the idea of seasoning my soup by stirring it with my fingers, and half expected that the fresh roast would turn to corned beef in my mouth.

CHAPTER XXVII.

A GLANCE AT WARSAW.

BEFORE leaving Cracow, we visited the monument to Kosciusko, which is about a mile and a half from the city It is a simple mound of earth, thrown together by the Poles, in memory of the hero of two hemispheres. They are proud of the renown of Sobieski, but they treasure the name of Kosciusko within their heart of hearts. Probably no man was ever before honored with such a monument. It was not raised by subscription and hired labor, but by the spontaneous work of thousands of hands. Old and young, male and female, the noble and the peasant, carried their loads of earth, until the mound arose to be a beacon to the little Free State of Cracow—so long as that Free State existed. The account of its erection is truly touching, and one cannot look upon it without hoping that it may last to tell the story to distant ages and nations yet unformed.

When the Austrian Government determined to fortify Cracow, the commanding position which this mound occu-

Warsaw, a distance of two hundred miles. At first, you pass through a region of sand and pine wood, the very counterpart of New Jersey or North Carolina; then broad plains, partially cultivated; then pasture steppes, pine wood, and cultivation again. The villages are scattering clusters of thatched cottages resembling Irish cabins, except that they are always neatly whitewashed and have a more tidy appearance. This is rather in contrast to the people, who are very dirty. The common, coarse Slavonic type is here universal—low, square forehead, heavy brows, prominent cheek-bones, flattish nose, with broad nostrils and full lips. With the addition of a projecting mouth, many of the faces would be completely Irish. The refined Slavonic face, as one sees it among the Polish gentry, is nevertheless very handsome. The forehead becomes nigh and arched, the nose straight and regular, and the face shows an approach to the classic oval. This is even more striking in the female than in the male countenance. At Granitza we were charmed by a vision of perfect loveliness, which shone on us from time to time, from the upper window of an adjoining mansion. It was a woman of twenty-two, of ripe and yet tender beauty—features exquisitely regular, complexion like a blush rose, large, soft eyes, rather violet than blue, and a rippling crown of magnificent hair, "brown in the shadow and gold in the sun." I confess to watching this beautiful creature for half an hour through the window-blinds. The face of Kosciusko is pure Slavonic, of the peasant type, as is also that of Copernicus, if the portraits of him are correct.

The only place of any interest which we passed was

Czenstochau, celebrated for a miracle-working image of the Madonna. It is a pretty little town, partly built upon a hill which is at least fifty feet high. The station-houses on the road are similar to those in Germany, except that in the refreshment-room one sees, instead of multitudinous *seidl* of beer, the Russian *samovar*, and tumblers of hot tea, in which float slices of lemon. There are long delays at each station, which make the journey tedious, notwithstanding the speed of the trains, when in motion, is very good. Several thunder-storms passed over us, cooling the air and laying the frightful dust; night came on, and it was past midnight before we reached Warsaw. We were like a couple of lost sheep in the crowd, all of whom were hurrying to get to their beds, for the only language heard was Polish, and the officials shook their heads when I addressed them in French or German. Finally, by imitating the majority, we got rid of our passports, had our trunks examined again, and reached the Hotel d'Europe before daybreak.

The forenoon was devoted to preparations for our further journey. Fortunately, the diligence which was to leave for Moscow the next evening was vacant, and we at once engaged places. The passport was a more serious affair, as our own would avail us no further, but we must take out Russian ones instead. The Jew valet-de-place whispered to me, as we entered the office: "Speak French" The Poles hate the Germans much worse than they do their Russian conquerors, and although many of them understand the language, it is considered that of business, while French is the fashionable tongue. The officer asked a few ques tions—what was our object in coming to Russia—whether we had any acquaintances in the country—whether we had ever been there before—whether we were engaged in any business, etc., and then sent us with a checked certificate into another room, where the same questions were repeated and a document made out, which we were requested to sign. Our conductor slipped a ruble note between the two papers, and handed them to a third official, who adroitly removed the bribe and completed the necessary forms. These were petitions to the Governor of Warsaw, praying him to grant us passports to Moscow. On calling at the Governor's office, a secretary informed us that the passports would be ready the next day, but added, as we were leaving: "You had better pay for them now." Hereupon the valet handed over the money, adding a ruble above the proper amount, and then observed to me: "Now you are sure of getting them in time." True enough, they were furnished at the appointed hour. The entire outlay was about four rubles.

It was a sweltering day, the thermometer 90° in the shade, and we could do nothing more than lounge through some of the principal streets. Warsaw is indeed a spacious, stately city, but I had heard it overpraised, and was a little disappointed. It resembles Berlin more than any other European capital, but is less monotonously laid out, and more gay and animated in its aspects. At the time of my visit (June 14th), owing to the annual races, there was a large influx of visitors from the country, and the streets were thronged with a motley multitude. The numerous public squares—fifteen in all, I think—picturesquely irregular, form an agreeable feature of the city. The palaces of the Polish nobles, massive and desolate, remind one of Florence, but without the Palladian grace of the latter. But few of them are inhabited by the original families. Some of them are appropriated to civil and military uses, and in one of them I resided during my stay. The churches of St. John and the Holy Cross, and the Lutheran church, are rather large and lofty than imposing, but rise finely above the level masses of buildings, and furnish landmarks to the city. Decidedly the most impressive picture in Warsaw is that from the edge of the river bank, where the Zamek—the ancient citadel and palace of the Polish kings—rises with its towers and long walls on your left, while under you lies the older part of the city, with its narrow streets and ancient houses, crowded between the Vistula and the foot of the hill.

In the afternoon we took an omnibus to the race-course, which is about two miles distant. The whole city was wending thither, and there could not have been less than forty or fifty thousand persons on the ground. It was a thoroughly Polish crowd, there being but few Russians or Germans present. Peasants from the country with sunbrowned faces, and long, light-brown hair, with round Chinese caps and petticoat trowsers; mechanics and petty tradesmen of either honestly coarse or shabby-genteel appearance; Jews, with long greased locks hanging from their temples, lank, unctuous, and far-smelling figures; Cossacks, with their long lances, heavy caps of black sheepskin, and breasts covered with cartridge pockets; prosperous burghers, sleek and proper, and straight as the figure columns in their ledgers; noblemen, poor and with a melancholy air of fallen greatness, or rich and flaunting in the careless freedom of secured position. Besides, there were itinerant peddlers, by hundreds, selling oranges, sweetmeats, cigars done up in sealed packages, which offered an agreeable hazard in buying them, beer, and even water, in large stone jugs. The crowd formed a compact inclosure nearly around the whole course of two miles. Outside of it extended a wide belt of carriages, hacks, omnibuses, and rough country carts, and as the soil was six inches deep in fine dust, the continual arrivals of vehicles raised such clouds that at times a man could scarcely see his nearest neighbor.

We held out with difficulty long enough to see the first race, which was to have taken place at five, but, with oriental punctuality, commenced at half-past six. The horses, although of mixed English blood, fell considerably below the English standard. There were eight in all, but the race was not exciting, as a fine bay animal, ridden by an English jockey, took the lead at the start, and kept it to the end. During the second heat a Polish jockey was thrown from his horse, breaking his neck instantly. What more interested me than the speed of the horses, was the beauty of the Polish women of the better class. During two years in Europe, I did not see so great a number of handsome faces, as I there saw in an hour. It would be difficult to furnish a larger proportion from the acknowledged loveliness of Philadelphia, Baltimore, or Louisville These maids of Warsaw are not only radiant blondes, whose eyes and hair remind you of corn-flowers among ripe grain.

his heroic grandson, Thaddeus Sobieski!"—or something quite like it. But the lying Jew valet declared that it was a journey of eight hours, and I have discovered, wner too late, that it might be accomplished in three. The pianist, however, accompanied us to Lazinski, the park and palace of Stanislaus Augustus, on the banks of the Vistula. The building stands in the midst of an artificial lake, which is inclosed in a framework of forests. The white statues which stud the banks gleam in strong relief against the dark green background. "There is nothing so beautiful as this in existence," proudly asserted the pianist, "and yet you see the place is deserted. There is no taste in Warsaw; nobody comes here." In the palace there is a picture gallery; all copies, with the exception of portraits of Stanislaus Augustus, the nobles of his court, and his many mistresses. As we descended the steps, we met the son of Kotzebue, the dramatist. He is now an officer (a General, I believe) in the Russian service, more than sixty years old, and of a very ill-favored physiognomy.

So far as I may judge (and my opportunities, I must confess, were slight), the Poles are gradually acquiescing in the rule of Russia. The course pursued by the present Emperor has already given him much popularity among them, and the plan of the regeneration of Poland is indefinitely postponed. Those with whom I conversed admit, if reluctantly, in some instances, that Alexander II. has made many changes for the better. "The best thing he has done for us," said an intelligent Pole, "is the abolition of espionage. Warsaw is now full of former spies, whose business is at an end; and it must be confessed that they are no longer necessary." The feeling of nationality survives, however, long after a nation is dead and buried. The Jews in Poland call themselves Jews, and the Poles in Russia will call themselves Poles, centuries hence.

but also dark-eyed beauties, with faces of a full Southern oval, lips round and delicate as those of an Amorette, and a pure golden transparency of complexion. The connoisseur of woman's beauty can nowhere better compare these two rival styles, nor have so great a difficulty in deciding between them.

We made our way back to the city in a blinding cloud of dust, between a double row of clamorous beggars. They were wonderfully picturesque creatures, where some repulsive deformity was not exposed. There were the hoary heads of saints, which seemed to have come direct from Italian canvas, sun-burnt boys from Murillo, and skinny hags drawn by the hand of Michael Angelo. Over the noiseless bed of dust rushed the country carts, filled with peasants drunk enough to be jolly, the funny little horses going in a frolicsome, irregular gallop, as if they too had taken a drop too much. Now and then some overladen pedestrian, beating a zigzag course against the gale, would fall and disappear in a cloud, like a bursting shell. I saw but one specimen of the picturesque Polish costume—a servant-girl in red petticoat and boots, and the trim jacket which we all know in the Cracovienne. The poorer women, generally, were shabby and slovenly imitations of the rich.

Wandering along the streets, with throats full of dust, we were attracted to the sign of "*Pivo Bavarski*" (Bavarian beer). Entering a court littered with the refuse of the kitchen, we discovered a sort of German restaurant, of suspicious cleanliness. The proprietor who served us with an insipid beverage—a slander on the admirable brewage of Munich—soon learned that we were strangers.

"But how did you happen to find my place?" he asked. "All the other beer-saloons in the city are dirty, low places: mine is the only *noble* establishment." He was very desirous of importing a negro girl from America, for a barmaid. "I should have all the nobility of the city here," said he. "She would be a great curiosity. There is that woman Pastrana, with the hair all over her face—she has made a great fortune, they say. There are not many of the kind, and I could not afford it, but if I could get one quite black, with a woolly head, I should make more money in a day than I now do in a month." He wished to engage me to send him such an attraction, but I respectfully declined.

At this place we fell in with a Polish pianist, a virtuoso in pictures and old furniture. He took us to his room, a charming artistic and antiquarian den. Among other things he had a few undoubted originals—a small Rembrandt, a Gerard Dow, a very fine Matsys, two Bourguignons, and a landscape which appeared to be an early work of Claude. He wanted to sell these, of course at a good price, and likewise commissioned me to furnish him with a purchaser in America. The man fondled his treasures with a genuine attachment and delight, and I am sure that nothing but necessity induced him to part with them.

I wanted to visit Villanow, the residence of John Sobieski. Do you remember the passage in dear old Miss Porter's "Thaddeus of Warsaw," where the hero contemplates the moon? "'How often have I walked with my departed mother upon the ramparts of Villanow, and gazed upon that resplendent orb!' 'Villanow!' exclaimed the Countess; 'surely that is the residence of Sobieski, and you must be

The distinguished Polish poet, Adam Mickiewicz, he stated, was a great admirer of Emerson, whom he frequently cites in his prose writings. The Emperor Alexander has recently authorized the publication of the collected works of Mickiewicz (with the exception of some political papers) at Warsaw, for the benefit of the poet's family, and has also permitted contributions to be taken up for the same purpose.

The post stations on this road are at intervals of from twelve to twenty-two versts, and the diligence usually stops barely long enough to change horses. At the larger towns, however, there is a halt of half an hour, which allows the passenger time to get a hasty meal. The Pole assisted us during the first twelve hours, but after that we were entirely adrift, as the conductor spoke only in Russian. A smattering of the language was necessary in order to support life. I therefore went to work, and with the assistance of an imperfect vocabulary in Murray, learned the numerals up to one-hundred, the words "*how much?*" and "*immediately*," and beef-steak is the same in all languages, and "tea" in Russian (*tschaï*) is the same as in Chinese. I had no difficulty in supplying our wants. This vocabulary, however, like most of those in guide-books, teaches you just what you don't want to say. It gives you the Russian for a "floating preserve for fish," and "I am a nobleman," &c., and omits such vulgar necessities as a basin and towel, and even the verb "to have." Fortunately, the people at the station-houses are tolerably quick of comprehension. We were always served with very little delay, and with dishes of which no reasonable traveller could complain. The prices varied greatly, being treble at some stations what they were at others. Whether this was a sliding scale of honesty or of actual value, I was unable to ascertain

All day we rolled along, over the rich plains of Poland, stopping at the large country towns of Siedlce, Miedzyrzic, Biala, and others whose names the reader has probably never heard and never could pronounce. The country may be described in a few words—woods of pine and birch, fields of rye, rape-seed and turnips, broad, swampy pastures, and scattering one-story villages, with thatched roofs and white-washed walls. Sunburnt peasants in the fields, dressed in round black felt caps, dirt-colored shirts, and wide trowsers: Jews in the villages, disgusting to behold, with shocking bad hats of the stove-pipe breed, greasy love-locks hanging from their temples, and shabby black caftans reaching to their heels. These people justify the former middle age superstition that the Jew is distinguished from the Christian by a peculiar bodily odor. You can scent them quite as far as you can see them. Moses would have hewn them limb from limb, for their foulness. The worst of it is, they hover round the post-stations and pounce upon a stranger, in the hope of making something out of him, be it ever so little. I was surprised to find that they all speak a little German, but afterwards learned that they do more or less of smuggling, in the Baltic provinces. "They are such a timid and cowardly race," said my informant, "and yet, when detected in the act of smuggling, they will sometimes fight desperately, rather than lose what they have." Many of them carry on a trade in segars, done up in sealed packages, which you are expected to buy without opening.

CHAPTER XXVIII.

A JOURNEY THROUGH CENTRAL RUSSIA.

THERE is a diligence three or four times a week between Warsaw and Moscow. The trip—a distance of eight hundred English miles—is made in five days by the fast coach, which leaves the former place every Monday evening, and in six days by the others. The fare is fifty silver rubles ($37½) for an outside, and seventy ($52½) for an inside seat. On account of the intense heat, we took outside places, but as there happened to be no other through passengers we were allowed the range of the entire vehicle. It was a strongly built, substantial affair, resembling a French diligence, but smaller and more comfortable in every way. A traveller who had made this journey recommended us to take a supply of provisions, asserting that it was impossible to procure anything on the way; but as a Russian official contradicted this statement, we took his word, and had no reason to regret it afterwards. In fact, I have never made a journey by diligence with more ease and less fatigue.

At seven o'clock on Monday evening, we took our places beside the Russian conductor, who, in his coat braided with gold, resembled an officer of cavalry, and started on our long voyage through unknown regions. The postilion sounded a charge on his trumpet as we rattled through the streets of Warsaw, past the stately Zamek, and down the long hill upon which the city is proudly lifted, to the Vistula. A bridge of boats crosses to the suburb of Praga, whence all traces of the blood spilt by Suwarrow, Skryznecki, and Diebitsch have long since been washed away. It is now a very quiet, dull sort of a place, with no vestiges of its former defences. Beyond it stretches that vast plain of Central Europe and Asia, whose limits are the British Channel and the Chinese Wall. In traversing it, I was continually reminded of Humboldt's description of the Kirghiz Steppes—"Ten miles give you the picture of a thousand." Straight before us, cutting the belted tracts of pine-forest and grain land, the road ran to the horizon, where its white floor met the sky. Four horses abreast, with two leaders, carried us past the verst-posts at the rate of eight or nine miles an hour, and the postilion's horn sounded incessant warnings to the slow teams laden with hay or other country produce, with which the road was filled. The night was warm and balmy, and the long summer twilight connected sunset and sunrise with its bridge of boreal light.

A young Pole was our companion the first night. I was interested in hearing from him that Longfellow's poems had been published in the Polish language, at Lublin, a large city about a hundred miles south-east of Warsaw

The towns through which one passes are built upon one model, and present very little difference in their general features. In the centre is usually a spacious square, which serves as a market place. The shops and Government offices front upon it, and broad streets diverge from the four corners. Most of the houses are one-story, and built of wood, painted red, white or yellow. Standing in the centre of the square, one looks over its low barrier upon some groups of ash, poplar or linden trees, which rise from the gardens beyond, the heavy, half-Asiatic spire of a church, and the sky, whose large, unbroken vault rests upon the circle of the horizon. In summer, when many of the inhabitants are in the fields, the place has a silent, sleepy air, and you are glad to exchange it for the rippling of grain, the shadows of the dark pines, and the smell of blossoming grasses, which await you at its very door.

In the afternoon, we crossed the Bug, the eastern frontier of the *last* kingdom of Poland, although the language is heard as far as the Dnieper, and the Polish *zlots* accepted as currency. Here is an immense fortified camp, adjoining the city of Brzesc. Some hundreds of soldiers were bathing in the stream and washing their clothes at the sam time. The fortifications are built of brick, of great extent, but not of remarkable strength. There are also small military stations at intervals along the whole length of the road. The soldiers are employed in keeping in order little ornamental gardens attached to the buildings, and these bits of gravel walk, thicket and flower-bed are so many cheerful oases in the long waste of a half-cultivated country.

For more than a hundred and fifty miles, we traversed the swampy region between the Bug and the Dnieper There is almost an uninterrupted extent of marshy land—varying greatly in breadth, however—from the Baltic to the Black Sea. The streams which form the Dnieper and the Dwina, flowing in contrary directions, are interlaced like the fingers of two clasping hands, so that there is in reality no watershed, but a level plateau, over which the waters go wandering as if in search of some accident to determine their future course. In this region the villages are few and far apart, and the rank, dark woods more frequent. Malignant gnats bit us at night, and huge yellow gad-flies came in swarms by day, to madden our horses and attack ourselves. The country was monotonous as the sea, and so close was the general resemblance between the districts through which we passed, that we seemed to make no headway whatever. Every morning, we opened our eyes on the same landscape, or the same wide, low village, and the same abominable Hebrews. After two or three days of such travel, we hailed the first mole-hill of an elevation with much the same feeling as if it had been Mount Blanc. I could easily understand why the Russian peasants, when they draw a mountain, place its summit among the very stars.

The country, nevertheless, through all Central Russia, is evidently of great fertility, although, under an imperfect system of cultivation, it does not yield half of what it is capable. The same character of soil, in England, would be a garden. What Russia greatly needs is a class of enter-prising agriculturists, who would live upon their land,

and devote themselves to its proper development. During the whole journey, I did not notice ten country residences. The road, however, is comparatively new, and the old highway, via Wilna and Smolensk, which it has superceded, no doubt presents a better picture in this respect. Drainage, manuring, and a judicious rotation of crops, would work wonders with such a mellow and bounteous soil. Some travellers speak of the waste and desolate appearance of the Russian plains; the French describe them as a savage wilderness; but they are in fact far more naturally productive than the plains of Northern Germany.

The road to Moscow is not surpassed by any highway in the world. It is macadamized for the whole distance, kept in admirable order, deviates but little from a right line, and, except at some river-crossings, has no grade too heavy for a railroad. Build six or eight bridges and you might lay down the rails upon it, from Warsaw to Moscow. At every verst, there is a post with the distance from both these cities and St. Petersburg, and from the first station on either hand. Each verst, again, is divided into fifths. The station houses are built of brick, and all on the same plan. The house fronts the road, flanked by a high brick wall, through a gate in which you enter a spacious court yard, surrounded by stables and the dwellings for servants. In the main building, there are three or four clean, well-furnished rooms for travellers, who find everything which they may need except beds. The Russians carry their own bedding with them, and the broad sofas, with leather cushions, make excellent couches. Those who do not take the diligence are obliged to have a *padaroshna*, or Govern ment order for horses, from post to post, as in Sweden. A foreigner, to travel in this style, must have his own vehicle, and, moreover, must know a little of the language.

On the third morning, we reached the town of Bobruisk, n the Beresina. It was some distance further up the river at the bridge of Borisoff, that the French army met with such a terrible disaster during the retreat from Moscow. The Beresina is now a deep, full, quiet stream, flowing between low, curving banks, on his way to join the Dnieper. Below the town are some beautiful clumps of birch and ash, among which rises the round red mass of a new brick fort. A stalwart soldier, leaning on Crimean crutches, begged of us as we descended to the bridge, and two muscular, clean-limbed grooms stripped, sprang naked upon their horses, and swam them like Tritons in the centre of the river. Three more stations brought us to the Dnieper, at the town of Rogatcheff. Here he is already a strong stream, and the flock of heavy, flat-bottomed barges moored along his banks had no doubt seen the Black Sea. The town is a small but lively place. A stranger is struck with the great width of the streets in all these places, through which they acquire a neat, respectable appearance, n spite of the low houses. The frequency of fires probably gave rise to this method of building, as we passed two villages which were more than half in ashes, where the conflagration had been stopped by the road.

After passing the Dnieper, the marshes cease, and the country becomes slightly undulating—very slightly, indeed, but still perceptible without the aid of a theodolite. The fir is less and less frequent, and the birch increases in the same proportion, so that before reaching Moscow the forests are almost entirely composed of this delicate, graceful, shivering tree—the scantily-clothed Dryad of the North. Its hues are always cold, and where it abounds one cannot have full faith in summer. The weather, besides, had changed, and in place of the sultry air of Warsaw, we had a strong north wind, with a temperature of only 40° in the mornings. Our overcoats were bearable the whole day, and a thick Scotch plaid was no unwelcome addition at night. Nevertheless, there was little difference in the soil and vegetation, and the silver-headed rye rolled in as rich waves as ever, to break upon the shores of harvest.

On Friday we entered Old Russia—Holy Russia, as it is sometimes called, in the fond veneration of the people. The country became more thickly populated, and from every village rose a picturesque church, white as snow, and crowned with as many bright green domes and spires as its proportions would allow. These gay, graceful structures, towering at intervals above the birchen groves, and sparkling in the sunshine, gave a peculiar charm to the otherwise monotonous landscape. The Jews, with their greasy ringlets, disappeared, Polish money was refused at the stations, and the peasantry showed the pure Russian type, in face and costume. Every man of them wore his beard unshorn, and the commonest visage received a sort of character and dignity thereby. Whenever the diligence stopped, a company of venerable and very dirty figures appeared before us, bowing incessantly with Oriental gravity, and urging their claims to charity in what I have no doubt were very choice and elegant expressions. They were pertinacious, but not clamorous, and it was impossible to look anywhere within thirty degrees of them, without occasioning new demonstrations of reverence and supplication.

After leaving the streams of the Dnieper and coming upon those of the Oka, whose waters flow with the Volga to the far Caspian Sea, the country can no longer be called a plain. It is rather a rolling prairie, like those of Southern Wisconsin, but with still gentler undulations. Our horses dashed down the gradual descents at a mad gallop, which carried them nearly to the top of the next rise, and we frequently accomplished fifteen versts within the hour. On Saturday morning we breakfasted at Malo Jaroslavitz, where an obelisk has been erected to commemorate Murat's defeat, and in the afternoon reached the lively little town of Podolsk, on the great southern highway from Moscow to Tula and Orel, and further to Odessa and the Crimea. We were now within thirty-five versts of Moscow, which we were anxious to see before dark. Five days and nights of travel had cramped us a little, but we felt capable of as much more upon such a superb road. The sun set upon the silvery birchen forests, and the long swells and slopes of grain. Heavy clouds covered the sky, except along the north, where the lurid yellow twilight moved slowly around towards sunrise, and we were sinking into a wearied sleep, when a long line of dark towers and Oriental domes appeared in the distance, drawn sharp and hard against the angry lustre. This was Moscow! Ere long we descended into the valley of the Moskva, rattled for many and many a verst through gloomy streets, caught a midnight glimpse of the majestic pile of the Kremlin, and after a seemingly endless cruize in a Russian droshky, reached the welcome haven of a good hotel

CHAPTER XXIX.

A PANORAMIC VIEW OF MOSCOW.

It was Madame de Stael, I believe, who, on first seeing Moscow, exclaimed: "*Voilà Rome. Tartare!*" This may have been true before the destruction of the ancient city, but it would hardly apply at the present day. In its immense extent Moscow may well rival Rome, as in this respect it is surpassed by no modern capital except London; but, although its Asiatic character is quite as strongly marked as that of Constantinople, it is by no means Tartar. No other city in the world presents so cosmopolitan an aspect. The gilded domes of Lucknow—the pagodas of China—Byzantine churches—Grecian temples—palaces in the style of Versailles—heavy inexpressive German buildings—wooden country cottages—glaring American signs—boulevards, gardens, silent lanes, roaring streets, open markets, Turkish bazaars, French cafés, German beer cellars, and Chinese tea-houses—all are found here, not grouped exclusively into separate cantons, but mixed and jumbled together, until Europe and Asia, the Past and

Present, the Old World and the New, are so blended and confounded, that it is impossible to say which predominates. Another city so bizarre and so picturesque as Moscow does not exist. To call it Russian would be too narrow a distinction: it suggests the world.

Its position, near the imaginary line where one continent is merged into the other, accounts for this. The waters of the Moskva seek an Asiatic Sea, yet the nearest ports of the city are those of Central Europe. Its fibres of commerce branch eastward across the Tartar steppes to Mongolia and China: southward to Samarcand and Bokhara, to Cashmere and Persia; northward to Archangel and the Polar Ocean; and on the west, to all the rest of Europe. The race who founded it came from the south-east, and brought with them the minaret and the swelling Oriental dome, the love of gilding and glaring colors; its religion came from Constantinople, with the Byzantine pillar and the Greek cross; and the founder of Russian power learned his trade in the West. On every one of its thousand spires and domes glitters the crescent (as a token that they were once in the hands of the Tartars), but now surmounted by the triumphant cross. At its southern end the muezzin calls to prayer from the roof of his mosque, while at the northern, the whistle of the locomotive announces the departure of the train for St. Petersburg.

When you overlook the city from an elevated point, it loses nothing of its originality in the broader compass of your vision. On the contrary, many clashing impressions naturally arising from the incongruity of its features, are forgotten, and the vast, dazzling panorama assumes a grand dramatic character. It is an immense show, gotten up for a temporary effect, and you can scarcely believe that it may not be taken to pieces and removed as soon as its purpose has been attained. Whence this array of grass-green roofs, out of which rise by hundreds spires and towers stranger and more fantastic than ever were builded in a mad architect's dream? Whence these gilded and silvered domes, which blind your eyes with reflected suns, and seem to dance and totter in their own splendor, as you move? It can be no city of trade and government, of pleasure and scandal, of crime and religion, which you look upon; it was built when the Arabian Nights were true, and the Prince of the Hundred Islands reigns in its central palace.

And yet there are few cities in Europe (Berlin excepted) which have not greater advantages of position than Moscow. Accident or whim seems to have suggested the choice of the site to its founders. The little Moskva is not navigable in summer for steamers drawing eighteen inches of water. It is an insignificant tributary, not of the Volga, but of the Oka, which falls into the Volga at Nijni-Novgorod, and here is the spot pointed at by Nature for the commercial emporium of Central Russia and Western Asia. But in the days of Vladimir, this point was too near the Tartars, and though Peter the Great at one time seriously designed to make it his capital, his rivalry with Sweden, and his desire to approach Europe rather than Asia, finally prevailed, and St. Petersburg arose from the Finland swamps. Moscow, since then, has lost the rank and advantages of a capital, although it continues to be the Holy City of the Russians, and the favorite residence of many of the ancient noble families. The rapid growth of the manufacturing interest in this part of Russia has recently given it a start, but its growth is slow, and its population (350,000) is probably not much greater than in the days of Ivan or Michael Romanoff.

The Moskva, in passing through the city, divides it into two unequal parts, about three-fourths occupying the northern bank and one-fourth the southern. The river is so tortuous that it may be said to flow toward all points of the compass before reaching the Kremlin, whence its course is eastward toward the Oka. In the centre, and rising directly from the water, is the isolated hill of the Kremlin, a natural mound, about a mile in circumference, and less than a hundred feet in height. On either side of it, the northern bank ascends very gradually for the distance of a mile or more, where it melts into the long undulations of the country. On the southern side of the Moskva, at the south-western extremity of the city, are the Sparrow Hills, which, running nearly due east and west, form a chord to the great winding curve of the river, and inclose the whole southern portion of Moscow, which is built on the level bottom between it and their bases. These hills are steep and abrupt on the northern side, and though rising less than two hundred feet above the water, overtop every other elevation, far and near. Every stranger who wishes to see the panorama of Moscow should first mount the tower of Ivan Veliki, on the Kremlin, and then make an excursion to the Sparrow Hills.

The conflagration of 1812, though, with the exception of

the *Kitai Gorod*, or Chinese City, which wholly escaped, it left scarcely fifty houses standing, contributed very little to modernize the aspect of Moscow. A few of the principal streets were widened, and two concentric circles of boulevards introduced in the restoration of the city, but most of the old streets and lanes were rebuilt on the same plan, and in much the same character as before. Inside the outer boulevard, which embraces the business portion of the city, the houses are almost exclusively of brick, covered with stucco, and painted yellow, light blue, pink, or pale red. Outside of it, for many a verst, stretch the rows of private residences, interspersed with garden plots, while the outskirts are made up of the houses of the poorer classes, one-story cottages of boards or logs, gaudily painted, as in the country villages. Many of the better dwellings are also of wood, which material is recommended both by its cheapness and comfort. Stone is scarce and dear, and there does not seem to be sufficient to pave the streets properly. A shallow bed of small cobble-stones, so lightly rolled that it soon becomes uneven, jolts the life out of you, even in summer, but in the spring it is said to be far worse.

The diameter of the city, from north to south, cannot be less than eight miles, while its circumference will fall little short of twenty-five. Its low houses, broad, rambling streets, large interior courts, market-places, and gardens, account for this extent. It is truly a city of magnificent distances, and its people have their own peculiar ideas of what is near and what is far. I was greatly taken in until I discovered this fact. "Close at hand" proved to be a mile off, and when one man says of another, "We are neighbors," you may depend that they live an hour's walk apart. Another difficulty is, there are so few right lines, that it is next to impossible to go directly from one given point to another. Your course is either a right angle, semicircle, an elliptical curve, or the letter S. I have had considerable practice in *orientiren*, but have never yet had so much trouble to learn the topography of a town. It is full of those scarcely perceptible curves and deflections which gradually carry you out of your direction, while you imagine you are going straight ahead. If you have ever tried to trundle a wheelbarrow to a mark blindfold, you will know how easily one may be baffled in this way.

Just this circumstance, however, prolongs the impression of novelty, which, to an old traveller like myself, is a rare charm. There are reminiscences from all parts of the world which I have already seen, but, in addition, a stamp and character of picturesque incongruity entirely peculiar to Moscow. But two streets—the *Twerskaia Oulitza*, leading from the Kremlin towards the St. Petersburg gate, and the *Kuznetskoi Most*, or Smiths' Bridge—have a busy metropolitan aspect, and preserve the same character throughout their whole extent; the others are full of transformations and surprises. You pass between palaces, with lofty porticos, and find yourself in a country village; still further, you enter a thronged market-place; beyond are churches with blue domes, bespangled with golden stars; then rows of shops, displaying fashionable European goods and wares. These cease suddenly, and you are in the midst of gardens, but not a hundred paces from their green seclusion you find yourself in the bustle of an Oriental bazaar. In Moscow no man, except an old inhabitant, knows what a street may bring forth.

The population, also, exhibits a corresponding diversity. The European gentlemen, with cylinder hats and tight kid gloves, do not appear more out of place under those crescent-tipped domes of gold than the sallow Persians and silken-robed Armenians beside yonder French palace. The Russian peasant, with his thick brown beard, red shirt, and wide trowsers stuck into his boots, elbows you on the narrow sidewalk. After him comes a lady, with the smallest of bonnets and the largest of crinolines, respectfully followed by a man-servant, whose presence attests her respectability. Alone, she would be subject to suspicion. A fair Circassian, with blue eyes and the build of an Adonis, next meets you; then, perhaps, a Tartar in his round cap of black lamb's wool, or a Chinese, resembling a faulty image of yellow clay, cast aside before the true Adam was made; then European bagmen, smirking and impertinent a Russian nurse, with a head-dress like the spread tail of a red peacock; a priest in flowing hair and black cassock; a money-changer, whose beardless face proclaims his neuter gender: a company of *istvostchiks* (hackmen) in squat black hats and long blue caftans; officers in the imperial uniform; firemen in gilded helmets, saintly old beggars children in natural costume, fallen women, gypsies, cossack —all succeed each other in endless and ever-changing procession.

The best point for a bird's-eye view of the city is from the tower of Ivan Veliki, on the Kremlin. This is a belfry

200 feet high, surmounted by a golden dome. When you have passed the Tzar Kolokol, or King of Bells, which rests on a granite pedestal at its base, and have climbed through some half a dozen bell chambers to the upper gallery, you see nearly the whole of Moscow—for the northern part goes beyond your horizon. On all other sides it stretches far, far away, leaving only a narrow ring of dark-green woods between it and the sky. The Moskva twists like a wounded snake at your feet, his little stream almost swallowed up in the immense sea of the pale-green roofs. This vast green ring is checkered with the pink and yellow fronts of the buildings which rise above the general level, while all over it, far and near, singly or in clusters, shoot up the painted, reed-like towers, and open to the day the golden and silver blossoms of their domes. How the sun flashes back, angrily or triumphantly, from the dazzling hemispheres, until this northern capital shines in more than tropic fire! What a blaze, and brilliance, and rainbow variegation under this pale-blue sky!

The view from the Sparrow Hills is still more beautiful. You are inclosed with a belt of birch and pine woods. Under you the river reflects the sky, and beyond it sweep blossoming meadows up to the suburban gardens, over which rises the long line of the gilded city, whose neares domes seem to flash in your very face, and whose farthest towers fade against the sky. Their long array fills one-third of the horizon. I counted between five and six hundred, one-third of which were either gilded or silvered. The dome of the new cathedral, as large as that of St. Paul's, London, burned in the centre like a globe of flame—

like the sun itself, with stars and constellations sparkling around it far and wide. From this point the advanced guard of Napoleon's army first saw Moscow—a vast, silent, glittering city, fired by the sunset, and with the seeds of a more awful splendor in its heart. No wonder that the soldiers stood still, by a spontaneous impulse, grounded their arms, and exclaimed, as one man : " Moscow ! Moscow !"

I saw this wonderful picture on a still sultry, afternoon The woods and meadows, the thousand towers of the city, were bathed in bright sunshine; but beyond the latter lowered, black as ink, a pile of thunder-clouds. The threatening background rose, letting fall a shifting curtain of dark gray, from the feet of which whirled clouds of tawny dust, veiling the splendor of the distant domes. As the storm advanced, columns of dust arose, here and there, all over the city; a shadow, as of night, crept across it, leaving only the nearer spires to blaze with double splendor against the black chaos. Presently the more distant portions of the city were blotted out. The brighter towers remained for a time visible, shining spectrally through the falling cloud, and seeming to be removed far back into the depths of the atmosphere. The sound of hail and rain, crashing on the metal roofs, reached our ears; the last golden dome stood yet a moment in the sunshine, and then everything swam in a chaos of dust and storm. So veil by veil fell over the magical scene, and as the whirlwind reached us, a void, black and impenetrable, hid it from our eyes. We had again witnessed the destruction of Moscow

CHAPTER XXX.

THE KREMLIN.

If Moscow is the Mecca of the Russians, the Kremlin is its Kaaba. Within its ancient walls is gathered all that is holiest in religion or most cherished in historical tradition. Kiev and Novgorod retain but a dim halo of their former sanctity; their glory lies wholly in the Past. The kingdoms of which they were the centres had ceased to exist before the foundation of Russian power. On the hill of the Kremlin was first planted that mighty tree whose branches now overshadow two Continents. The fact that Tartar, Swede, and Frenchman have laid their axes at its very root, without being able to lop off a single bough, though the world awaited its fall, only endears this spot the more to the Russian people, and strengthens their superstitious faith in the Divine protection vouchsafed to it. The Tartar planted his crescent on its holy spires, and there it still glitters, but *under* the conquering cross. Napoleon housed in its ancient palace, and a thousand of his cannon are now piled in the court-yard. Its very gates are pro tected by miracles, and the peasant from a distant province enters them with much the same feeling as a Jewish pilgrim enters the long-lost City of Zion.

The Kremlin hill stands very nearly in the centre of the city. It is triangular in form, the longest side facing the Moskva, about a mile in circumference and somewhat less than a hundred feet in height. Adjoining it on the east is the *Kitai Gorod* (Chinese City), still inclosed within its ancient walls. The original walls of the Kremlin were built by Demetrius Donskoi, in the fourteenth century, and though frequently repaired, if not wholly rebuilt, since that time, they still retain their ancient character. Rising directly from the Moskva, at the foot of the hill, on the southern side, they climb it at either end, and crown it on the north. Thus, when you stand on the opposite bank of the river, you see before you the long notched wall, interrupted with picturesque Tartar towers, like an antique frame to the green slope of the hill, whose level top bears aloft its crown of palaces, churches, and towers. This is the only general view one gets of the Kremlin, although its clustered golden domes are visible from almost every part of the city. There was formerly a lake-like moat around the northern side of the hill; but Alexander I. drained and planted it, and it is now a pleasant garden.

The main entrance is at the north-eastern angle, through a double-towered portal, called the Sunday Gate. As I propose acting as a *valet de place* for my fellow-traveller-readers, I shall describe to them the notable sights of the Kremlin, in the order in which they meet us. We shall not enter, therefore, without pausing a moment before this gate, to inspect more closely a little chapel, or rather shrine, built against the wall, between two archways. Before the shrine is a platform, thronged with a bare-headed crowd, whose heads are continually bobbing up and down as they cross themselves. Every one who passes, going in or out, does the same, and many an officer, grave citizen or resplendent lady descends from the droshky, presses through the throng, and falls on his or her knees before the holy picture inside the sanctuary. We press in, among hackmen, beggars, merchants, and high officials, all so intent on their manipulations that they do not even see us, and finally reach a niche lighted with silver lamps, before a screen dazzling with gold, silver, and precious stones. A high-born lady in silk and lace, and a lousy-bearded serf are kneeling side by side, and kissing with passionate devotion the glass cover over a Byzantine mother and child, of dark mulatto complexion, whose hands and faces alone are visible through the gilded and jeweled mantles. This is the "Iberian Mother of God"—a miraculous picture, which, after working wonders on Georgia and on Mount Athos, has for the last two hundred years been the protectress of the Moscovites. Her aid is invoked by high and low, in all the circumstances of life, and I doubt whether any other shrine in the world is the witness of such general and so much real devotion.

Once within the Sunday Gate, we see before us the long *Krasnoi Ploshad*, or Red Square stretching southward to the bank of the Moskva. Close on our right towers the gray wall of the Kremlin—for, although on the hill, we are not yet fairly within the sacred citadel—while on the left, parallel to it, is the long, low front of the *Gostinnoi Dvor*, or Great Bazaar. In the centre of the square is a bronze monument to Minim and Pojarski, the Russian heroes, who in 1610 aroused the people, stormed Moscow, and drove out Vladislas of Poland, who had been called to the throne by the Boyards. But for this act the relative destiny of the two powers might have been reversed. The Russians, therefore, deservedly honor the memory of the sturdy butcher of Nijni Novgorod, who, like the Roman Ciceronaccio, seems to have been the master-spirit of the Revolution. He is represented as addressing Pojarski, the General, who sits before him, listening, one hand on his sword. The figures are colossal, and full of fire and vigor. A short distance beyond this monument is a small circular platform of masonry, which is said to have been a throne, or public judgment-seat, of the early Tzars.

Proceeding down the square to its southern extremity, we halt at last before the most astonishing structure our eyes have ever beheld. What is it?—a church, a pavilion, or an immense toy? All the colors of the rainbow, all the forms and combinations which straight and curved lines can produce, are here compounded. It seems to be the product of some architectural kaleidoscope, in which the most incongruous things assume a certain order and system, for surely such another bewildering pile does not exist. It is not beautiful, for Beauty requires at least a suggestion of symmetry, and here the idea of proportion or adaptation is wholly lost. Neither is the effect offensive, because the maze of colors, in which red, green, and gold, predominate, attracts, and cajoles the eye. The purposed incongruity of the building is seen in the minutest details, and where there is an accidental resemblance in form, it is balanced by a difference in color.

This is the Cathedral of St. Basil, built during the reign of Ivan the Terrible, who is said to have been so charmed with the work, that he caused the eyes of the architect to be blinded, to prevent him from ever building another such. The same story, however, is told of various buildings, clocks, and pieces of mechanism, in Europe, and is doubtless false. Examining the Cathedral more closely, we find it to be an agglomeration of towers, no two of which are alike, either in height, shape, or any other particular. Some are round, some square, some hexagonal, some octagonal: one ends in a pyramidal spire, another in a cone, and others in bulging domes of the most fantastic pattern—twisted in spiral bands of yellow and green like an ancient Moslem turban, vertically ribbed with green and silver, checkered with squares of blue and gold, covered with knobbed scales, like a pine-cone, or with overlapping leaves of crimson, purple, gold, and green. Between the bases of these towers galleries are introduced, which, again, differ in style and ornament as much as the towers themselves. The interior walls are covered with a grotesque maze of painting, consisting of flower-pots, thistles, roses, vines, birds, beasts, and scroll-work, twined together in inextricable confusion, as we often see in Byzantine capitals and friezes.

The interior of the Cathedral is no less curious than the outside. Every tower incloses a chapel, so that twelve or fifteen saints here have their shrines under one roof, yet enjoy the tapers, the incense, and the prayers of their worshippers in private, no one interfering with the other. The chapels, owing to their narrow bases and great height, resemble flues. Their sides are covered with sacred frescoes, and all manner of ornamental painting on a golden ground, and as you look up the diminishing shaft, the colossal face of Christ, the Virgin, or the protecting Saint, stares down upon you from the hollow of the capping dome. The central tower is one hundred and twenty feet high, while the diameter of the chapel inside it cannot be more than thirty feet at the base. I cannot better describe this singular structure than by calling it the Apotheosis of Chimneys.

Let us now turn back a few steps, and pass through the Kremlin wall by the *Spass Vorota*, or Gate of the Redeemer. This is even more peculiarly sacred than the chapel of the Iberian Mother. Over the hollow arch hangs a picture of the Saviour, which looks with benignity upon the Russians, but breathes fire and thunder upon their foes. The Tartars, so says tradition, have been driven back again and again from this gate by miraculous resistance, and, though the French entered at last, all their attempts to blow it up were in vain. The other entrance, the Gate of St. Nicholas has also its picture, but of lesser sanctity. Here the French succeeded in cracking the arch, as far as the picture-frame, where the rent suddenly stopped. No man dare pass through the Gate of the Redeemer without uncovering his head—not even the Emperor. The common Russians commence at twenty paces off, and very few of them pass through the Red Square, on their way to and from the Moskva, without turning towards the Gate, bowing, and crossing themselves. This is not the only shrine in Moscow whose holiness irradiates a wide circle around it. I have frequently seen men performing their devotions in the market-place or the middle of the street, and, by following the direction of their eyes, have discovered at a considerable distance, the object of reverence.

At last we tread the paved court of the Kremlin. Before us rises the tower of Ivan Veliki, whose massive, sturdy walls seem to groan under its load of monster bells. Beyond it are the Cathedral of St. Michael, the Church of the Assumption, and the ancient church of the Tzars, all crowded with tiaras of gilded domes. To the right rises another cluster of dark-blue, pear-shaped domes, over the House of the Holy Synod, while the new Palace (Granovitaya Palata), with its heavy French front and wings, above which

"The light aerial gallery, golden-railed,
Burns like a fringe of fire,"

fills up the background. The Tartar towers of the Kremlin wall shoot up, on our left, from under the edge of the platform whereon we stand, and away and beyond them glitters the southern part of the wonderful city—a vast semicircle of red, green, and gold. I know not when this picture is most beautiful—when it blinds you in the glare of sunshine, when the shadows of clouds soften its piercing colors and extinguish half its reflected fires, when evening wraps it in a violet mist, repainting it with sober tints, or when it lies pale and gray, yet sprinkled with points of silver light, under the midnight moon.

At the foot of the tower stands on a granite pedestal the

Tzar Kolokol, or Emperor of Bells, whose renown is worldwide. It was cast by order of the Empress Anne in 1730, but was broken seven years afterward, through the burning of the wooden tower in which it hung. It is a little over 21 feet in hight, 22 feet in diameter at the bottom, weighs 120 tons, and the estimated value of the gold, silver, and copper contained in it is $1,500,000. In one of the lower stories of the tower hangs another bell cast more than a century before the Tzar Kolokol, and weighing 64 tons. Its iron tongue is swung from side to side by the united exertions of three men. It is only rung thrice a year, and when it speaks all other bells are silent. To those who stand near the tower, the vibration of the air is said to be like that which follows the simultaneous discharge of a hundred cannon. In the other stories hang at least forty or fifty bells, varying in weight from 36 tons to a thousand pounds: some of them are one-third silver. When they all sound at once, as on Easter morn, the very tower must rock on its foundation. In those parts of Russia where the Eastern Church is predominant, no other sect is allowed to possess bells. In Austria the same prohibition is extended to the Protestant churches. The sound of the bell is a part of the act of worship, and therefore no heterodox tongue, though of iron, must be permitted to preach false doctrine to half the city.

The Empress Anne seems to have had a fondness for monster castings. Turning to the right into an adjoining courtyard, we behold a tremendous piece of artillery, familiarly known as the "pocket-piece" of this Tzarina. The diameter of the bore is three feet, but it is evident that the gun never could have been used. It was no doubt made for show, from the bronze of captured cannon. In the same court are arranged the spoils of 1812, consisting of nearly a thousand cannon, French and German. They are mostly small field pieces, and hence make but little display, in spite of their number. The Turkish and Persian guns, some of which are highly ornamented, occupy the opposite side of the court, and are much the finest of all the trophies here.

We will now enter the churches in the palace court. They are but of modern dimensions, and very plain, outwardly, except in their crowns of far-shining golden domes. Undoubtedly they were once painted in the style of the Cathedral of St. Basil, but the rainbow frescoes are now covered with a uniform coat of whitewash. One is therefore all the more dazzled by the pomp and glare of the interior. The walls, the five domes, resting on four tall pillars at their intersections, the pillars themselves, everything but the floor, is covered with a coating of flashing gold; the *ikonostast*, or screen before the Holy of Holies, is of gilded silver and rises to the roof; the altars are of massive silver, and the shrine-pictures are set in a blaze of diamonds, emeralds, and rubies. A multitude of saints are painted on the walls, and seem to float in a golden sky. And not saints alone, but—strange to say—classic philosophers and historians. Thucydides and Plutarch, in company with Sts. Anthony and Jerome! There are said to be 2,300 figures in this church, which is much more than the number of worshippers who can find place within it. I have been there on Sunday, when it was thronged, and really there was less diversity of visage, costume, and character among the pictures above than among the human beings below. It was a wonderful crowd! I could have picked out the representatives of fifty nations and the facial stamp of three centuries. The singing was sublime. The choir was unseen, behind the silver screen, and the sweetness and purity of the boy sopranos swelled and sank like a chorus of angels heard through the fitful gusts of a storm. Devotional music nowhere receives such glorious expression as in the Russian churches.

The Cathedral of the Archangel Michael, but a few paces distant from that of the Assumption, resembles it in its internal structure. It is more dimly lighted, however, the gold is not so glaring, and, in place of the army of saints, there are large frescoes of Heaven, Hell, Judgment, &c. On the floor, arranged in rows, are the sarcophagi of the early Tzars, from Ivan I. to Alexis, father of Peter the Great. They are covered with dusty, mouldering palls of cloth or velvet, each one inscribed with his name. In the middle of the church in a splendid silver coffin, is the body of a boy seven or eight years of age, which is universally believed to be that of the young Demetrius, the last prince of the race of Rurik, who was put to death by Boris Gudonoff. The lid of the coffin is open, and on the inner side is a portrait of the boy, in a frame of massive gold studded with jewels. The body is wrapped in cloth of gold, and a cushion covers the face. The attendant priest was about to remove this cushion, when our guide whispered to me, "You are expected to kiss the forehead," and I turned away. These relics are ranked among the holiest in Moscow, and are most devoutly worshipped, although it is by no means certain that they belong to the true Demetrius.

Close at hand is the House of the Holy Synod, and as we are accompanied by our obliging Consul, Col. Claxton, to whom all doors are open, we are admitted into the sanctuary where are preserved the robes worn by Russian Patriarchs during the last six hundred years, as well as the silver jars containing the sacred oil, used for solemn sacraments throughout the whole Empire. The robes are of the heaviest silk, inwoven with gold and silver thread, and so sown with jewels that they would stand stiff upright with their own richness. The Patriarchs seem to have had an especial fondness for pearls, of which, in some instances, the embroidered figures are entirely composed. In strong contrast to these dazzling vestments are the coarse brown hat and mantle of the Patriarch Nichon. The holy oil is preserved in thirty-three jars, which, as well as the larger vessels used in preparing it, are of massive silver. About two gallons a year are necessary to supply Russia. The council hall of the Holy Synod is in the same building. It is evidently the ancient place of assembly—a long low room, with sacred frescoes on a golden ground, and raised seats along the wall for the principal personages.

Let us now turn from the sacred to the secular sights of the Kremlin, although some of the latter are not less sacred, to Russian eyes. The palace doors open to the special permit presented by Col. Claxton, and we ascend the broad, noble staircase. The plain exterior of the building gives no hint of the splendors within. I have seen all the palaces of Europe (with the exception of the Escurial), but I cannot recall one in which the highest possible magnificence is so subservient to good taste, as here. Inlaid floors, of such beautiful design and such precious wood, that you tread upon them with regret; capitals, cornices, and ceiling-soffits of gold; walls overlaid with fluted silk; giant candelabra of silver and malachite, and the soft gleam of many-tinted marbles, combine to make this a truly Imperial residence. The grand hall of St. George, all in white and gold, is literally incrusted with ornamented carved-work; that of St. Alexander Nevsky is sumptuous in blue and gold; of St. Wladimar in crimson and gold; while in that of St. Elizabeth, the walls are not only overlaid with gold, and the furniture of massive silver, but in the centre of every door is a Maltese cross, formed of the largest diamonds! The eye does not tire of this unwonted splendor, nor does it seem difficult to dwell even in such dazzling halls. In a lower story is the banqueting-hall, hung with crimson velvet, studded with golden eagles. Here the Emperor feasts with his nobles on the day of coronation—the only occasion on which it is used.

The dwelling rooms are fitted up with equal magnificence, except those occupied by the Emperor himself, in which the furniture is very plain and serviceable. In some of these rooms we found everything topsy-turvy. Officers were busy in taking an inventory of the furniture, even to the smallest articles, in order that a stop may be put to the wholesale plunder which has been carried on in the imperial household, since the death of Peter the Great. The dishonesty of Russian officials is a matter of universal noto riety, and Alexander II. is doing his part to check and punish it. He has not been the slightest sufferer. During the coronation, 40,000 lamps were bought for the illumination of the Kremlin, and now, not one is to be found! Thousands of yards of crimson cloth, furnished on the same occasion, have disappeared, and enormous charges appear in the bills for articles which were never bought at all. All Moscow was laughing over one of these discoveries, which is too amusing not to tell, although I may offend strict ideas of propriety in relating it. In the suite of the Empress were fifty chosen Ladies of Honor, who, of course, were lodged and entertained at the Imperial expense. When the bills came to be settled it was found that, in furnishing the bed-chambers of these fifty ladies, 4,500 utensils of a useful character had been purchased, or no less than *ninety* apiece!

A part of the ancient Palace of the Tzars—all that was left by fire and Frenchmen—forms the rear wing of the building. It is very much in the style of the Cathedral of St. Basil—irregular, fantastic, and covered with a painted tangle of scrolls, vines, flowers, and birds. The apartments of the Tzarina and children, the private chapel, audience-room, and *terema* or inclosed balcony, are still quite perfect. From the latter, it is said, Napoleon watched the progress of the fire, the night after his arrival in Moscow. On the ancient tables stand the treasure-chests of the Tzar Alexis—five large boxes of massive gold, covered with inscriptions in the old Slavonian character. If such were the chests, what must have been the treasure? But really, before one gets through with the Kremlin, gold and jewels become drugs. You still delight in their blaze and beauty, but you cease to be impressed by their value.

This warns me that the words, too, in which I have been endeavoring to describe these things, may at last lose their color and force, from sheer repetition. I shall there fore barely mention the last, and perhaps the most interesting sight of all—The Treasury. I know no historical museum in Europe of such magnificence, although there may be others more technically complete. Here, crowns and thrones are as plenty as mineralogical specimens elsewhere. In one hall are the jewelled thrones of Ivan III., Boris Gudonoff, Michael Romanoff, Peter the Great and his brother, and of Poland; while between them, each resting on a crimson cushion, on its separate pillar, are the crowns of those monarchs, and of the subject kingdoms of Siberia, Poland, Kazan, Novgorod, and the Crimea. In another case is the sceptre of Poland, broken in the centre, and the Constitution of that ill-fated country lies in a box at the feet of Alexander I.'s portrait. There are also the litter of Charles XII., taken at Pultava; the heavy jack-boots of the great Peter; the jewelled horse-trappings of Catharine II., her equestrian portrait in male attire (and a gallant, dashing, strapping cavalier she is!), the helmet of Michael Romanoff—curiously enough, with an Arabic sentence over the brow—and a superb collection of arms, armor, military trappings, golden and silver vessels, and antique jewelry. A lower room contains the imperial coaches and sleds, for nearly two centuries back.

Can you wonder now, even after the little I have found room to say, that the Kremlin is looked upon by the Russian people with fond and faithful veneration?

CHAPTER XXXI.

A VISIT TO THE FOUNDLING HOSPITAL.

It was a pleasant change to me to turn my eyes, dazzled by the splendors of the Kremlin, upon an edifice which has neither gold nor jewels to show, but which illustrates the patriarchal, or rather *paternal*, character of the Russian Government, on the grandest scale. This is the *Vospitatelnoi Dom*, or Foundling Hospital—but the title conveys no idea of the extent and completeness of this imperial charity. There are similar institutions in Paris, Stockholm, Vienna, and other cities, on a much more contracted scale. Our New York asylum for children, on Randall's Island, though a most beneficent establishment, is still more limited in its operations than the latter. In Russia the Foundling Hospital is characterized by some peculiar and very intersting features, which deserve to be generally known, as they are intimately connected with one of those tender moral questions *our* civilization is afraid to handle.

In every general view of Moscow, the eye is struck by an immense quadrangular building, or collection of build ings, on the northern bank of the Moskva, directly east of the Kremlin. The white front towers high over all the neighboring part of the city, and quite eclipses, in its imposing appearance, every palace, church, military barrack, or other public building whatever. It cannot be much less than a thousand feet in length, and, at a venture, I should estimate its size at three times that of the Capitol at Washington. The Governorship of this institution is only second in importance to that of the city itself, and is always conferred upon a nobleman of distinguished rank and attainments. The importance of the post may be estimated when I state that the annual expenses of the hospital amount to $5,000,000. A portion of the Government revenues are set aside for this purpose, in addition to which successive Tzars, as well as private individuals, have richly endowed it. The entire property devoted to the support, maintenance, and education of foundlings in Russia, is said to amount to the enormous sum of five hundred millions of dollars.

This stupendous institution was founded by Catharine II., immediately after her accession to the throne in 1762. Eight years afterwards, she established a branch at St. Petersburg, which has now outgrown the parent concern, and is conducted on a still more magnificent scale. The original design appears to have been to furnish an asylum for illegitimate children and destitute orphans. A lying-in hospital was connected with it, so that nothing might be left undone to suppress crime and misery in a humane and charitable way. The plan, however, was soon enlarged so as to embrace *all* children who might be offered, without question or stipulation, the parents, naturally, giving up their offspring to the service of the Government which had reared them. Russia offers herself as midwife, wet-nurse, mother, and teacher, to every new soul for whom there is no place among the homes of her people, and nobly and conscientiously does she discharge her self-imposed duty. She not only takes no life (capital punishment, I believe, does not exist), but she saves thousands annually. She, therefore, autocracy as she is, practically carries into effect one of the first articles of the ultra-socialistic code.

Through Col. Claxton's kindness, I obtained permission to visit the Foundling Hospital. We were received by the Superintendent, a lively intelligent gentleman, with half a dozen orders at his button-hole. Before conducting us through the building, he stated that we would see it to less advantage than usual, all the children being in the country for the summer, with the exception of those which had been received during the last few weeks. There is a large village about thirty versts from Moscow, whose inhabitants devote themselves entirely to the bringing up of these foundlings. We first entered a wing of the building, appropriated to the orphan children of officers. There were then one thousand two hundred in the institution, but all of them, with the exception of the sucklings, were enjoying their summer holidays in the country. It was the hour for their mid-day nap, and in the large, airy halls lay a hundred and fifty babes, each in its little white cot, covered with curtains of fine gauze. Only one whimpered a little; all the others slept quietly. The apartments were in the highest possible state of neatness, and the nurses, who stood silently, with hands folded on their breasts, bowing as we passed, were also remarkably neat in person.

These children enjoy some privileges over the foundlings and poorer orphans. The boys are taught some practical science or profession, and not unfrequently receive places as officers in the army. The girls receive an excellent education, including music and modern languages, and become teachers or governesses. As the larger children were all absent, I could form no idea of the manner of their instruction, except from an inspection of the school and class rooms, the appearance of which gave a good report. The Superintendents and Teachers are particularly required to watch the signs of any decided talent in the children, and, where such appears to develop it in the proper direction. Thus, excellent musicians, actors, painters, engineers, and mechanics of various kinds, have been produced, and the poor and nameless children of Russia have risen to wealth and distinction.

On our way to the Hospital proper, we passed through the Church, which is as cheerful and beautiful a place of devotion as I had seen since leaving the Parthenon. The walls are of scagliola, peach-blossom color, brightened, but not overloaded with golden ornaments. The dome, well painted in fresco, rests on pillars of the same material, and the tall altar screen, though gilded, is not glaring, nor are the Saints abnormal creatures, whose like is not to be found in Heaven or Earth. The *prestol*, or inmost shrine, stands under a dome, whose inner side contains a choral circle of lovely blonde-haired angels, floating in a blue, starry sky. All parts of the vast building are most substantially and carefully constructed. The walls are of brick or stone, the floors of marble or glazed tiles in the corridors, and the stair-cases of iron. The courts inclose garden-plots, radiant with flowers. The arrangements for heating and ventilation are admirable. With such care, one would think that a naturally healthy child would be as sure to live as a sound egg to be hatched in the Egyptian ovens.

We passed through hall after hall, filled with rows of little white cots, beside each of which stood a nurse, either watching her sleeping charge, or gently rocking it in her arms. Twelve hundred nurses and twelve hundred babies! This is homoculture on a large scale. Not all the plants would thrive; some helpless little ones would perhaps that day give up the unequal struggle, and, before men and women are produced from the crop there sown, the number will be diminished by one-third. The condition in which they arrive, often brought from a long distance, in rough weather, accounts for the mortality. When we consider, however, that the deaths, both in Moscow and St. Petersburg, annually exceed the births, it is evident that the Government takes better care of its children than do the parents themselves. Of the babies we saw, seven had been brought in on the day of our visit, up to the time of our arrival, and fourteen the previous day. The nurses were stout, healthy, ugly women, varying from twenty to forty years of age. They all wore the national costume— a dress bordered with scarlet, white apron, and a large, fan-shaped head-dress of white and red. In every hall there was a lady-like, intelligent overseeress. In spite of the multitude of babies, there was very little noise, and the most nervous old bachelor might have gone the round without once having his teeth set on edge.

The superintendent then conducted us to the office of agency, on the lower story, where the children are received The number of clerks and desks, and the library of records showed the extent of the business done. I looked over a report of the operations of the institution, from its foundation to the present time. The number of children confided to its care has increased from a few hundred in 1762 to 14,000 in 1857. Since the commencement of the year (Jan. 13, O. S.) 6,032 had arrived. The entire number received in ninety-six years is 330,000, to which may be added 60,000 more, born in the lying-in hospital during the same period—making 390,000 in all. The Petersburg branch affords still larger returns, so that at present 30,000 children are annually given into the care of the Government. A very large proportion of them are the offspring of poor married people, in all parts of the country. As the children may afterward be reclaimed, on certain conditions, and are in any case assured of as fortunate a lot, at least, as would have been theirs at home, the parents are the more easily led to take advantage of this charity. The child is taken without question, and therefore no reliable statistics of the public morality can be obtained from this source.

The office is kept open night and day, and no living child which is offered can be refused. The only question asked is, whether it has been baptized. If not, the ceremony is immediately performed in an adjoining room, by a priest connected with the institution, one of the oldest nurses, generally, acting as godmother. Its name and number are then entered in the official book, a card containing their and the date of its arrival is attached to its neck, and another given to the mother, so that it may afterwards be identified and reclaimed. Very frequently, the mother is allowed to become its nurse, in which case she receives pay like the other nurses. After six weeks or two months in the institution, it is sent into the country, where it remains until old enough to receive instruction. The regular nurses are paid at the rate of about $50 a year, in addition to their board and lodging. If the parents pay a sum equal to $25 on the deposition of the infant, they are entitled to have it brought up exclusively within the walls of the institution, where it is more carefully attended to than elsewhere. The payment of $200 procures for it, if a boy, the rank of an officer. The parents are allowed to see their children at stated times, and many of them take advantage of this permission. The greater part, however, live in the provinces, and virtually give up their children to the State; though it is always possible by consulting the Hospital directory, to find where the latter are, and to recover them.

In the lying-in hospital, all women are received who apply. They are allowed to enter one month before their confinement, and to remain afterwards until their health is entirely restored. Those who wish to be unknown are concealed by a curtain which falls across the middle of th bed, so that their faces are never seen. Besides this, no one is allowed to enter the hospital except the persons actually employed within it. The late Emperor, even, respected its privacy, and at once gave up his desire to enter, on the representations of the Governor. The arrange ments are said to be so excellent that not only poor married women, but many who are quite above the necessity of such a charity, take advantage of it. In this case, also, the number of children brought forth is no evidence as to the proportion of illegitimate births. It is not obligatory upon the mother to leave her child in the hospital; she may take it with her if she chooses, but it will of course be received, if offered.

Besides the soldiers, common mechanics, and factory girls, which the children of merely ordinary capacity become, the Government has, of late years, established many of them as farmers and colonists on the uncultivated crown lands. They are mated, married, and comfortably settle in villages, where, in addition to their agricultural labors, they frequently take charge of a younger generation of foundlings. I have seen some of these villages where the houses were all neat Swiss cottages, under the projecting eaves of which the families sat in the mild evening air, while groups of sprightly children, too nearly of an age to belong to the occupants, sported before them. The people looked happy and prosperous. If there is a patriotic peasantry on earth, they should certainly belong to it. They are, in the fullest sense of the term, children of their country.

The St. Petersburg Hospital, though in the heart of the city, covers, with its dependencies, twenty-eight acres of ground. Upwards of five hundred teachers are employed many of them on very high salaries. The number of nurses, servants, and other persons employed in the establishment, amounts to upward of five thousand. The boys and girls, both there and in Moscow, are taught separately. The cost of their education, alone, is more than $1,000,000 annually. In a word, Russia spends on her orphans and castaways as much as the entire revenues of Sweden, Norway, and Greece.

Let us not be so dazzled, however, by the splendid liberality of this charity, as to lose sight of the moral question which it involves. No other nation has yet instituted such a system; few other governments would dare do it at present. What effect has it had on public morals? It has existed for nearly a century, and whatever influence it may exercise, either for good or evil, must now be manifest. One fact is certain—that the number of children delivered into its keeping, has steadily increased from year to year; but this, as I have already shown, is no indication whatever. The growth of its resources, the perfection of its arrangements, and the liberal education which it bestows sufficiently explain this increase. In the absence of reliable moral statistics, we are obliged, simply, to draw a parallel between the condition of the Russians, in this respect, at present, and the accounts given of them in the last century. Judging from these data, I do not hesitate to declare that the effect of the system has *not* been detrimental to the general morality of the Russian people. On the contrary they have improved with the improvement in their condition and the gradual advance of civilization. When I compare the chronicles of Richard Chancellor, and of Sir John Chardin, two and a half centuries ago, with what I see now, I can scarcely realize that they are the same people

"But," cries a Pharisee, "this Hospital affords an easy and secret relief to the sinner. By saving her from public shame, it encourages her in private vice! It removes the righteous penalty placed upon incontinence, and thereby gradually demoralizes society!" I do not deny that the relief here afforded *may* increase the number of individuals who need it, but I assert, in all earnestness, that the moral tone of "Society" would not be lowered thereby, seeing that, where one licentious act *may be* encouraged, one awful crime is certainly prevented. *In Russia, infanticides and abortions are almost unknown.* In America, one need but look at what is *discovered.* God only knows how many additional cases of the crime most abhorent to human nature are perpetrated in secret. And yet, if some benevolent millionare should propose to build such a foundling hospital in New-York, pulpit and press would riddle him with the red-hot shot of holy indignation. Oh, no! Let the subject alone—your fingers, of course, are white, and were not meant to handle pitch. No matter what crimes are eating their way into the moral heart of Society, so long as all is fair on the outside. Let the unwedded mother finding no pity or relief for her, and no place in the world for her unlawful offspring, murder it before it is born! This is better than to stretch out a helping hand to her and so prevent the crime. Ten to one, the act is never found out; appearances are preserved, and our sanctified prudery is unruffled.

It is a great mistake to suppose that the moral tone of Society can only be preserved by making desperate outcasts of all who sin. So long as we preserve a genuine domestic life—so long as we have virtuous homes, liberal education and religious influences—we need not fear that a Christian charity like that which I have described will touch our purity. It will only cleanse us from the stain of the blackest of crimes. The number of illegitimate births would be ncreased by the diminution in the number of abortions Who will dare to say that the reverse is preferable? We boast, and with some justice, of the superior morality of our population, as compared with that of the nations of Europe; but we should know that in none of the latter is infanticide (both before and after birth) so common as with us. We should remember that a morality which is uncharitable, cruel, and Pharisaic, inevitably breeds a secret immorality. The Spartan holiness of the New England pilgrims was followed by a shocking prevalence of unnatural vice, which diminished in proportion as their iron discipline was relaxed.

At any rate, we can never err by helping those who are in trouble, even though that trouble have come through vice. I have never heard that the Magdalen Societies have increased the number of prostitutes, and I do not believe that a foundling hospital would encourage seduction or adultery. To change one word in the immortal lines of Burns:

"What's done, we partly may compute,
But know not what's *prevented.*"

CHAPTER XXXII.

MOSCOW, IN-DOORS AND OUT.

WERE I a painter of the Dutch or Flemish school, I could bring you many a characteristic sketch of Moscow life. Here, especially, such subjects require form and color, and their accompanying "still life," and are therefore only to be made intelligible by the pen after the pencil has gone before. But there are few, if any, *genre* pictures in Russia. The most distinguished artist the country has yet produced —Bruloff—painted goddesses, nymphs, saints, and the Destruction of Pompeii. The streets of Moscow are full of subjects, many of which are peculiarly interesting, as they illustrate features of Russian life which must soon change or disappear. The istvostchiks, with their squat black hats, splendid beards, and blue caftans; the double-waisted peasant women at the street shrines; the bare-headed serf, bowing and crossing himself, with his eyes fixed on a distant church; the shabby merchants in the second-hand markets, with their tables of heterogeneous wares; the vaulted avenues of the Gostinnoi Dvor, and the curious stalls in the Kitai Gorod; the vegetable markets, the sellers of *qvass*, the wood-boatmen on the Moskva and the Tartars at their mosque, all furnish studies to the stranger, whether he be painter or author. It would require a long residence, to exhaust the interest of the city, in this respect.

To one who has seen the bazaars of Constantinople, the Gostinnoi Dvor presents no new features. It is low, arched above and paved under foot, and each avenue or part of an avenue is devoted to a particular kind of merchandise. The inside is a perfect labyrinth, and no little time is necessary in order to learn the geographical arrangement of the shops. If you want nails you may wander through the various departments devoted to linen, woollen, silk, and cotton goods, jewels, wax candles, tar, and turpentine, before you get to iron. Buttons are in one direction and tape in another; sugar behind you, and spoons far ahead. As you walk down the dimly-lighted passages, you are hailed with invitations to buy, on all sides; the merchants hang with expectation on the turning of your head, and receive with ecstacy the accidental glance of your eye. This desire to have you for a customer does not prevent them from asking much more than they expect to receive, and if you have the least inclination to buy, no one is so stony-hearted as to let you go away empty-handed.

The shops of the jewelers are interesting, from the variety of precious stones, chiefly from the mountains of Siberia, which are to be found in them. The jewels most fashionable in Moscow at present are diamonds, emeralds, pearls, and turquoises. Opals also bring a large price, but stones of secondary order, such as topaz, garnet, amethyst, onyx, and aqua-marine, are plentiful and cheap Siberia produces superb emeralds, and the finest amethysts, aqua-marines, and topazes I ever saw. The Siberian diamond, which is found in abundance in the Ural Mountains, appears to be neither more nor less than a white topaz. A necklace of seventy-five of these stones, the size of a cherry, costs a little less than $20. I noticed a few fine sapphires, but suspect that they found their way thither from India, through Persia. One jeweler showed me a jacinth, a rather rare stone with a splendid scarlet fire, for which he demanded fifty rubles. There were also some glorious opals, darting their lambent rays of pink, green, blue and pearl-white, but their value was equal to their beauty. Malachite and lapiz-lazuli, so common in Russian palaces and churches, are dear, and good specimens are not easy to be had.

In this bazaar you are struck by the smooth, sallow faces of the money-changers, and a certain mixture of weakness and cunning in their expression. You are therefore not surprised when you learn that they are all eunuchs. I endeavored, but in vain, to discover the cause of this singular fact. The money-changers, so say the people, have for centuries past constituted a peculiar class, or guild. They are very rich, naturally clannish on account of their mutilation, and accept no new member into their body who has not undergone a like preparation. As voluntary converts to such a sect must be very scarce, they would in time become extinct if they did not purchase, at a heavy cost, the sons of poor parents, who are qualified at an age when they can neither understand nor resist their fate.

The Government has prohibited this practice under very severe penalties, and the vile brotherhood will probably soon cease to exist.

The Riadi, an open bazaar in the Kitai Gorod, deserves to be next visited. It is less ostentatious in its character, but exhibits even a greater diversity of shops and wares, and is thronged from sunrise until sunset with purchasers and traders. Here you find everything which the common Russian requires for his domestic life, his religion, his birth, marriage, and death. For a few copeks you may drink a ladle of *qvass,* eat a basin of the national *shtshee* (cabbage soup) or *botvinia* (an iced soup full of raw cucumbers and various other indigestibles), and finish with a glass of the fiery *vodki*. The latter, however, generally comes first, as in Sweden. Wax candles of all sizes are here displayed, and the collection of patron saints is truly astonishing. Brown Virgins predominate, but St. Nicholas, in a scarlet mantle, and St. George slaying the Dragon, are also great favorites. As in Russia no house is built and no room occupied, without the presence of a saint, the trade in the Byzantine Lares and Penates is very great. No Russian, of whatever rank, enters a house, however humble, without uncovering his head. It is an act of religion rather than of courtesy.

The fondness of the common people for pictures is remarkable. To say nothing of the saints and illustrations of Biblical history which you meet with on all sides, there are shops and booths filled entirely with caricatures or allegorical subjects. The most favorite of these seems to be the punishment of avarice. Rich old sinners, with puffy cheeks and fat round bellies, grasping a bag of specie in each hand, are seized by devils, pricked with pitchforks, or torn limb from limb. Another picture illustrates the two ways—one broad and easy, the other winding and difficult, one terminating in flames and devils, and the other at the feet of a dark-brown Virgin. Crinoline, even, is satirized in some of the caricatures. Others, again, are more than broad in their fun, and, if there are ladies in your company, you would do best not to look at them. The drawing in these pictures is of the rudest and wretchedest kind; but there is always a printed explanation at the foot of the sheet, so that you cannot fail to know what is meant.

At the Second-Hand Markets, of which there are several, one finds the oddest collection of old articles, from English novels to Arabic seal-rings, from French hats to Chinese shoes, from ancient crucifixes to damaged modern crinolines. The world's refuse seems to have been swept together here. It would be difficut to name any article which you could not find. I wandered for an hour through one of these markets, near the Soukhoreff Tower, and the only things which I could think of and did not see, were a coal-scuttle and an oyster-knife. However, I made but a partial survey, and do not doubt but that both the articles were there somewhere. One of the stupidest and greasiest of the merchants had a second-hand mineralogical collection for sale. A boy who could not read offered me some German theological books, of the most orthodox character. Looking up from my inspection of them, I saw around me grass, soap, wagon-gear, garlic, sofas, crockery, guitars, crucifixes, oil cloth, and cheese! Singularly enough, the buyers represented all classes of society, from serfs up to officers in full uniform and ladies of the widest periphery.

Let us escape from this variegated and somewhat bewildered crowd, and seek a little fresh air further from the busy heart of the city. A friend proposes a ride to Astankina and Petroffskoi, which lie a short distance outside the barrier, on the northern side. We have but to cry "*davai!*" (here!) and a dozen istvostchiks answer to the call. They are very jolly fellows, and their hats—like the old bell-crown of thirty years ago, razeed—give them a smart and jaunty air, in spite of the blue cloth caftan, which reaches to their heels. They have all ruddy faces, stumpy noses, bluish-gray eyes, and beards of exactly the same cut and color, whatever their build and physiognomy. The old national droshky, which most of them drive, is a hybrid between the Norwegian cariole and the Irish jaunting car—a light, low, jolting thing, but cheap and sufficiently convenient. If there is one passenger he sits astride; if two, side-wise. The istvostchik sits also astride, in front, and it is not the most agreeable feature of his nature, that he always eats garlic. His feet rest on the frame of the vehicle, close to the horse's heels, from which, or from the mud, he is not protected by any dashboard. I inferred from this fact that the Russian horses are unusually well-behaved, and am told that it is really the case. It is a very unusual thing for one of them to kick while in harness. There are no such hack-horses in the world. Without an exception they are handsome, well-conditioned spirited animals. The istvostchik differs from all other hackmen, in the circumstance that it is impossible for him to drive slowly. If you are not in a hurry, he always is. As there is no established tax, the fare must be agreed upon beforehand, but it does not usually amount to more than twelve cents a mile. A handsome open calèche, with two orses, can be had for three dollars a day. There is more or less Ukraine blood in the common Moscow horses.

The fields around the city are principally devoted to the cultivation of vegetables. Companies of women, singing in shrill chorus, were hoeing and weeding among them, as we drove over the rolling swell towards Astankina. This is a summer palace and park belonging to Count Cheremetieff. The grounds are laid out in the style of Versailles, and kept in excellent order. One is astonished at the richness and luxuriance of the foliage, and the great variety of trees which are found in this severe climate. The poplar, the linden, the locust, the elm, the ash, and the horse-chesnut thrive very well, with a little care and protection. Around the garden, with its clipped hedges, flower-beds and statues, stretches for many a verst a forest of tall firs, which breaks the violence of the winter winds. Here was the scene of one of those gigantic pieces of flattery, by which the courtiers of Catharine II. sought to win or keep her favor. During a visit of that Empress to Astankina, she remarked to the proprietor: "Were it not for the forest, you would be able to see Moscow." The latter immediately set some thousands of serfs to work, and in a few days afterwards prevailed upon the Empress to pay him another visit. "Your Majesty," he said, "regretted that the forest should shut out my view of Moscow. It shall do so no longer." He thereupon waved his hand, and there was a movement among the trees. They rocked backward and forward a moment, tottered, and fell crashing together, breaking a wide avenue through the forest, at the end of which glittered in the distance the golden domes of the city.

Petroffskoi is a a glaring, fantastic palace, on the St. Petersburg road, about two miles from Moscow. It was built by the Empress Elizabeth, and its architecture seems to have been borrowed from that of the Kremlin. Here Napoleon took up his quarters, after being roasted out of the latter place. Hence also started the coronation procession of Alexander II., probably one of the grandest pageants ever witnessed in Europe. The park, which is traversed by handsome carriage-roads, is at all times open to the public, and on a clear summer evening, when whole families of the middle class come hither, bringing their samovars, and drinking their tumblers of tea flavored with lemonpeel, in the shade of the birch and linden groves, the spectacle is exceedingly animated and cheerful. There is also in this park a summer theatre, in which French vaudevilles are given.

Moscow, however, can boast of possessing a spot for summer recreation, the like of which is not to be found in Paris. The Hermitage, the principal resort of the fashionable world, is a remarkably picturesque garden, with a theatre and concert hall in the open air. It lies upon the side of a hill, at the foot of which is a little lake, embowered in trees. Beyond the water rise massive zigzag walls, the fortifications of a Tartar city, whose peaked roofs climb an opposite hill, and stretch far away into the distance, the farthest towers melting into the air. And yet the whole thing is a scenic illusion. Three canvas frames, not a hundred yards from your eye, contain the whole of it. Thousands of crimson lamps illuminate the embowered walks, and on the top of the hill is a spacious auditorium, inclosed by lamp-lit arches. On a stage at one end are assembled a company of Russian gipsies, whose songs are as popular here as the Ethiopian melodies are with us. The gipsies are born singers, and among the young girls who sing tonight there are two or three voices which would create an excitement even on the boards of the Italian Opera. The prima donna is a superb contralto, whom the Russians consider second only to Alboni. She is a girl of twenty-two, with magnificent hair of raven blackness, and flashing black eyes.

There are from twenty-five to thirty singers, in all, of whom two-thirds are females. A portion, only, appear to be of pure gipsy blood, with the small deep-set eyes and the tawny skin of Egypt. Others are bright blond, with blue eyes, betraying at once their parentage and the immorality of the tribe. The leader, a tall, slender, swarthy man with a silver belt around his waist, and a guitar in his hand, takes his station in front of the women, who are seated in a row across the stage, and strikes up a wild, barbaric melody, to which the whole troop sing in chorus. It is music of a perfectly original character, with an undertone of sadness, such as one remarks in the songs of all rude nations, yet with recurring melodies which delight the ear, and with a complete harmony in the arrangement of the parts. Afterwards the swarthy soprano sings the favorite "*Troika*" (three-horse team), gliding through the singular breaks and undulations of the melody with a careless ease, to which the exquisite purity of her voice gives the highest charm. In the course of the evening there was a dance, which resembled in many respects that of the Arab ghawazees, although not quite so suggestive.

My time was so much occupied by the many sights which I have been endeavoring to paint for the reader, that I saw but little of Moscow society. Besides, my visit happened at an unfavorable time, so many families being absent in the country or on their travels. The breaking down of the obstacles which the late Emperor threw in the way of Russians leaving their country, immediately poured a flood of Russian travel upon the rest of Europe. Of the persons to whom I had letters of introduction—among them the distinguished author, Pawlow—not one was at home. Through the kindness of Col. Claxton, however, I made some very pleasant acquaintances, and had a glimpse, at least, of Russian society.

At a soirée one evening I was very agreeably impressed with the manners of the ladies. French is still the language of society, even with the Russians themselves, and a knowledge of it is quite indispensable to the stranger. English and German are occasionally spoken, and with that ease and purity of accent for which the Russians are distinguished. I was glad to find that those whom I met, ladies as well as gentlemen, were thoroughly familiar with their own authors. A number of names, which I had never heard of before, were mentioned with enthusiasm. There are several literary papers in Moscow, with a circulation of from twelve to fourteen thousand copies each.

Among the editors and literary men of Moscow I found some very intelligent gentlemen. I was agreeably surprised at the freedom with which the political condition of the country, and the reforms in progress, are discussed. The prevailing sentiment was that of entire satisfaction—a satisfaction best expressed by the earnestness and brevity of the exclamation: "If it will only last!" With regard to the emancipation of the serfs, I was told that public opinion is decidedly in favor of it, including a large majority of the proprietors. The fact that the serfs themselves, under the knowledge of the great change which awaits them, are so quiet and patient, is considered a promising sign. The most difficult question connected with the reform is that of attaching the latter, for a time at least, to the domains. They have the Nomadic blood of the Tartars, and the attempt is being made to achieve by *self-interest* what has been hitherto done by force. But the nobles will not give their land for nothing, and the serfs will not pay for what they now have gratis. A compromise is therefore proposed, by which the serfs receive their houses, and will be allowed to purchase a certain portion of land on easy terms, if they choose.

In Russia old things are now passing away, and a new order of things is coming into existence. Many curious characteristics and customs which bear the stamp of five centuries, are beginning to disappear, and this change is at last making itself felt even in Moscow—the very focus of Russian nationality. When the Locomotive once enters a city the ghosts of the Past take flight for ever. Those sounding highways of international communication are more potent than any ukase of Peter the Great to wean the people from their cherished superstitions. Moscow may thus, gradually, lose its power of reproducing the past conditions of the Russian people, but it will always faithfully reflect their character. It will always remain the illuminated title-page to the history of the empire. Other capitals may, in the course of time, be built on the shores of the Caspian or the banks of the Amoor, but they will never take away from Moscow its peculiar distinction of representing and illustrating the history, the growth, the religion, the many-sided individuality of Russia.

CHAPTER XXXIII.

RAILROADS IN RUSSIA.

On leaving Moscow for St. Petersburg we were obliged to take out fresh passports, giving up those which we had obtained in Warsaw. As one is required to appear personally, this formality is a little troublesome, but we were subjected to no questioning, and the documents were ready at the time promised. After paying the fees, we were about to leave, when the official whispered: "You have forgotten my tea-money." The readiness with which he changed a note, while the subordinates looked the other way, proved to me that this system of gratuities (to use a mild term) is not only general, but permitted by the higher authorities. Many of the civil officers have salaries ranging from six to ten rubles a month—barely enough to clothe them—so that without this "tea-money," the machinery of government would move very slowly.

I also went to the office of the Censor, to inquire concerning the fate of the books taken from me on the Polish frontier. Here I was very politely received, and was in formed that the books had not arrived. The Censor seemed a little embarrassed, and I half suspected that the books might be on the prohibited list. Kohl's work, I was informed, belongs to this class, although I saw, in the shop-windows, books which I should have supposed were much more objectionable than his. It is permitted to all literary and scientific men, however, to import freely whatever works they choose. The list of foreign newspapers admitted into Russia has recently been much enlarged, but they also pass through the Censor's hands, and one frequently sees paragraphs or whole columns either covered with a coating of black paste, or so nicely erased that no sign of printer's ink is left.

During our stay in Moscow we lodged at the *Hotel de Dresde*, which I can conscientiously recommend to future travellers. It is a large, low building on the Government square, at the corner of the Tverskaia Oulitza, and convenient to the Kremlin. The only discomfort, which it shares in common with the other hotels, is, that the servants are all Russian. We obtained a large, pleasant room for two rubles a-day, and a dinner, cooked in the most admirable style, for a ruble each. Other charges were in the same proportion; so that the daily expense was about $3. As there is no *table d'hôte*, the meals being served in one's own room, this is rather below New York prices. A German author, who resided two years in Moscow, gave me $1,000 as a fair estimate of the annual expense of living for a bachelor. House-rent and the ordinary necessaries of life are cheap; but luxuries of all kinds, clothing, etc., are very dear.

On the northern side of the city, just outside the low earthen barrier, stands the great Railroad Station. The principal train for St. Petersburg leaves daily at noon, and reaches its destination the next morning at eight—600 versts, or 400 English miles, in twenty hours. The fares are respectively 19, 13 and 9 rubles, for the first, second and third class. The station building is on the most imposing scale, and all the operations of the road are conducted with the utmost precision and regularity, although perhaps a little slower than in other countries. The first class carriages are divided into compartments, and luxuriously cushioned, as in England; the second-class are arranged exactly on the American plan (in fact, I believe they are built in America), except that the seats are not so closely crowded together. The entrance is at the end, over a platform on which the brakeman stands, as with us. As the day of our departure happened to be Monday, which is considered so unlucky a day among the Russians that they never travel when they can avoid it, there was just a comfortable number of passengers. We bade adieu to our obliging friend, Col. Claxton, whose kindness had contributed so much to the interest of our visit, and, as the dial marked noon, steamed off for St. Petersburg.

Straight as sunbeams, the four parallel lines of rail shoot away to the north-west, and vanish far off in a sharp point on the horizon. Woods, hills, swamps, ravines, rivers, may intersect the road, but it swerves not a hair from the direct course, except where such deflection is necessary to keep the general level between Moscow and the Volga. After passing the Valdai Hills, about half-way to St. Petersburg, the course is almost as straight as if drawn with a ruler for the remaining two hundred miles. The Russians say this road is only to be looked upon as an article of luxury. The Emperor Nicholas consulted his own convenience and the facility of conveying troops rather than the convenience of the country and the development of its resources. By insisting upon the shortest possible distance between the two cities, he carried the road for hundreds of versts through swamps where an artificial foundation of piles was necessary; while, by bending its course a little to the south, nearer the line of the highway, not only would these swamps have been avoided, but the cities of Novgorod, Valdai, and Torshok, with the settled and cultivated regions around them, would have shared in the advantages and added to the profits of the road.

In its construction and accessories, one can truly say that this is the finest railway in the world. Its only drawback is an occasional roughness, the cause of which, I suspect, lies in the cars rather than the road itself. There are thirty-three stations between Moscow and St. Petersburg. At the most of these, the station-houses are palaces, all built exactly alike, and on a scale of magnificence which scorns expense. A great deal of needless luxury has been wasted upon them. The bridges, also, are models of solidity and durability. Everything is on the grandest scale, and the punctuality and exactness of the running arrangements are worthy of all praise. But at what a cost has all this been accomplished! This road, 400 miles in length, over a level country, with very few cuts, embankments, and bridges, except between Moscow and Tver (about one-fourth of the distance), has been built at an expense of 120,000,000 of rubles ($90,000,000) or $225,000 per mile. When one takes into consideration the cheapness of labor in Russia, the sum becomes still more enormous.

The work was not only conducted by American engineers but Mr. Winans, the chief-engineer, is at present carrying on the running business under a contract with the Government. His principal assistants are also Americans. This contract, which was originally for ten years, has yet three years to run, at the end of which time Mr. Winans will be able to live upon what he has earned. His annual profit upon the contract is said to be *one million* rubles. Some idea of its liberal character may be obtained from the fact that his allowance for grease alone is three silver copeks a verst for each wheel—about 3½ cents a mile; or, with an ordinary train, some $700 for the run from Moscow to St. Petersburg. His own part of the contract is faithfully and admirably discharged, and he is of course fairly entitled to all he can make. It is not to be wondered at, however, that the receipts of the road in 1857 exceeded the expenditures by a few thousand rubles only.

The fact is, even yet, the road does not appear to be conducted with a view to profit. The way traffic and travel which railroad companies elsewhere make it a point to encourage, is here entirely neglected. There are none but through trains, and but a single passenger train daily. Besides this, no freight is taken at the way stations, **unless** there should happen to be a little room to spare, after the through freight is cared for. Tver, through which the road passes, is at the head of navigation on the Volga, and after Nijni Novgorod, the chief centre of trade with the regions watered by that mighty river, as far as the Caspian Sea; yet, I am informed, there is no special provision made for affording the facilities of communication which the place so much needs.

Russia, however, is soon to be covered with a general system of railroad communication, which, when completed, must exercise a vast influence on her productive and commercial activity. A road from Moscow to Nijni Novgorod on the Volga, where the grand annual fair is held, has been commenced, and will probably be finished in from three to five years. The distance is about 250 miles, and the estimated expense $50,000 per mile. The road from St. Petersburg to Warsaw—a little over 700 miles in length—has been in progress for some years past, and will be finished, it is said, by the close of the year 1860. In September, 1858, it was opened as far as Pskov (German "Pleskow"), at the head of Lake Peipus, and will probably reach Dwinaburg, whence a branch road to Riga is now building, in the course of 1859. Near Kovno it will be intersected by another branch from Königsburg, via Tilsit and Gumbinnen, whereby there will be a direct communication between St. Petersburg and Berlin.

The other projected roads, the building of which has been contracted for by a French company, but not yet commenced, are from Libau, on the Baltic, easterly through Witepsk and Smolensk to the large manufacturing town of Tula, 112 miles south of Moscow; and another from the latter city to Charkoff, in the Ukraine, with branches to

Odessa and the Crimea. The former of these will be nearly 700 miles in length, and the latter at least 1,000. The cheapest plan for the Russian Government to build railroads, would undoubtedly be, to permit the formation of private companies for that purpose. In Middle and Southern Russia, the cost of construction would certainly be no greater than in Illinois, where, if I remember rightly, the roads are built for half the amount of the lowest estimate I heard given in Moscow. The effect of these improvements upon the internal condition of Russia can hardly be overvalued. They are in fact but the commencement of a still grander system of communication, which, little by little, will thrust its iron feelers into Asia, and grapple with the inertia of four thousand years.

To return to our journey. The halts at the way stations were rather long—five, ten, fifteen minutes, and at Tver, where we arrived at five o'clock, half an hour for dinner. In this respect, as in every other, the arrangements were most convenient and complete. We had a good meal at a reasonable price, and were allowed a rational time to eat it. At every one of the other stations there was a neat booth provided with beer, qvass, soda water, lemonade, cigars, and pastry. Most of the passengers got out and smoked their cigarettes at these places, as the practice is not allowed inside the cars. There is a second-class carriage especially for smokers, but one is obliged to take out a license to smoke there, for which he pays ten rubles. The Russians are nearly all smokers, but the custom is very strictly prohibited in the streets of cities, and even in the small country villages.

The country, slightly undulating in the neighborhood of Moscow, becomes level as you approach the Volga. The monotony of which I have spoken in a previous chapter, is its prevailing characteristic. Great stretches of swamp or of pasture-ground, fields of rye and barley, and forests of fir and birch, succeed one another, in unvarying sameness. Now and then you have a wide sweep of horizon—a green sea, streaked with rosy foam-drifts of flowers—a luxuriant summer-tangle of copse and woodland, or a white village church, with green domes, rising over a silvery lake of rye; and these pictures, beautiful in themselves, do not become less so by repetition. The Volga is certainly the most interesting object in the whole course of the journey. Tver, a city of 20,000 inhabitants, on its right bank, is conspicuous from the number of its spires and domes. Along the bank lie scores of flat-bottomed barges, rafts, and vessels of light draft. The river here is scarcely so large as the Hudson at Albany, flowing in a sandy bed, with frequent shallows. But, like the Danube at Ulm, it is not the smallness of the stream which occupies your thoughts. You follow the waters, in imagination, to the old towns of Yaroslav and Nijni Novgorod, to the Tartar Kazan and the ruins of Bulgar, through the steppes of the Cossacks and Kirghizes, to the Caspian Sea and the foot of ancient Caucasus.

The sky was heavily overcast, so that, in spite of our high latitude, the night was dark. I therefore did not see the Valdai hills, which we passed towards midnight—the only real hills in Russia proper, west of the Ural Mountains. It was among these hills that Alexander I. intrenched himself, to await Napoleon. When the morning twilight came, we were in the midst of the swampy region, careering straight forward, on and on, over the boundless level. The only object of note was the large and rapid river Volchoff, flowing from the Ilmen Lake at Novgorod northward into Lake Ladoga. The road crosses it by a magnificent American bridge.

Some fifty or sixty versts before reaching St. Petersburg, we passed through a large estate belonging to the rich Russian, Kokoreff, who has lately been distinguishing himself by the prominent part he has taken in all measures tending to the improvement of his country—the emancipation of the serfs, the steamboat companies of the Dnieper and Dniester, the formation of a moneyed association for encouraging manufactures, &c. This Kokoreff was the son of a common peasant, and commenced life by keeping a cheap brandy-shop. He gradually prospered, and, being a man of much natural shrewdness and energy, took the contract for the brandy revenue of the whole Empire, which is farmed out. He is worth about seven millions of rubles, much of which he has invested in landed property. He has now set himself to work to introduce improvements in agriculture, and his estate presents a striking contrast to that of his neighbors. Neat, comfortable houses for the laborers, spacious barns for the grain, forests trimmed and protected, meadows drained, rough land cleared and prepared for culture—these were some of the features which struck my eye, as we rushed along. Kokoreff is charged by some with being extravagant and fantastic in his views, and therefore an unsafe example to follow; but a man who makes such an employment of his means, cannot do otherwise than work real and lasting good for his country.

By and by vegetable gardens succeeded to the swamps, villages became more frequent, houses, smoking factories, and workshops on our right, then a level, uniform mass of buildings, over which towered some golden-tipped spires, and at eight o'clock, precisely, we landed in the station at St. Petersburg.

CHAPTER XXXIV.

ST. PETERSBURG AND ITS PALACES.

No two cities can be more unlike than Moscow and St. Petersburg; they scarcely appear to have been built by the same people. Were it not for some of the older churches, which seem curiously out of place, a traveller coming from the former city, would imagine that he had already left Russia. The strange, fantastic, picturesque, Tartar character has disappeared, and all that one sees is suggestive of Western Europe. This is but the first impression, however. The second is that of a power so colossal as to coerce nature herself—a power which can only be developed when unbounded resources are placed under the direction of a single will—and herein we again recognise Russia. St. Petersburg is also a marvel in its way, and if the interest which it excites is of a totally different character from that which one feels in Moscow, it is no less imposing and permanent.

No man except Peter the Great would have conceived the idea of building a city here. Yet, if we leave out of sight the physical difficulties against which he had to contend, and consider not only the character of his ambition, but the inadequateness of any other site on the Baltic coast to meet its designs, we cannot see that he could have done otherwise. Had he selected Nijni Novgorod, as he first intended, the heart of Russian power would have been placed on the borders of Asia, still further from the influence of European civilization. Russia, in this case, would never have attained to a first place in the councils of European nations. It was necessary to approach the west. Finland and Livonia were at that time in the possession of Sweden, and Poland was still a nation. Peter's choice, therefore, was restricted to the shores of the Gulf of Finland. Here, truly, he might have found other sites presenting fewer natural obstacles, but at the same time fewer natural advantages. The Neva, through which the largest lake in Europe pours its waters into the sea, afforded a ready-made communication, not only with Novgorod and Onega, but with a large portion of that Finland whose acquisition he even then foresaw, while the island of Cronstadt, guarding the entrance from the Gulf, offered a fitting station for his infant navy. The extreme high latitude of the new capital was even an advantage: winter was his ally then, as it has been the best ally of Russia in later times. And the wisdom of his selection has just again been demonstrated, when the combined naval strength of Europe lay before Cronstadt and did not dare to attack it.

But nothing short of that genius, which is the same thing as madness in the eyes of the world, would have undertaken the work. Here, where the Neva, a broad, full, rapid stream, spreads itself out among swampy islands, completely flooding them when the spring freshets have burst the ice and where a strong south-west wind drives the waters of the Gulf high over the highest land the city stands upon, have arisen clusters of gigantic edifices, mountains of masonry, in their solid durability bidding defiance to the unstable soil. The marshy shores of the river are hidden under league-long quays of massive granite; millions of piles bear aloft the tremendous weight of palaces, churches, obelisks, and bridges; and four grand canals, passing through and around the city, so tap the Neva of his menacing strength that the fearful inundations of former years cannot be repeated. One hundred and fifty years have passed away since Peter built his cottage in the midst of an uninhabited wilderness, and now there stands on the spot one of the first of European capitals, with a population of more than half a million.

The town was first commenced on the northern bank of the Neva, on the *Aptekarskoi*, or Apothecary's Island. In cold climates, a man always builds his house fronting the south. Very soon, however, the southern bank received the preference, on account of its convenience and its proximity to a little rising ground. At present three-quarters of the city, if not more, are south of the Neva, the remaining portion being scattered over the two large islands of Aptekarskoi and Vassili Ostrov. Those who know Berlin, can form a tolerable idea of those parts of St. Petersburg distant from the river. The streets are alike broad and regular, the houses high, massive, and plain. But there is not the sameness and tameness of the Prussian capital.

Even in July, when the Court was absent, the fashionable world off on its travels, and nobody at home, it was as lively a city as one could well wish to see. Five thousand droshkies and as many carriages rattle hither and thither from morning till night—or rather, continuously, for you can see to read in the streets at midnight, and they are then by no means deserted. Where the summer is so fleeting it is doubly enjoyed, and during those long, delicious twilights, especially, no one remains indoors who can get out.

The approach to the city from the land side is particularly tame. On such a dead level the first block of buildings shuts out the view of everything beyond, and even when you reach the *Nevskoi Prospekt*—the Broadway of St. Petersburg—and look down its vista of three miles, the only thing you see is the gilded spire of the Admiralty Building, at the end. On the Neva, only, and the Admiralty Square, can you get anything like a picture broad enough to copy and carry away in your mind. Proceeding down the Nevskoi Prospekt to this central point, you are not particularly struck with the architecture on either hand. Everything is large, substantial, and imposing, but nothing more. Even the Annitshkoff Palace, which you see on the right, as you approach the Fontanka Canal, does not particularly impress you. The bridge over the canal, however, demands more than a passing glance. At each end are two groups in bronze by a Russian sculptor, whose name I am sorry not to know. They are called the Horse-Tamers, each representing a man and horse, engaged in a violent struggle for the mastership. The style of taming has no resemblance to Mr. Rarey's, but the figures are very bold and spirited. The Emperor Nicholas presented copies of two of these groups to the King of Prussia, who placed them on the corners of the Museum front, in Berlin, where they have been christened by the people, "Progress Prevented" and "Reaction Encouraged."

Continuing our course down the Nevskoi Prospekt, we pass in succession, on the right, the Alexander Theatre, the Gostinnoi Dvor, or Great Bazaar, and the Cathedral of Our Lady of Kazan. The latter is built of gray Finland granite, with a circular colonnade in front, copied from that of St. Peter's at Rome. In the open space inclosed by the colonnade are bronze statues of Kutusoff and Barclay de Tolly. The buildings on either hand become more lofty and imposing, the throng in the street greater, and soon after crossing the last of the canals, the Moika, we enter the famous Admiralty Square—the grand centre of St. Petersburg, around which are grouped its most important buildings and monuments. Here everything is on such a grand scale, that the magnitude of the different objects is at first not apparent to the eye. The Square is about a mile in length, by a quarter of a mile in breadth. In front of us is the Admiralty Building, with a front of 1,500 feet, and wings resting on the Neva, 650 feet in length. To the right of it is the Winter Palace, with 700 feet front, and still further the Hermitage, nearly as large. Opposite these two is the Hotel de l'Etat Major, of corresponding proportions, while the Alexander Column—a monolith of red granite, 160 feet in height, including pedestal and capital—rises from the centre of the square between.

Turning to the left, we see the huge golden dome of the Izaak's Cathedral lifted between three and four hundred feet into the air, and gleaming like a fallen sun on the summit of granite mountain. The western end of the great square is taken up by the Synod and Senate Houses, whose fronts are united in one long façade by a sort of triumphal arch. Between them and the Admiralty, on the bank of the Neva, is the celebrated equestrian statue of Peter the Great.

Here are the elements of an architectural panorama of the grandest kind, yet the general effect is by no means such as one would anticipate, and simply because one indispensable condition has been overlooked—proportion. With the exception of the Izaak's Cathedral, there is not a single edifice in this square which is not much too low for the extent of its base. Hence they all appear to be lower than is really the fact, and as they are of very nearly uniform height, the eye ranges around the square seeking in vain for some picturesque break in the splendid monotony. A skilful architect might have at least mitigated this fault, but those who planned the Admiralty and the Winter Palace seem to have been even incapable of perceiving it. The latter building is quite disfigured by the placing of a sort of half-story above the true cornice. On the other hand, the Izaak's Cathedral, of which I shall have more to say presently, is one of the very finest specimens of modern architecture in existence. It stands in the centre of a small square of its own, opening into that of the Admiralty at its western end; and here, decidedly, is the most striking view in St. Petersburg. On one side is the Cathedral, on the other the Neva, against whose sparkling current and the long line of buildings on the northern bank gallops Peter on his huge block of granite; while far in front the Alexander Column, soaring high above the surrounding buildings, is seen in its true proportions.

Crossing the Square, between the Admiralty Building and the Winter Palace, we stand upon the bank of the Neva. Directly opposite opens the main branch, or little Neva, dividing Vassili Ostrov and the Aptekarskoi Islands. The river is here more than a third of a mile in breadth, of a clear, pale green color, and rapid current. At the intersection of the two arms, on Vassili Ostrov, stands the Exchange, a square building with a Grecian façade. To the left of it is the long front of the Academy of Sciences, then the Academy of Arts, and at the extremity of our view, where the main branch of the Neva turns northward into the Gulf of Finland, the School of Mines. In front of the Aptekarskoi, and separated from it only by a moat, is the old fortress of Peter and Paul, now a prison for nobles, with its tall-spired church, in the vaults of which rest Peter the Great and all the monarchs since his time. On the southern bank, on which we stand, a row of palaces stretches away on our right to the Trinity Bridge, beyond which we see the green linden-trees of the Summer Gardens. From either shore of the river, or from the bridges which span it, the pictures are always broad, bright, and cheerful. Splendid granite stairways lead down to the water, gayly-painted boats dart to and fro, little steamers keep up a communication with the further islands, and the miles of massive quay on either side are thronged with a busy populace. Here the midsummer heat is always tempered by a delightful breeze, and the very sight of the dancing water is cooling, under the pale, hot, quiet sky. I do not wonder at the enthusiasm of the St. Petersburgers for the Neva. Its water is so remarkably soft and sweet that they prefer it to all other water in the world. The Emperor Alexander always carried a supply with him, bottled, when he was absent from the capital. The stranger, however, cannot drink it with impunity, as its effect on an unaccustomed body is medicinal in the highest degree.

The Winter Palace stands upon the site of the old one, which was destroyed by fire in 1837. Kohl's account of this latter structure is worth quoting. "The suits of apartments were perfect labyrinths, and even the chief of the Imperial household, who had filled that post for twelve years, was not perfectly acquainted with all the nooks and corners of the building. As in the forests of great landholders, many colonies are settled of which the owner takes no notice, so there nestled many a one in this palace not included among the regular inhabitants. For example, the watchmen on the roof, placed there for different purposes, among others to keep the water in the tanks from freezing during the winter, by casting in red-hot balls, built themselves huts between the chimneys, took their wives and children there, and even kept poultry and goats, which fed on the grass of the roof: it is said that at last some cows were introduced, but this abuse had been corrected before the palace was burnt." Fortunately, the new palace is not so labyrinthine, though of equal extent. During the residence of Nicholas there, 6,000 persons frequently lived in it at one time. Strangers are freely allowed to visit all parts of it, on presenting a ticket, which the major domo gives on application. Formerly, the visitor was obliged to appear in full dress, but in the general relaxation of laws and customs which has followed the accession of Alexander II., this rule has also been given up. Our Minister, Mr. Seymour, informed me that the Emperor receives American citizens in ordinary civil dress, not requiring them to appear in Court costume.

There is no other Court in Europe which, with such immense means and such magnificent appointments, preserves so great a simplicity. The freedom from ostentation or parade in the Imperial Family of Russia, except upon stated occasions, is a very agreeable feature. Nowhere else does the monarch walk about his capital, unattended. The Empress, even, may take a stroll, if she likes. We met one day the *Czarevitch*, or Crown Prince, with two of his younger brothers, in a plain two-horse carriage, with a single soldier as footman. These fine, fresh, handsome boys were quite alone, and looked as if they were competent to take care of themselves. The grandfather of the reigning Empress was a *Stallmeister* (Master of the Horse) in Darmstadt, and she is probably indebted to him for her prudent, amiable, sensible character. Nicholas was aware of her descent, but he wisely gave his sons perfect freedom to choose their own wives, and welcomed her as cordially as if her ancestry dated from Julius Cæsar. In visiting the palace, I was particularly struck with the cheerful plainness of the private apartments, which contrasted remarkably with the pomp and dazzle of those for state occasions.

To describe minutely all that I saw in the Winter Palace would take up several chapters. We were between two and three hours in walking slowly through the principal halls and chambers. A large number of these are devoted to pictures, principally portraits and battle scenes. A large room contains several hundred portraits of the officers who served against Napoleon in 1813–14. Then follows the Hall of the Marshals, with few and full-length figures, some of which are of great historical interest. Potemkin is here represented in full armor, a tall, Apollonian figure, over six feet in height, with a fine oval head, regular and handsome features, soft blue eyes, and curly golden hair. Suwarrow is a short man, with large benevolent head, very broad in the temples, where phrenologists place the organ of constructiveness. He wears a plain leather jacket and breeches, and resembles nothing so much as an old Quaker preacher. Barclay de Tolly is tall, slender, stern, and thoughtful, with a prematurely bald head; Kutusoff short, thick, coarse, and heavy-featured. In striking contrast with these personages is Wellington, with his cold, prim, English face and small head.

The battle pieces represent all the noted fields in which Russian arms have been engaged, from Narva to Inkermann—not merely an ostentatious display of victories, but important defeats as well, so that the series presents a true historical interest. Narva receives as prominent a place as Pultava, Borodino as Leipzig, Silistria as Ismail. Many of the later pictures are fine works of art: the illustrations of the Persian and Circassian wars, especially, are full of rich dramatic effect. Altogether, this gallery will compare very well with that of Versailles. One of the most interesting halls is that devoted to the coronation gifts received by Alexander, Nicholas, and the present Emperor. The ancient custom is still preserved, of each province throughout the Empire sending bread and salt as a token of welcome. But the loaf is carried upon a massive salver of gold and silver, of the rarest workmanship, and the salt in a box or cup of the same material, studded with jewels. The salvers presented to the two former Emperors rise in dazling pyramids from the floor nearly to the ceiling, but they are far outshone by those of Alexander II., who received just as much as his father and uncle together. If the wealth lavished upon these offerings is an index to the popular feeling, it is a happy omen for his reign. The taste, richness, and variety of the ornaments bestowed upon the mighty golden salvers exceeds anything of the kind I ever saw. Their value can only be estimated by millions It is significant, perhaps, that the largest and most superb, which occupies the place of honor, in the centre of the glorious pile, is the offering of the serfs of the Imperial domains.

We were admitted into the room containing the crown jewels, which are arranged in glass cases, according to their character and value. In the centre is the crown of Alexander, a hemisphere of the purest diamonds: beside it the sceptre, containing the famous brilliant purchased by Catherine II. from a Greek slave, and for a time supposed to be the largest in the world. It turns out to be smaller than the Koh-i-nor, though (to my eyes, at least,) of a purer water. There is not a quarter so many jewels here as in the Treasury at Moscow, yet their value far exceeds that of the latter. The stones are of the largest and rarest kind, and the splendor of their tints is a delicious intoxication to the eye. The soul of all the fiery roses of Persia lives in these rubies; the freshness of all velvet sward, whether in Alpine valley or English lawn, in these emeralds; the bloom of southern seas in these sapphires, and the essence of a thousand harvest moons in these necklaces of pearl.

Before leaving the Palace we were conducted to a small room in the first story, in the north-western corner. Two Imperial guardsmen stood at the door, and two old servants in livery were in a little ante-room, one of whom accompanied us into the narrow chamber where Nicholas lived and died. Nothing has been changed since his body was carried out of it. The hard camp-bed (so small and narrow that I should not wish to sleep upon it) stands there, beside his writing-table. On a stool at the foot lies his dressing-gown. His comb, brushes, gloves, pocket-handkerchief, knife, and pencil are carelessly laid upon a small toilet-table under a very moderate-sized looking-glass. A plain, green carpet covers the floor, and the half dozen chairs are lined with green leather. The walls are almost concealed by pictures, either landscapes or battle-pieces, and few of them of any value. Just over his pillow is a picture of a very pretty young girl dressed as a soldier. It was scarcely possible to believe that the occupant of this room had been dead for more than three years. Every object suggests life, and while we are examining them we half expect to see that colossal figure, which all Europe knew so well, appear at the door. The only thing which has been added is a very beautiful drawing of the Emperor's head, after death. The expression upon the face is that of pain and trouble, not the serene, impenetrable calm which it wore during life.

The Hermitage, adjoining the Winter Palace, was built by Catherine, as a place of escape from the fatigue of Court ceremonials, and of quiet conversation with a few privileged persons. The name seems to have been jestingly or ironically given. Who would not be a hermit in this immense pile, whose walls are of marble, blazing with gold, whose floors are of the choicest inlaid woods, and whose furniture is of the rarest and most costly workmanship in porphpry, jasper, lapiz-lazuli and malachite? Such splendor is now out of place, since the palace has been given up to the Arts. The vast collection of pictures accumulated by the Russian Emperors is here displayed, together with a gallery of sculpture, one of the finest assortments of antique gems in the world, a collection of Grecian and Etruscan antiquities, and a library of rare books and manuscripts. The picture gallery is particularly rich in the works of Rubens, Vandyke, Rembrandt, Murillo, and the Dutch school, and though it contains few celebrated master-pieces, the number of really good pictures is remarkable. They occupy between forty and fifty large halls, and a man cannot say that he **really knows** the collection in less time than **a week**.

CHAPTER XXXV

TZARSKO SELO, PAULOVSK AND THE ISLANDS.

One of my first excursions, after reaching St. Petersburg, was to the hill of Pulkowa, seventeen versts south of the city. There, in the magnificent astronomical Observatory built during the reign of Nicholas, dwelt a brother-in-law whom I had never seen, and there was born the first child who has a right to call me uncle. Procuring an open calêche with three horses—the Russian *troika*—we left St. Petersburg by the Moscow road, which issues from the city through a tall triumphal arch. The main road is a hundred feet broad, with a narrower highway on each side, divided from it by a double row of trees. At the end of the seventh verst, the road to Moscow strikes off to the left, while that to Pulkowa preserves its mathematical straightness, so that its termini, the triumphal arch and the dome of the Observatory, are visible from all parts of it. About half-way there is a German colony settled, and the comfort of the houses, no less than the blooming appearance of the little gardens and orchards, presents an agreeable contrast to the bare, unadorned Russian villages.

The hill of Pulkowa is the nearest rising ground to St. Petersburg, and though the highest point is only some two hundred and fifty feet above the level of the Baltic, this elevation is sufficient to command a panorama of between forty and fifty miles in diameter. On the summit, surrounded by scattered groves of fir and birch trees, is the Observatory, probably the most perfectly appointed institution of the kind in the world. The cost of its erection must have exceeded a million of dollars. On passing through the spacious halls, rotundas, and towers with moveable cupolas, I had cause to regret my inability to appreciate the peculiar excellence of the splendid instruments, and the ingenious mechanical contrivances for using them. In the chief tower was the colossal refractor of Frauenhofer, of which our Cambridge Observatory (if I remember rightly) possesses the only counterpart. The grand hall is hung with portraits of distinguished astronomers, among whom I recognised Hansen and Airy.

I had the pleasure of passing an evening with the Director of the Observatory, the venerable Von Struve, whose name is well known in America. He was then slowly recovering from an illness which for a time threatened his life, and was still comparatively feeble. He is between sixty-five and seventy years old, of medium stature, with a large, symmetrical head, and a remarkably benign and genial expression of countenance. In addition to his astronomical acquirements he is a profound Greek scholar, and understands the principal modern languages, including English, which he speaks with unusual fluency and correctness He is perfectly familiar with all that has been done of late years in America for the encouragement of Astronomy and kindred sciences, and mentioned the names of Gould, Pierce, Gilliss, and Maury with great admiration. Von Struve is another example of the truth that the study of the stars need not, as in Newton's case, make a man indifferent to the amenities of our insignificant terrestrial life. Like other astronomers of my acquaintance, he is particularly happy in his family relations and takes a hearty enjoyment in society. Leverrier is the very reverse of this, if what I have heard of him be true. He is said to be exceedingly proud, reserved, and ostentatious in his manner. A distinguished German recently visited him in Paris, with a letter of introduction. After reading it, Leverrier looked up, measured the bearer from head to foot, and asked, in a rude impertinent tone: " *Que voulez-vous?*" " *Rien,*" coolly answered the German, as he bowed and withdrew.

At the western end of the hill is a pile of granite boulders, on which, Tradition says, Peter the Great sat and planned the building of his capital. The distance from the city is too great to make the story probable. It is very likely, however, that this may have been one of the Tzar's favorite spots. The eye, weary of a narrow horizon, inclosed by a ring of dark woods, more or less distinct, here roves with delight over the expanding plain, whose far rim is lost in the blue evening mists of the Neva. The many spires of St. Petersburg sparkle with shifting lustres in the sunset, the great dome of St. Izaak blazing over the lesser lights like the moon among stars. Wher the air is clear Cronstadt may be seen in the west, floating on the sea-horizon.

The celebrated Summer Palace and park of Tzarsko Selo are seven versts beyond Pulkowa. The grounds, which are of immense extent—eighteen miles in circumference, it is said—are always open to the public. My newly-found relative had been kind enough to procure tickets of admission to the palace and armory, and we made choice of a warm Sunday afternoon, when tens of thousands come out by railroad from St. Petersburg, for our visit. Entering the park from the western side, we found ourselves in the midst of gently undulating fields, dotted with groves of fir, ash, and birch—an English landscape, were the green a little more dark and juicy. Here was a dairy farm, there a stable for elephants, and a little further an asylum for pensioned horses. The favorite steeds of the Emperor, after his death, are withdrawn from active service and pass their days here in comfort and indolence. One or two of the horses of Alexander I. are still on the list, although their age cannot be less than forty years. At each of these institutions we received very polite invitations from the servants in attendance to enter and inspect them. The invitation was sometimes accompanied by the words: "I am a married man," or "I have a family," which in Russia means: "I should not object to receive a gratuity." I was not a little perplexed, occasionally, until I ascertained this fact. One day, while standing before the house of Peter the Great, in the Summer Gardens, a soldier came up to me and said: "Pray go into the house, my lord: the keeper is married."

The Armory is a brick building in the Gothic style, standing on a wooded knoll in the Park. The collection of armor is one of the finest in Europe, and its arrangement would delight the eye of an antiquary. From the ninth century to the nineteenth, no characteristic weapon or piece of defensive mail is wanting, from the heavy, unwieldy accoutrements of the German knights to the chain shirts of the Saracens and the pomp of Milanese armor, inlaid with gold. One of the cabinets contains two sets of horse trappings presented by the Sultan of Turkey—the first on concluding the peace of Adrianople, after Diebitsch had crossed the Balkan, and the second when Ibrahim Pasha menaced Constantinople and the Sultan invoked the aid of Russia. The latter, naturally, is much the more splendid of the two: the housings and pistol holsters blaze with arabesques of the largest diamonds There are many very interesting historical relics in the collection, but I cannot give the catalogue. Suffice it to say that a volume of illustrations has been published, and may be had for 500 rubles.

As we advanced toward the palace the grounds gradually became more artificial in their design and more carefully tended. The sward had a veritable "pile," like imperial velvet: it appeared to have been *combed* rather than raked. Not a dead leaf was visible on the exquisitely smooth gravel of the walks, not a defective bough had been suffered to remain on the arching avenues of linden or elm. Nature seemed to have taken a Turkish bath and put on a clean Sunday dress. There is not an ill weed, an awkward plant, a frog, toad, snake, or bug, in this expensive Eden. Usually, a gardener walks after you with a broom, to efface any footprints you may have left behind you, but for some reason or other we were spared this attention. Woe unto you if you touch a flower! But there is little danger of that: you would as soon think of cutting a rose out of a drawing-room carpet, as of thus meddling with this super-human order.

In the course of our walk we came upon a ruined abbey, so capitally imitated that if it stood anywhere else even an old traveller might be deceived by it. One square tower alone is standing, and in this tower, which you reach by a wooden staircase built over the ruins, is the famous statue of Christ, by Dannecker, the sculptor of Ariadne and the Panther. This is no traditionary Christ, with low forehead and straight, insipid features: the head is rather that of a scholar and a thinker. You are at once struck with the individuality of the figure. He is repesented as speaking, turning towards the left and slightly leaning forward. A single flowing garment, hanging from his neck to his feet, partly conceals the symmetrical yet somewhat delicate form. The head is large, nobly rounded and balanced, with a preponderance of development in the intellectual and moral regions of the brain, his hair long, but very fine and thin, as if prematurely thinned by thought, the beard scanty, and the expression of the countenance at once grave, gentle, and spiritual The longer I looked upon it the more I was penetrated with its wonderful representation of the attributes of Christ—Wisdom and Love. The face calmly surveys and comprehends all forms of human passion, with pity for the erring, joy in the good, and tenderness for all.

It is that transcendent purity in whose presence the sinner feels no repellant reproof, but only consolation.

I have seen few statues like this, where the form is lost sight of in the presence of the idea. In this respect it is Dannecker's greatest, as it was his favorite work. He devoted many a day of labor, thought, and aspiration to the modelling of the head. When, at length, it was completed in clay, a sudden distrust in his success overwhelmed him. Having no longer confidence in his own judgment or that of his artistic friends, he one day took a little uneducated child into his studio, placed the head before it, and said: "Who is this?" The child looked steadfastly upon the features, so unlike the conventional Christ of artists, and without hesitation answered: "It is the Saviour." The old man, himself a child in his simplicity and sincerity, accepted this answer as a final judgment, and completed his work in marble.

Our way led on over straight Dutch canals, past artificial hills and rock-work, through a Chinese village which resembles nothing in China, and under Babylonian hanging gardens, to the front of the palace, which is 1,200 feet in length, and rises from the crest of a long knoll, gently sloping down to a lake. Some fine oak trees adorn the lawn; on the top of a granite rock a bronze nymph is crying over her broken pitcher, out of which rushes a stream of sparkling water; and on the lake itself a pretty little cutter lies at anchor. Arsenals and fortresses in miniature stud the opposite shore, and on a wooded point stands a Turkish kiosk and minaret, the interior of which is a sumptuous oriental bath, presented by the Sultan. The park beyond the palace, toward the village of Tzarsko Selo is in even more rigid full dress than that through which we had already passed, and I verily believe that if a leaf gets accidentally twisted on its stem, some one is on hand to set it right again.

All the pillars, statues, cornices, and ornaments on the long palace front were covered with heavy gilding in the time of Catharine II. When they began to look a little shabby and the gold needed replacing, the Empress was offered half a million of rubles for the scrapings, but she replied with a magnificent scorn: "I am not in the habit of selling my old rags." The Imperial banner of Russia, floating at the mast-head, showed that the family were at home, but we were nevertheless allowed to enter. A "married" servant conducted us through the apartments once occupied by Catharine and Alexander I. Here there is much that is curious, though no splendor comparable to that of the Winter Palace, or the Imperial apartments in the Kremlin. One room is lined entirely with amber, a present from Frederick the Great. The effect is soft, rich, and waxy, without being glaring. In others the panelling is of malachite or lapiz-lazuli. Catherine's bedchamber has not been changed since she left it: the bed-posts are of purple glass, and the walls lined with porcelain.

Most interesting of all, however, are the apartments occupied by Alexander I., in which every article has been preserved with religious veneration. His bed is a very narrow mattress of leather stuffed with straw, and the entire furniture of the room would not fetch more than fifty dollars if sold at auction. On the toilet table lie his comb breeches, razor, and a clear pocket-handkerchief; his cloak hangs over a chair, and his well-worn writing-desk still shows the pens, pencils, bits of sealing-wax, and paper-weights, as he left them. His boots, I noticed, were of very thin leather—too thin either for health or comfort—and had been cracked through and patched in several places. His Majesty had evidently discovered how much more agreeable to the feet are old boots than new ones. But he is quite thrown into the shade by Peter the Great, whose boots, at Moscow, would weigh ten pounds apiece, and might be warranted to wear ten years without mending.

Towards evening we took droshkies and drove to Paulovsk, which is about three miles to the eastward of Tzarsko, Selo. This is at present the summer residence of the Grand Duke Constantine, but the park is at all times free to the public. It is of great extent, the aggregate length of the walks being estimated at a hundred miles. Here Nature is released from curling-tongs and stays: her garments adorn without pinching her, and her hair is loosened to the wind. For this reason, Paulovsk pleased me better than Tzarsko Selo. Its deep, winding dells, threaded by natural streams; its opulent woods of ash, birch, and elm; its sequestered walks, branching away into neglected forest solitudes, and its open, sunny lawns, sweet with the breath of the half-raked hay, speak of genial culture rather than art. There is here an artificial lake, surrounded by low but steep hills, which are covered with summer villas and terraced gardens. A cutter on the water and a full-rigged mizenmast planted on the hill behind the palace, give evidence of the

Grand Duke's naval tastes. Braisted, with a sailor's eye, criticised the rigging of the mast rather sharply, but the princely boys who run up and down these shrouds are not expected to do duty before the mast, and so, perhaps, it makes little difference. Besides, to learn seamanship on a mizenmast planted in the woods, is like learning to swim upon your dining-table.

In the evening some thousands of Petersburghers assembled around a pavilion attached to the railroad station where the orchestra of the younger Strauss added music to the unbroken twilight. This is a speculation of the railroad company, which pays Strauss 15,000 rubles for his own services during the summer months. I had heard better music performed under the direction of his celebrated father, and looked at the crowd rather than listened to the band. Here were civil and military gentlemen mixing like oil and vinegar in a salad; noble ladies, some beautiful and all well-dressed; *filles de joie*, rouged and crinolined, hunting alone or in couples; countless nurses, looking after children in fancy peasant costume—red shirt, sash, wide trowsers, and boots; pale, slender Circassian officers, resembling antique Grecian bas-reliefs; Persians in plenty, each with an entire black sheep towering over his fox-like face, and a lively sprinkling of Armenians, Cossacks, and Tartars. When the Emperor is at home, he may often be seen here, with the Empress on his arm and the older children following, walking in the crowd.

We devoted one evening to a tour of the islands, the beauties of which have not been overpraised by travellers. There are forty, altogether, in the delta of the Neva, all of which are included within the precincts of the city, but only seven of them are of any considerable size. Many of the smaller ones are still wild, uninhabited swamps, frequented only by the seal in summer and by the wolf in winter. The others, lying beside them, crowded with palaces, villas, and gardens, exhibit the difference between civilization and barbarism, in Nature. Crossing the Troitska Bridge, to the large Aptekarskoi Island, we pass on the right the first church built in St. Petersburg, an old wooden structure, with green domes, such as may be seen in many a country village. Even before leaving this island, the city proper is gradually transformed into a garden suburb, with scattered houses buried in foilage. Following the throng of carriages and droshkies, we cross to Kammenoi Island, where the suburban character is complete. Every dwelling, be it only a wooden cottage no bigger than a tollman's box, sits in a nest of flowers and hides itself under a covert of trees. The farther north you go, the greater the fondness for flowers. In the Tropics, gardens are planted for shade, but here for the bloom and odor, the bright, transient coloring, for which the eye hungers after six months of snow. Nowhere is so much of summer crowded into the space of three months.

I was going to compare the roads on these islands to the eastern part of Euclid street, in Cleveland, Ohio, but there the dwellings and grounds are altogether of a more stately character. The Russian villas—*datchas*, they are called—are built of wood, generally without regard to architectural style, but quaint, cozy, irregular, and picturesque. Now and then you see a genuine Swiss farm-house, with project ing eaves and balconies of carved wood. Some of the handsomest residences are veritable log-houses, the trunks of equal size, overlapping at the corners, and simply barked and painted. There could be no finer model for an American farm-house, especially in the West, but with us the taste for glaring brick predominates. Some traveller has said that in Russia the expressions "*red*" and "*beautiful*" are synonymous. The same thing might be said of us. I remember one house between Milwaukee and Racine which was pure vermilion, and resembled a red-hot lime-kiln. Many of these *datchas*, also, are touched up with red, and have summer awnings of striped canvass, fashioned like tents or pavilions, over the entrance. Before every window there is a shelf studded with pots of exotic flowers.

At the end of Kammenoi Island is a Summer theatre, where French vaudevilles are performed. Beyond is Yelaginskoi Island, whereon the Emperor has a villa and garden, which are marvels of scrupulous neatness and elegance. Through every break in the embowering woods you catch glimpses of the clear green arms of the Neva on either hand, and, as if this mixture of land and water were not sufficiently labyrinthine, artificial lakes are hollowed in the islands, the earth being employed to form mounds and ridges beyond their uniform level. After a drive of five or six miles through these enchanting island-suburbs, you reach the shore of the Gulf, on Krestoffskoi, and may watch the sunset moving across Finland, until it becomes morning over Lake Ladoga.

If you would see all this, take your over-coat with you for, although the thermometer may stand all day at 90° in the shade, with evening comes a fresh, cold air. By disregarding the custom of the country in this respect, I received a beautiful cold in the head. Until midnight the islands are alive with a merry multitude. There are pavilions where artificial mineral waters are drunk, artificial Tyrolese and real gipsies sing, and the national dances of Russia are danced: smoking is permitted in the open air and brandy, qvass, champagne and German beer are sold. The little steamers running to the Summer Gardens are laden to the water's edge, and it is morning before all the pleasure-seekers are brought home again.

CHAPTER XXXVI.

VARIETIES OF THE RUSSIAN CAPITAL.

BEFORE leaving Russia, let me add a few detached sketches to the general picture which I have endeavored to give the reader, of St. Petersburg and its environs. My description, however, will be far from exhaustive, because I purposely refrained from making my visit so. I hope to see Russia again in the course of a few years, less hurriedly and with better preparation.

The finest building in Russia—in all Northern Europe, indeed—is the Cathedral of St. Izaak. Commenced in the year 1826, in the place of a former structure erected by Catharine II. and Paul, it received its final consecration in June, 1858. Thirty-two years of uninterrupted labor, backed by the unlimited resources of the Empire, were required to complete this gigantic work. Its cost is estimated at 90,000,000 rubles, or $67,500,000, but a large slice out of this sum (as in our own Government contracts) may be put under the head of "pickings and stealings." To make a firm foundation in the swampy soil, piles to the value of a million of dollars were driven. Upon them rose a basement of granite, supporting a mighty granite structure, in the form of a Greek cross, crowned by a huge dome of gilded iron. The design is simple and majestic, and the various parts are so nicely balanced and harmonized that at first sight the Cathedral appears smaller than is really the case. It grows upon the eye with each visit, but can only be seen in its full magnitude at a considerable distance.

The four sides are fronts of exactly similar design and dimensions—a Grecian pediment, resting on sixteen monolith columns of red Finnish granite, sixty feet in height and seven feet in diameter, with Corinthian capitals in bronze. These tremendous shafts emulate the marvels of Dendera and Karnak. In fact, the great hall of columns in the latter temple does not represent as much art, labor and wealth. The dome, which is a little less than that of St. Paul's, in London, rests upon a circular colonnade of similar monoliths, of smaller dimensions. The body of the edifice is of gray granite, and upon each of the four corners are groups of kneeling angels, with candelabra, in bronze. Crowning this sublime pile is the golden hemisphere of the dome, which so flashes in the sunlight that the eye can scarcely bear its splendor. Far out on the Gulf of Finland, it glitters over the evening horizon like a rising star.

The interior is divided into five vaulted halls, the central one, under the dome, soaring to a height of 292 feet. The massive piers which support them, the walls, the ceiling, and the recesses for shrines, are lined with the most precious marbles, whose exquisite beauty of coloring reconciles the eye to their somewhat ostentatious magnificence. The richest and loveliest tints are here combined—pink, lilac, pale-green, purple, dark-blue, brown, orange, and violet—and with so much skill that the lavish display of gold loses half its disagreeable glare. The *ikonostast*, or screen before the Holy of Holies, is a giant wall of wealth. Eight pillars of malachite, fifty feet high, bear aloft its golden cornice and divide its surface of gilded silver into compartments, whereon are painted the favorite saints of Russia. The altar canopy is supported by two pillars of lapiz-lazuli, bluer than the ice of Polar seas. But wealth, uncombined with taste, can only impress a vulgar mind: you are overwhelmed by the glare, not touched by the beauty. Aladdin's Palace may be built of clay, when the genie is Ictinus or Palladio.

Across the Neva, on the eastern point of Vassili Ostrov, are two immense plastered buildings—the Academy of Arts and the Academy of Sciences. Before visiting them, however, let us pause a moment before Falconet's famous statue of Peter the Great. After having seen Clark Mills's statue of Gen. Jackson rearing on his hind legs, which our enlightened legislators have pronounced to be the greates thing of the kind in the world, I had very limited expectations of Peter, seeing that the latter does not rear so high, and that his horse's tail touches the ground—which is a great fault, according to the aforesaid judges of Art When I found, however, that Peter sits his horse like a man, and not like a wooden effigy, and that the horse is arrested in a position which he can maintain for an instant without tumbling backward, I decided that I had been a little too hasty in forming my conclusions. The long tail of the horse, and the writhing serpent upon which he tramples, are obviously introduced for the purpose of maintaining the equilibrium of the figure, which is thus secured without too great exaggeration. Gen. Jackson, on the other hand, disdains any such aid. Having borrowed one of Franconi's horses, trained to walk on its hind legs, he needs neither serpent nor long tail. And yet, I fear, Peter will be pronounced the better rider by every impartial judge.

The Academy of Sciences is only open to the public on Mondays. Not being aware of this, I timed my visit so unfortunately that I was not able to see its interesting zoological collections, which contain, among other things, the remains of the Siberian mammoth, found imbedded in the ice of the Lena. In the zoological cabinet at Moscow there is also the entire skeleton of a mastodon, but of rather smaller size than that which was formerly in Peale's Museum, in Philadelphia. The Russian Academy of Sciences is a Government institution, and is intrusted with the organization and superintendence of all geological, topographical, and astronomical undertakings. Its President is Count Bludoff, to whom I had a letter of introduction, but, as he was absent on his travels, I was not so fortunate as to make his acquaintance.

The Academy of Arts has accomplished but little, as yet. Russia has furnished some good sculptors, but no painter who could fairly be admitted to a first place. Even Brüloff, who is generally reckoned the greatest, and who really was an artist of no ordinary power, appears meretricious beside the grand old masters. In the gallery of Russian paintings in the Hermitage, I was particularly struck by the crude, exaggerated manner of the various artists—a distinction which applied to landscapes as well as figures. There was a gale on the Black Sea, which was one mass of raw pink and pea-green. Some Circassian landscapes, however, were very finely and boldly drawn, though still deficient in the main charm of color. No people are prouder of their great men than the Russians, and in no other country, probably, would a truly great artist receive more generous support—but Academies alone are not sufficient to create artists. On the contrary, they rather hinder that free, spontaneous development and growth which all Art demands, and without which it will never produce anything great and permanent.

Toward the western end of Vassili Ostrov stands another institution, which is unquestionably the most perfect of its kind in the world—the School of Mines. It was originally founded by Peter the Great, for the purpose of training a corps of mining engineers, and with the gradual development of the mineral resources of Russia, its importance and efficiency can now scarcely be over-estimated. Nearly the whole of the immense building is devoted to collections of minerals, models of all kinds of machinery used in mining, and fac-similes of all the principal mines, with their shafts, galleries, and veins of ore, constructed with the most wonderful labor and skill. The minerals form a dazzling gallery of crude wealth. There is the famous nugget of the Ural—an 80 lb. lump of pure gold; a mass of malachite, weighing 4,000 lbs.; a single perfect beryl, weighing six pounds, and valued at $30,000; crusted sheets of deep violet amethysts; huge blocks of jasper, of all imaginable hues; slabs of precious marble, and boulders of granite and porphyry, together with ores of platina, silver, copper, and iron—bright and beautiful spirits, waiting for the touch of fire to be released from their dusky prisons. The specimens are of the rarest and most costly character, filling several large halls.

After we had inspected the models of machines, buildings, and mines, an old soldier conducted us into the cellar, gave us each a long wax candle, and unlocked a heavy iron door. We entered, and the hinges closed behind us. As if by magic we stood in the bowels of a coal mine—in a winding, narrow shaft, traversed by strata of clay, coal, and crumbling slate-rock. All the various dips, positions, and characters of coal-beds are here displayed in turn. A labyrinth of mines succeeded—silver, lead, copper, gold, and iron, imitated with astonishing fidelity to nature. The dampness of the soil, which filled the passages with a raw, chill air, completed the resemblance. At intervals, shafts from above (of very trifling depth, naturally) penetrated this subterranean region, and illustrated the various means of communication with the surface. In fact, the School of Mines, from beginning to end, is one of the most thoroughly sensible and practical institutions I have ever seen.

On the Aptekarskoi Island, just above the Troitzka Bridge, is the cottage of Peter the Great—his first residence in the young capital. It is built of logs, and contains only three small rooms. In order the more effectu ally to preserve it, a brick house has been built around and over it, and the rude old hut has thus become a sort of shrine, whither the devout Russians flock in crowds. The main room is in fact a religious sanctuary, hung with holy pictures, and hot with the flames of a dozen wax candles. At the time of my visit it was filled with a crowd of common people, bowing and crossing themselves, muttering prayers and lighting tapers, in an atmosphere so unctuous and stifling that I was obliged to retire immediately. The custode, who was evidently a married man, unlocked the inner rooms at the sight of a silver piece, and showed me the rough table and stools, made by Peter's own hand, as well as the tattered sail which belonged to his boat. At one end of the house is the boat itself, a light, trim, sharp craft about fifteen feet long, which Braisted, after carefully inspecting with a seaman's eye, pronounced "well done!" It would be well if all apprentices nowadays learned their trades as well as Master Peter of Saardam. It is curious to find, however, that the man who first broke the power of the Russian priesthood, and forcibly uprooted so many old customs and superstitions, should now, although un-canonized, receive the honors due to a saint.

I will not ask the reader to accompany me to the Cathedral of our Lady of Kazan, or to the Preobrajensky, Smolnoi, and St. Alexander Nevsky churches. They are all quite modern in character, with the exception of the Tartaresque, bespangled spires on the three latter. The last named contains the tomb of Suwarrow, and the body of the saint to whom it is dedicated, in a coffin of massive silver, weighing five thousand pounds. This relic was for merly preserved in a monastery on the banks of the Volga, whence Peter the Great transferred it to the capital. Very soon afterwards the saint disappeared, and was found again in his old place, being dissatisfied (so said the monks) with his removal. Nevertheless, Peter had him brought back a second time, and threatened the monks with the severest penalties if they allowed him to escape. It is needless to add that the saint kept perfectly quiet after that. At Naples, during the French occupation, the blood of St. Januarius was once made to liquefy in the same arbitrary manner.

Behind the Gostinnoi Dvor is a curious market, known through Petersburg as the *Apraxin Rinok*, or "Louse Exchange," from the questionable cleanliness of its booths, occupants, and customers. But let not the stranger be deterred from entering by the natural hesitation which the name inspires. It is a second-hand market, or bazaar, similar to those in Moscow, but of much greater extent, containing upwards of five thousand booths. A few paces after leaving the noisy Garden street, you are in the midst of a queer, shabby, ruinous-looking town, where the silence is broken only by such cries as: "What would please you, my lord?" "Here are excellent mattresses!" "A very cheap carriage!" "Pictures! Behold the beautiful St. Nicholas!" "Iron wheel-tires—here they are!" "Here are the swords!" "Brass kettles—please to step in!" etc. The wares are arranged in separate streets, but without regard to their fitness or resemblance, and everybody offers you what he has, though it might be something which you never buy. We were simply curious strangers, as any one could see; yet we were pressingly solicited to buy old bedding, leather, rusty iron, household furniture, sleds, salt fish, shrines, crosses, and pictures, to say nothing of shabby greasy caftans, and damaged hats, which could not even be touched without a heroic effort. To judge from the great extent and multifarious character of the various bazaars, the Russians must be a people passionately fond of shopping. Several rows of booths in the Louse Exchange are devoted to cheap refreshments, principally tea, qvass, fish boiled in oil, black bread and raw cucumbers. Others again are filled with every variety of dried fruits and vegetables, and these are decidedly the most agreeable districts.

The fruit shops in the Nevisko Prospekt are an agreeable surprise to the stranger. Passing before the windows, you are saluted by the musky odor of golden melons, the breath of peaches, plums, grapes, oranges, and fresh figs, which are here displayed in as much profusion as if they were the ordinary growths of the soil. The fruit is all raised in hot-houses, and I did not venture to ask the price. This is one of those luxuries which are most easily excused.

The Botanical Garden, in which I spent an afternoon, contains one of the finest collections of tropical plants in Europe. Here, in lat. 60°, you may walk through an avenue of palm-trees sixty feet high, under tree-ferns and bananas, by ponds of lotus and Indian lily, and banks of splendid orchids, breathing an air heavy with the richest and warmest odors. The extent of these giant hot-houses cannot be less than a mile and a half. The short summer, and long dark winter of the north requires a peculiar course of treatment for those children of the sun. During the three warm months they are forced as much as possible, so that the growth of six months is obtained in that time, and the productive forces of the plant are kept up to their normal standard. After this result is obtained, it thrives as steadily as in a more favorable climate. The palms, in particular, are noble specimens. One of them (a *phœnix*, I believe) was in blossom, which is an unheard of event in such a latitude.

CHAPTER XXXVII.

JOURNEY THROUGH THE BALTIC PROVINCES.

The steamers from Cronstadt to Stettin and Lübeck were crowded with Russian families, bound abroad, and all places were taken weeks beforehand. I therefore shortened my stay by a few days, and took seats in the Government diligence to the Prussian frontier, via Narva and Riga. A special passport for leaving Russia is necessary, and the old formality of having your name published three times in the newspapers is still adhered to. We duly appeared in the list of departing travellers, with names slightly misspelled and the designation of "American subjects," after which, furnished with a stamped certificate to the effect that no creditors had appeared against us, we repaired to the Passport Office. The formalities were long and somewhat tedious, but the officials, most of whom spoke three or four languages, were exceedingly courteous and gentlemanly, and in the course of a few hours we were put *en regle*. No "tea-money" was here demanded; the legal fees, however, were high enough, amounting, in all, to about ten rubles

After receiving the passport, one is allowed to remain three weeks, so that the publication of the name for the benefit of creditors is of no practical use.

The passport system of Russia has hitherto been far more onerous to the subjects of the Empire than to foreigners. Under the reign of Nicholas, the minimum cost of a permission to travel abroad was fifty rubles, and was even then arbitrarily withheld in many instances. Nobles and gentlemen of fortune were obliged to pay proportionately more. I met a Russian in Germany in 1845, who had paid five hundred rubles for one year's leave, and Prince Demidoff, it is stated was taxed no less than fifty thousand rubles annually. Although Nicholas himself travelled a great deal, he appears to have desired exclusion for his subjects, fearing the influence of new habits and ideas upon them. Alexander, on the other hand, trusts the deep-rooted national feeling of the Russians, and not only permits, without reserve, but encourages travel. A passport now costs five rubles, for burgher or noble, while a merchant, travelling for the sake of his business, pays but one. As a consequence there was in the summer of 1858, a general stampede to France, Germany, and Italy, and of all the gentlemen whom I hoped to meet, not one was at home.

The distance from St. Petersburg to Tauroggen, on the Prussian frontier, is seven hundred and eighty versts, or about five hundred and twenty miles. The slow post which we took, is four days and nights in traversing it, including long delays at the principal stations. We took our seats at six o'clock, on a hot summer evening, the sun still three hours distance above the horizon. My com panion on the inside was a young French merchant from Moscow, a fellow of twenty-four, pale, hollow-eyed, knock-kneed, and already showing signs of baldness. It is not pleasant to have a body prematurely broken down by licentiousness so close to one; but travellers cannot alway choose their coach or bed-fellows. On applying the usual tests to the Frenchman's mind, in order to discover whether there were any sparks remaining in such a heap of ashes, I was not rewarded by any appreciable result. He venerated Louis Napoleon, and declared that to him alone was due the abolition of serfdom in Russia, he having secretly driven Alexander II. to adopt the measure. His statements on the commonest subjects concerning Russia were so wide of the mark that I soon dropped him in despair. Besides, he had a disagreeable habit of naming every other place than Moscow "down there." (*Là bas.*) Berlin, Paris, Constantinople, America, St. Petersburg—all were "down there." "Where?" I would ask, impatiently. "Why, down there." Twenty-four hours of this conversation was a surfeit, so I gradually withdrew into my shell, and before the journey's end we only spoke every three hours.

Braisted had a little better luck. His comrade in the coupé (the diligence only carries four persons) was a wealthy Russian, laboring under a violent attack of dyspepsia, which he endeavored to cure by drinking tea and eating immense quantities of sour milk. He was a hypochondriac on the subject of his stomach. He ate as much as the remaining three of us, and was continually lamenting his loss of appetite. There was a time, he said, when he had consumed an entire roast turkey at one meal, but now meat was fatal to him. Nevertheless at the next station, where a large dish of cutlets was placed before us, he set to with the determination of a suicide, and ate enough (according to his theory) to have caused his death. He frankly confessed that he had spent a large fortune in his younger days, and only took up business when he was driven to it, but he had since then prospered exceedingly. He was, withal, a man of much experience and intelligence, and the more we saw of him the more reason we found to like him. The story of his life, which, even in its most private aspects, he confided to me, had a deeper interest than was evident on the surface. He illustrated, without knowing it, more than one of the many puzzles which belong to his race and sex. It is a fact, the importance of which can never be diminished, that the full and true history of one man's life is worth all the books that ever were written about Human Nature.

For the first three hours after leaving the capital we followed the shore of the Gulf of Finland, toward Peterhof, passing a series of the most charming parks and villas, the the summer residences of the wealthy St. Peterburgers. A long ridge of gently rolling ground, studded with groves of birch and fir, offers natural advantages which the latte have not lost sight of. The dwellings are mostly of wood, not distinguished for their architecture, but look comfortable and homelike, and the grounds are almost universally laid out in the English style, with sloping lawns of the freshest turf, trees of unpruned growth, winding walks, and gay flower-beds of a single hue. For fifteen miles this fairy diorama of summer palaces passed by on our left, while on the right the Gulf expanded broad and blue, from the shining domes of the city to the dim, wave-washed fortresses of Cronstadt. At Strelna we left the coast, and struck inland over the low Esthonian plateau toward Narva. The post-stations on this old route were not to be compared to those on the new highway between Warsaw and Moscow, but they furnished everything we needed, and the landlords all spoke German better than Russian.

The sun set precisely at nine o'clock, but we slept through the splendid twilight, each jammed into his particular corner, until long after sunrise. At Jamburg, a considerable town on the river Luga, we took advantage of a half-hour's halt, to bathe. We were in the middle of the stream when the diligence passed. The conductor, however, was obliging enough to wait on the opposite bank, and apologized for leaving us, by stating that he did not recognise us without our clothes. He is not the only man who looks at the coat instead of the face. Two hours more brought us to Narva, the little town whose name rings so grandly in Swedish history and song. On the eastern bank of the river Narova stands the village and fortress of Ivangorod, built by Peter to secure the favorite turn in his fortunes, five years after his overthrow on the same spot. With such a beginning as this unparalleled victory, what might not Charles XII. have become, had he inherited the prudence as well as the military genius of Gustavus Adolphus? A boy of seventeen, at the head of 8,000 men, utterly routing an army of 50,000! When one sees the sloping bank of the Narova, on the top of which the Russians were intrenched, and pictures to himself the charge of that little band of Swedes as they swept up the hill in a blinding storm of snow and sleet, crying "*Ur vägen, Moskoviter!*" (Out of the way, Muscovites!) he cannot but acknowledge that there are few events in his tory so stirring and sublime.

Narva is an insignificant little place of 5,000 inhabitants still wholly Swedish in appearance. It is beginning to rise in importance, however, through its cotton factories. The Narova furnishes a splendid water-power, of which Baron Stieglitz has taken advantage, and in addition to the large mills which have been in operation for a few years past, is now building a new one to contain 150,000 spindles. Owing to the judicious protective policy of Russia, her manufactures of all kinds are rapidly increasing, and the cotton-mills are already so numerous as to sustain a direct trade with the United States. The number of American vessels in Russian ports last summer was probably four times what it was five years ago. At Narva the people told us with great exultation that an American ship, freighted with cotton bales, lay in the outer harbor—the first which had ever been seen there.

Through the hot, breathless middle hours of the day we traversed the shore of the Gulf, looking over the long undulating fields of ripening rye upon its blue surface. In the afternoon we left the direct road to Revel and struck southward over the cold, bare Esthonian plains toward Lake Peipus. From the higher ridges the eye saw only interminable forests of fir, and even in the hollows where broad tracts of cultivated land intervened, the character of the country was poor and cheerless. The post-stations were poverty-stricken places, where we could only obtain a little beer, bread, and cheese, and the night (or rather the nocturnal twilight) was the more welcome, since sleep was no loss. By the next morning we had entered Livonia and were descending toward Dorpat from the ridges above Lake Peipus, through a fertile and well-settled country. Splendid fields of rye, which appeared to be almost the only grain cultivated, lined the road, gleaming with changeable yellow and silver tints between the dark masses of the evergreen woods. Comfortable farm-houses and well-built villages dotted the landscape, which basked in the full glare of midsummer.

In Dorpat we had but an hour, the greater part of which was devoted to breakfast, so that we only saw the outside of the town. It is a very neat, cheerful place of about 15,000 inhabitants, picturesquely built over low hills, and divided by a river. On the old *Domberg,* crowned with trees, stand the Cathedral and the Observatory. The University is one of the first in Russia, but is attended principally by students from the Baltic provinces. That part of Livonia lying between Dorpat and the Dwina, embracing the valley of the river Aa, is said to be a very attractive region, rich in natural beauties and pictorial reminiscences. It is called the Livonian Switzerland, although none of its hills rise more than eight hundred feet above the sea-level. But such hills are Andes to those who have never seen anything but plains.

We were about thirty hours on the road from Dorpat to Riga. The country reminded me very much of that part of Sweden which lies opposite Livonia—long rolling up lands, belted with fir-woods, and warm, winding valleys threaded by swift, cold streams. The Aa, which we followed for a few stages, flows through a charming pastoral region, full of lovely and tranquil pictures. The Livonians are very much attached to their homes, an attachment which arises from their quiet domestic life and the comparative isolation of the province. There are many feudal ruins among these valleys, each of which has its traditions of siege and battle, love, and revenge. The chief interest however, will be found in the people, who, allied in many respects to the Germans, Swedes, and Russians, have yet characteristics quite peculiar to themselves.

We drove into Riga in the midst of a heavy thunder-shower, on the third afternoon after leaving St. Petersburg. The guide-book says there are many interesting things to be seen here—such as the Peter's Church, the Rathhaus, and other old buildings dating from the Hanseatic times—but we had no opportunity of visiting them. The city is now being greatly improved by the levelling of its massive walls. As the main outlet for the produce of Lithuania, Courland, Livonia, and a large portion of Poland, it has always enjoyed a very considerable trade, which will be largely increased in two years by the construction of the railroad to Dünaburg. We were gratified to see the American flag among the shipping.

We crossed the Dwina by a floating bridge a mile in length, and after a journey of three hours over a sandy plain, reached Mittau, the ancient capital of Courland. The grand castle built by Biron, the last Duke of Courland, looms over the quiet little town with an air of ostentatious mockery. The Courland nobles, though decayed and fallen, as compared with their former state, are said to be still a proud, chivalric, hospitable race. The branches of their family trees stretch through both Europe and America.

That night and all next day we journeyed over the monotonous, sandy swells of Lithuania—a dreary region of dark forests, scanty fields of flax and rye, dirty villages swarming with Jews and a population of Slavic type, who spoke only the unintelligible Lettish, with a few words of German. We had been four days and nights in the diligence and were beginning to feel fatigued. The Russian experienced still more violent attacks of dyspepsia and was unable to procure enough sour milk; the knock-kneed Frenchman ceased to make remarks about the people "down there," and stupidly dozed all day in his corner. We had, besides, a fifth passenger from Dorpat, who had bought the conductor's seat—an old fellow, whose gray, greasy beard, long shaggy surtout, and whining voice stamped him as a Jew in the minds of all of us. We were not a little surprised therefore, on parting with him in an obscure little village in Lithuania, to find that he belonged to a distinguished Swedish family of Esthonia.

In just ninety-six hours after leaving St. Petersburg, we entered Tauroggen, the last Russian station. Escaping from the hands of Jews who changed our remaining paper money at a ruinous rate, we took a fresh coach to Laugsargen, the first Prussian station, about seven versts distant. Two stone pillars, a bar across the road and a Cossack guard marked the frontier. When the bar had been lifted and again let down behind us, we were outside of Russia and in a land whose people and language were most familiar and most welcome, after those of our own. The Prussian officials greeted us like old friends; the neat, comfortable dwellings, with their gardens and leafy arbors, were a delightful and unexpected sight, after the bare, forlorn houses of Tauroggen, and all that was difficult or fatiguing in our summer trip was over.

We went on to Tilsit on the Niemen, by extra post the same night, caught three hours' sleep, and then took a fresh start for Königsberg, which we reached in five days from St. Petersburg. The journey is not very fatiguing, and though so rapid, enables one to see the outside, at least, of a large portion of the Baltic provinces. Hence, I would recommend the curious traveller to choose this route, rather than take the steamer direct from Stettin to Cronstadt. From Königsberg it is fifteen hours to Berlin by railroad.

THE END.

www.ingramcontent.com/pod-product-compliance
Lightning Source LLC
Chambersburg PA
CBHW051725300426
44115CB00007B/463